I0129126

DEFERENCE AND DIVERGENCE IN REGIONAL HUMAN RIGHTS COURTS

DEFERENCE AND DIVERGENCE IN REGIONAL HUMAN RIGHTS COURTS

Maria A. Sanchez

CORNELL UNIVERSITY PRESS

ITHACA AND LONDON

Copyright © 2026 by Maria A. Sanchez

All rights reserved. Except for brief quotations in a review, this book, or parts thereof, must not be reproduced in any form without permission in writing from the publisher. For information, address Cornell University Press, Sage House, 512 East State Street, Ithaca, New York 14850. Visit our website at cornellpress.cornell.edu.

First published 2026 by Cornell University Press

Librarians: A CIP catalog record for this book is available from the Library of Congress.

ISBN 9781501785504 (hardcover)
ISBN 9781501785535 (paperback)
ISBN 9781501785528 (epub)
ISBN 9781501785511 (pdf)

GPSR EU contact: Sam Thornton, Mare Nostrum Group B.V., Mauritskade 21D, 1091 GC, Amsterdam, NL, gpsr@mare-nostrum.co.uk.

To Joe, my parents (Steven Sanchez and Ann McCaslin Sanchez),
and Rosie

Contents

Abbreviations

ACtHPR   African Court on Human and Peoples' Rights
AU   African Union
CoE   Council of Europe
CoM   Committee of Ministers
ECtHR   European Court of Human Rights
IACtHR   Inter-American Court of Human Rights
IC   international court
ICC   International Criminal Court
IO   international organization
LGBT   lesbian, gay, transgender, bisexual
LGBTI   lesbian, gay, transgender, bisexual, intersex
MOA   margin of appreciation
OAS   Organization of American States
OAU   Organization of African Unity
PI   personal integrity
UDHR   Universal Declaration of Human Rights
UN   United Nations

INTRODUCTION

In November 2022, the Inter-American Court of Human Rights (IACtHR) issued a landmark ruling challenging controversial mandatory pretrial detention provisions in the Mexican Constitution. The case revolved around three men—Jorge Marcial Tzompaxtle Tecpile, Gerardo Tzompaxtle Tecpile, and Gustavo Robles López—whose ordeal began one January morning in 2006. Stranded by the side of the Mexico City–Veracruz highway after their car broke down, the men were approached by federal police agents. The police searched the men's personal belongings, an act that Mexican authorities now admit was performed illegally, without warrant or cause. The police allegedly found evidence of gang affiliation, marking the beginning of a long road back to freedom for the men.

Under Article 19 of the Mexican Constitution, individuals suspected of engaging in organized crime are subjected to mandatory pretrial detention without the possibility of bail. In Mexico's overwhelmingly backlogged judicial system, detainees are often imprisoned for years before a trial ever takes place.[1] Jorge, Gerardo, and Gustavo were held for over two and half years before being acquitted in 2008 of all charges of alleged gang affiliation. The men received no compensation for the years that had been stolen from them. Their case was far from unique: Nearly 40 percent of individuals currently imprisoned in Mexico have not been convicted of any crime, and half of that figure are behind bars as a result of mandatory pretrial detention measures codified in the Constitution.[2]

Seeking justice, Jorge, Gerardo, and Gustavo turned to the Inter-American Court. In its 2022 ruling on their case, the IACtHR ruled that Mexico had violated several provisions of the American Convention on Human Rights, including the rights to personal liberty and integrity, fair trial, and judicial protection. But the most stunning element of the ruling was contained in the orders of reparation that the Court imposed on the Mexican government. In addition to mandating that the government provide significant financial compensation and free medical and psychiatric treatment to the victims, the IACtHR judges declared Mexico's mandatory pretrial detention policies "incompatible" with international human rights law and ordered Mexico to amend several provisions of its Constitution to eliminate the practice.[3]

This bold directive asserted an expansive interpretation of the authority of international courts to intervene in domestic affairs. Constitutions are sacred manifestations of self-determination in democratic states, and external interference in their effectuation is liable to be perceived as an egregious assault on national sovereignty. While ordering a state to change its constitution might seem earth-shatteringly audacious to some, for the IACtHR it is actually a fairly conventional move. Throughout the Court's history, IACtHR judges have rarely shied away from imposing intensive remedial mandates on governments, including declaring domestic legislation to be null and void.

The generous scope of the IACtHR's self-interpreted authority, however, is by no means the status quo in international law, even among the IACtHR's fellow regional human rights courts. The European Court of Human Rights (ECtHR), an older, larger, and much wealthier court, has historically espoused a more restrained interpretation of the reach of its power into the domestic realm. Take, for example, an ECtHR case that, similar to the case discussed above, revolved around the contested international legality of legislation enabling prolonged pretrial detention. In *Stevan Petrovič v. Serbia* (2021), the applicant was detained by Serbian authorities on the suspicion of involvement in a robbery in 2013. Mr. Petrovič was held in pretrial detention for nearly three years. Among Petrovič's complaints before the ECtHR was his objection to provisions of the Serbian criminal code that permit judicial authorities to repeatedly extend pretrial detention periods without clear limitations.[4] While the ECtHR ultimately sided with Petrovič, ruling that Serbia had violated his right to liberty under the European Convention on Human Rights, the Court declined to mandate that Serbia implement any legislative reforms to revise its criminal code. Rather, it found that €6,000 constituted sufficient compensation for nonpecuniary damages. Exclusively mandating financial reparations is common practice for the ECtHR, which has historically targeted individual restitution rather than systemic domestic policy reform. This approach reflects the decidedly more limited role relative to the IACtHR that the ECtHR sees itself as playing in the melee of domestic politics.

The world's three regional human rights courts, the ECtHR, the IACtHR, and the African Court on Human and Peoples' Rights (ACtHPR), carry out similar judicial mandates to enforce similar human rights provisions. However, these courts have developed very different approaches to interpreting the boundaries of their authority over member state governments. The central aim of this work is to better understand the causes and consequences of regional divergence in exercise of international judicial authority through examining how the three courts have come to define and implement their unique missions. I investigate two main questions: Where do regional human rights courts' interpretations of the scope of their authority originate, and under what conditions do those interpretations change? In today's era of growing national backlash against international institutions, it is important to understand the implications of international courts' approaches to delineating appropriate deference to domestic sovereignty.

The histories of the three regional courts reveal a counterintuitive finding: The courts that were founded in the most inhospitable environments for human rights have ended up asserting the most expansive authority over governments. This phenomenon provides compelling evidence that international human rights law can actually fulfill the emancipatory mission that motivated its creation. While international law is often criticized as a mere tool that governments can manipulate to wield power, the three regional human rights courts have each exerted considerable authority to subjugate dominant political interests. These courts have done so through pioneering distinct conceptualizations of what "justice" looks like, rooted in social purposes forged during each court's founding moments.

Argument in Brief

This book demonstrates that international courts' interpretations of their authority are fundamentally shaped by those courts' founding senses of social purpose, or, in other words, the normative missions that drive court officials' perceptions of their institution's legitimacy. The historical contexts in which the European, Inter-American, and African courts emerged, in conjunction with the professional incentives of the actors who drafted the treaties that those courts enforce, led each court to perceive its legitimacy as arising from different sources. Relying on analysis of primary source documents from negotiations to establish each court, as well as early case law, I show how each court developed divergent founding interpretations of judges' authority. The European Court was founded on a "deferential" approach to interpreting its jurisdiction that prioritized respect for national sovereignty. The early Inter-American Court, in contrast, adopted a distinctly "interventionist" approach that has empowered it to assert broader authority in domestic affairs. The African Court, which was founded much more recently and thus benefited from observing the example of the other two courts, initially adopted a middle-ground position on the deferential-interventionist continuum of judicial authority. Subsequently, however, the African Court quickly aligned itself more closely with the Inter-American example, pushing the boundaries of its authority and igniting government ire in the process.

Having investigated the factors propelling the trajectory of regional courts' initial relationships to national sovereignty, this book then probes the conditions under which regional courts' interpretations of their authority *change*. What factors can cause international judges to expand or contract their interpretations of their authority over governments? I explore how each court has approached three central areas within international human rights law: freedom of expression, personal integrity rights (which include the right to life and the prohibition of torture), and anti-LGBT discrimination. I find that each court's founding interpretation of its authority has been generally durable. Still, shifts have occurred that have important implications for domestic human rights protections as well as the global coherence of international human rights law. First, the European Court has been uniquely deferential in response to government criticism relative to the Inter-American and African Courts. However, there is evidence that the European Court's deference has been tempered by two factors, particularly in recent years: (1) the severity of the rights violations in question, and (2) evolving social understandings of human rights norms, even without government consensus. The Inter-American Court has largely ignored accusations of judicial overreach, continuing to expand its jurisdiction and issue intensive remedial mandates even in the face of government backlash. But, as is particularly observable through the Inter-American Court's freedom of expression jurisprudence, the Court has demonstrated self-restraint and closer attention to emulating the European example in areas where the European Court has relatively more experience. As a much younger court with a comparatively small (but rapidly growing) body of case law, the African Court is still charting its path. Jurisprudence of the late 2010s–early 2020s, however, indicates that the African Court is following the Inter-American Court's lead, shrugging off government criticism and expansively interpreting its jurisdiction and remedial powers. It remains to be seen whether the ACtHPR's interventionism will be politically sustainable.

What is at Stake

Variation across regional courts' interpretations of the scope of their power is particularly consequential given an unprecedented trend toward transregional human rights cooperation that the three courts have themselves spearheaded in recent years. The ECtHR, IACtHR, and ACtHPR have increasingly cited one another's judgments over the past decade.[5] In October 2019, representatives from the three regional courts signed the Kampala Declaration, an agreement that committed the courts to strengthening coordination through jurisprudential dialogue, joint conferences, staff exchanges, and determination of common best practices.[6] In fulfillment of that declaration, judges and lawyers from the three courts have convened annually to discuss pressing human rights issues in their respective regions, recent case law developments, and avenues for achieving greater cooperation and cross-court jurisprudential coherence. At a May 2023 meeting hosted by the IACtHR in Costa Rica, the judges signed a new joint agreement reaffirming their commitment to "permanent dialogue and consultations mechanisms . . . to consolidate joint efforts" in the coming years.[7]

Regional human rights courts are increasingly recognized as the vanguards of international human rights law. Their rulings have important consequences not only for the citizens and governments involved in specific cases, but for evolving contemporary legal understandings of what "justice" for state-sponsored repression looks like. These courts are profoundly influential in defining what compliance with international law means in practice, as regional human rights systems have become more deeply embedded than the global United Nations system in domestic legal institutions.[8] The regional human rights courts are the only international courts in the world in which individuals and groups of citizens can independently submit cases alleging violations of their human rights at the hands of state actors and receive legally binding judgments. Individuals can also submit petitions to UN treaty bodies that enforce the various UN-sponsored human rights treaties, but these bodies do not have the authority to issue binding judgments. The International Court of Justice often deals with human rights concerns, but cases at that court must be submitted by government actors, not ordinary citizens. Likewise, the case referral process of the International Criminal Court (ICC) does not allow for cases to be initiated by ordinary citizens, and in any case the ICC is only able to prosecute individuals, limiting its ability hold governments accountable for systemic violations of international human rights law. In other words, if we are looking for hope that international legal institutions can empower disenfranchised communities to actualize their human rights in the face of government intransigence, the regional courts are our best bets. But the next decade will be crucial for determining whether that hope will be realized, and that realization fundamentally hinges on the three courts reconciling divergent interpretations of their judicial authority with each other's unique missions and with the imperative to discern appropriate deference to national sovereignty.

International judges can adopt varying perspectives on the boundaries of their authority relative to national institutions, driving divergence across when and how regional courts intervene in domestic affairs. This variation is consequential, first of all for victims of human rights violations and their families. For example, scholars have argued that the European Court's narrow interpretation of the temporal range of its jurisdiction relative to the Inter-American Court has blocked victims of human rights violations in post-conflict European states from accessing legal remedies that are available to victims of similar atrocities in Latin America.[9] As Russia's bloody invasion of Ukraine drags on, this question of how the European Court's relatively limited interpretation of its temporal jurisdiction might mitigate the Court's role in facilitating post-conflict justice becomes increasingly salient. Meanwhile, ACtHPR judges have embraced flexible interpretations of their Court's temporal jurisdiction in cases of political violence but provoked government backlash in the process, casting a hopeful but murky projection of the potential for the ACtHPR to be a formidable advocate for post-conflict accountability in Africa.[10]

On an empirical level, differences across the courts' approaches to ordering remedies in cases of established rights violations raise serious measurement issues for assessing compliance with rulings. Take, for example, one court that tends to mandate fewer remedies or types of remedies that are easier for a state to comply with, and another court that tends to order more remedies or remedies that involve significant domestic policy changes that are more difficult to comply with. We cannot meaningfully compare rates of state compliance across those two courts without accepting the fact that their disparate approaches to mandating remedies result in different definitions of what compliance means across those two contexts. Scholars have contended that compliance rates with IACtHR rulings are generally lower than compliance rates in the ECtHR,[11] while compliance rates with ACtHPR rulings have not yet been systematically assessed. But the fundamentally different nature of how those courts interpret the scope of their authority to order remedial measures raises doubts about whether it is productive to quantitatively compare compliance rates across courts in the first place.

Regional courts' varying approaches to ruling on the admissibility of cases impose selection effects on whether compliance with court judgments translates to actual improvements in domestic human rights practices. For example, one court may admit a category of cases involving violations for which it is difficult to get states to implement remedies. This widens the court's jurisdiction but ultimately lowers the overall rate of compliance with that court's judgments. Another court may tend to not admit that same category of cases, which limits that court's jurisdiction but results in better compliance rates. Without attention to how courts' different approaches to determining admissibility impact which cases receive rulings, it is difficult to infer anything about the relative effectiveness of these courts based on compliance rates alone.

Admissibility decisions provide unique opportunities for judges to express interpretations of the boundaries of their court's authority. The administrative nature of admissibility decisions renders them less visible and thus less likely to attract outside criticism compared to substantive judgments made in the final stages of cases. For example, Jed Odermatt finds that international courts tend to use procedural rules to subtly avoid ruling on politically sensitive cases.[12] Judges can use admissibility rulings to express normatively and strategically motivated interpretations of their authority while maintaining the optics of impartiality and thus preserving the court's legitimacy. Consequently, admissibility decisions provide useful outlets for judges to express how they interpret their authority. These processes have important implications for the extent to which international courts, including the regional human rights courts, encroach on state sovereignty.

Regional courts' different approaches to calibrating their authority can result in uneven regional application of purportedly global human rights principles, potentially threatening the coherence and legitimacy of international law. The three regional human rights courts are independent institutions operating in very different contexts; perfect harmony across their judicial approaches is not expected and likely would not be achievable or appropriate. Nevertheless, insofar as these courts are accessible to ordinary citizens and thus maintain a central role in modeling the deployment of international law in domestic life, inconsistencies across how the courts wield their authority can undermine claims to universality endemic to rhetorical legitimation of the modern human rights project. Furthermore, divergences might provide fodder for criticism by disenchanted governmental actors who point toward one court's approach in an effort to discredit another's. International institutions' failure to strike an amenable balance between exerting authority and respecting state sovereignty can have disastrous consequences, as has been seen with several governments withdrawing their citizens' right to submit petitions to the Inter-American and African human rights courts in recent years following critiques of judicial overreach. This challenge of exerting authority without causing governments to revolt is inherent to all sorts of international institutions, even beyond the realm of human rights.

The unique character of international human rights agreements relative to other types of international institutions makes variation across how human rights courts interpret their authority all the more puzzling. As Beth Simmons notes, human rights treaties are negotiated internationally but primarily aim to regulate relationships between citizens and national governments, relationships that almost exclusively unfold in the domestic arena. In other words, unlike most international treaties, which seek to govern state-state relations (for example, mutual defense pacts or trade commitments), human rights treaties focus on state-society relations. As such, and particularly considering the inherent power imbalance between ordinary citizens and government actors, the mechanisms available to human rights institutions for inducing compliance with international law are more limited than the mechanisms available in treaty regimes that primarily govern state-state relations.[13] Unlike economic or security-related arrangements, which may directly implicate the very survival of a state or particular regime, the incentives for governments to join and abide by human rights agreements are often less tangible and/or more difficult for leaders to perceive as essential for their survival. Material mechanisms for inducing compliance, such as reciprocity or retaliation,[14] while often effective in institutions governing state-state relations, may be overall less salient in human rights institutions governing state-society relations. Given the compliance challenges inherent to international human rights law, an area of law chronically lacking in enforcement mechanisms, it is perhaps surprising that regional human rights courts do not inherently trend toward deference as a way to cultivate cooperation with the governments upon whose goodwill these courts' very existence depends. Rather, even though the three regional courts operate under common constraints related to incentivizing government cooperation, we see each court developing its own approach to discerning appropriate deference and intervention in domestic affairs.

This book highlights the importance of institutional founding context in shaping the limitations and frontiers of international law. My hope is that this research can contribute to better understanding of how international institutions—even beyond the realm of human rights—define their missions, interact with governments, and learn from one another. In this age of increasing isolationism and resistance to international governance, it is imperative that actors working within international institutions figure out how to calibrate commitment to their normative agendas with the practical exigencies of sensitivity to sovereignty. Doing so requires awareness of how historically entrenched institutional norms impact actors' formulation of the menu of options they have to confront contemporary challenges.

Authority in International Courts

Before briefly introducing the three regional courts that this book examines, it is helpful to consider why international courts are created and the factors involved in shaping how judges within those courts interpret their mandates. The literature on state delegation to international organizations provides a starting point for investigating the origins of regional courts' interpretations of their authorities.

Understanding Delegation to International Organizations

International courts (ICs), like all international organizations (IOs), are first and foremost created to serve state interests. Acceding to any IO inherently entails sacrificing sovereignty on the part of governments. In turn, IO membership can provide governments with diverse benefits: for example, lowering the transaction costs associated with policymaking, assuaging information asymmetries between state and non-state actors, and providing forums in which states can make credible commitments to one another.[15] States must weigh the benefits of delegating authority to an IO against the costs of weakened policy autonomy. Rationalist theories of delegation maintain that when mechanisms of state control over an IO's autonomy are strong, the commitment embodied by delegation to that IO will be less credible, and vice versa. Thus, if barriers for commitment between member states are high, those states will delegate more authority to the IO to enhance the credibility of their commitments. If barriers to commitment between member states are lower, those states will prefer to keep the IO's decision-making powers limited to preserve their sovereignty.[16] States use delegation to IOs to make credible commitments not only to other states, but also to their domestic publics.[17]

Through codifying rules of procedure that govern how IOs can act and incentivizing adherence to those rules, governments can *ex ante* constrain IOs' actions. But IOs' preferences often diverge from those of their member states, for reasons anticipated and unanticipated by governments. *Ex ante* efforts to control IOs may prove ineffective when circumstances arise that governments did not anticipate or when the rules governing the IO–member state relationship are sufficiently vague as to allow the IO interpretational liberties.[18] Governments may also deliberately grant IOs discretion to formulate and execute their own preferences for the sake of increasing policy effectiveness or making commitments more credible.[19] The value that states place on judicial independence in international courts exemplifies one avenue through which governments constrain their own authority to enhance the credibility of commitments made through delegation.[20]

Regime type can influence barriers to commitment between states and consequently drive levels of delegation to IOs. For example, Barbara Koremenos finds that established democracies are less inclined to delegate power to IOs. She suggests that states with more tumultuous recent political histories may face internal commitment problems that make it difficult for them to credibly commit to future cooperation. Thus, such states will be more open to delegating authority to an IO.[21] This logic is supported in Simmons and Danner's study of delega-tion to the International Criminal Court, in which the authors find that the least democratic states were fastest to ratify the Rome Statute, despite the Statute's high "sovereignty costs." The authors propose that the states that most severely lack domestic mechanisms for holding government agents accountable are the most likely to seek out international mechanisms for doing so.[22] There is evidence that transitional democracies are more likely to seek membership in international human rights organizations than both autocracies and established democra-cies,[23] and furthermore that transitional democracies are particularly likely to seek membership in international human rights courts.[24] This phenomenon may be a result of the relatively high sovereignty costs that human rights courts are theorized to impose on member states, which boost the credibility of commit-ments signaled through delegation to such courts.

These findings suggest that the regime types present among an IO's founding member states influence the extent of the powers initially delegated to that IO. Member regime types may also impact whether and how IOs act independently of their constitutive governments once in operation. For example, an IO compris-ing diverse regime types may observe greater variation in member state prefer-ences as opposed to an IO comprising more similar regimes. Consequently, while an IO with a homogeneous membership body may be able to observe coherent signals indicating its member states' preferences, another IO with a relatively more heterogeneous membership body may observe more disjointed preferences across its member states. Lacking coherent signals of governments' preferences, an IO with relatively more heterogeneous membership may come to adopt its own preferences to fill that void and bolster its own sense of mission. Thus, even if homogeneous and heterogeneous IOs were imbued with similar potential to exercise discretion during the institutional design process, the heterogeneous IO would be more likely to actually act independently.

A two-step process could also occur in which regime type influences both the potential for discretion written into an IO's constitutive documents and the probability that the IO will actually use that discretion to act independently of its member states' preferences. First, variation in regime type and/or regime insta-bility across IO founding member states could increase the barriers to commit-ment between those states relative to a group of more homogeneous states. As a result, the heterogeneous group of states will create an IO with more discre-tionary authority in order to enhance the credibility of those states' collective commitments. Second, because of a lack of preference clarity among member states, the IO with a heterogeneous membership body may be more likely to actually utilize that discretionary authority and formulate independent prefer-ences. Importantly, this theory cannot tell us anything about (1) why states seek to impose specific boundaries on an IO's authority during the institutional design process or (2) whether any given IO is more or less likely to take independent action that expands its authority as opposed to contracting that authority. To address these issues, we must move beyond theories that conceptualize states and IOs as rational, unitary actors to better understand why an IO might develop more or less expansive interpretations of its authority.

Deconstructing "the State" to Explain Delegation to International Courts

Two limitations of theories of delegation that treat states and IOs as unitary actors are that (1) these theories "black box" both states and IOs, ignoring internal constituencies who comprise those actors and (2) these theories lack attention to third-party interventions in the IO–member state relationship—for example, the role of nongovernmental organizations (NGOs) or other non-state actors.[25] Third parties can provide information to governments that structures the alternatives government officials choose between when deciding whether and how to delegate power to an IO. Third parties also often engage in activism to interject new policy incentives into the IO–member state relationship.[26]

Designing an international court (IC) requires the participation of legal professionals who have specific expertise in international law and may or may not be concerned with accommodating states' political interests. These legal professionals occupy a unique, understudied position mediating the IO–member state relationship. The role of judges as IC "founders" is similarly overlooked in the delegation literature. An IC's founding judges establish the court's first precedents and, in most cases, are responsible for drafting the court's rules of procedure. Founding judges consequently have significant influence over how ICs implement certain delegated powers. This is particularly true when an IC's constitutive documents leave room for interpretation regarding the boundaries of the court's jurisdiction. This study addresses the delegation literature's disproportionate state-centrism by analyzing the various sub-state and non-state actors who participate in founding regional courts.

Nicole Deitelhoff's study of the negotiations to draft the Rome Statute reveals how powerful states' interests were subverted through normative appeals made by small and middling powers, assisted by NGOs, to delegate greater authority to the ICC. The majority of delegates that states sent to the ICC negotiations were legal advisers, while political advisers made up the minority in most delegations.[27] Initially, the negotiations were dominated by a major-power coalition that favored strong requirements for state consent to jurisdiction and extensive UN Security Council oversight of the Court. However, Deitelhoff identifies a turning point when a lesser-power coalition gained support by consolidating a narrative that framed the ICC negotiations as an unprecedented opportunity to create a highly autonomous court capable of overriding dominant power interests. This narrative called for nixing proposed Security Council oversight mechanisms. The lesser-power coalition persuaded a sufficient number of previously uncommitted states, and the majority of the coalition's demands were incorporated into the Rome Statute. This previously uncommitted group primarily comprised transitional democracies. These states' delegations lacked the resources to be fully present during drafting conferences and consequently had low rates of participation in the earlier stages of negotiations before they were targeted for greater involvement by the lesser-power coalition.[28]

Deitelhoff's study indicates that the final level of delegation to the ICC was not merely a function of barriers to commitment between states of diverse regime types, or a result of unstable regimes seeking to signal commitment to human rights in order to bolster their international reputations. Rather, the high level of delegation incorporated into the ICC's institutional design came about because particular actors, mostly legal professionals in delegations from less-powerful states, sought to create a highly legalized regime whose authority could transcend great power interests.

The Role of the International Bureaucracy in Constructing IO Authority

The legal professionals who participate in designing international courts can be considered "international bureaucrats." International bureaucrats are distinguished from political actors who represent states internationally by the fact that international bureaucrats derive their legitimacy not from their ability to execute state interests but from their technical expertise and independence from political forces. Jens Steffek claims that the international bureaucracy is the "perfect" representation of Weberian "rational-legal" bureaucratic rule.[29] The "objective" exercise of expert knowledge by bureaucrats creates depoliticization (or at least an appearance of depoliticization) within bureaucracies that bolsters those institutions' claims to legitimate authority. However, "bureaucracies are always created to defend or promote values," and bureaucracies' claims to authority also hinge on their ability to embody those values. Bureaucracies must constantly balance these competing narratives from which they derive authority and legitimacy: depoliticization and adherence to normative principles.[30] These principles, and particularly how they are articulated during the institutional design process, are critical for guiding the establishment, the embedding, and the development of any IO's interpretation of its authority. Bureaucracies are often compared to machines in that every action that bureaucrats take must align with clearly defined procedures and rules that result in consistent and predictable outcomes. However, "people will only accept the workings of the machinery if they accept its aims and the principles according to which it functions."[31] ICs exemplify this delicate balancing act. IC judges must carry out the normative mandate that prompted the creation of their court while eschewing political influence, deciding cases originating from often wildly disparate domestic contexts in a manner that is objective, consistent, transparent, and equitable. In this sense, we can consider IC judges as belonging to the community of international bureaucrats.

Several scholars have argued that international bureaucrats play an integral role in IO design and development that is often more independent from state interests than rationalist theories of delegation predict.[32] Tana Johnson documents how international bureaucrats working in preexisting IOs often use the institutional design process to insulate new IOs from states' interference. Johnson notes that this phenomenon may not extend to IO design negotiations that involve a highly capable group of states that do not face challenges such as a lack of resources or severe collective-action problems. In other words, negotiation delegations from technically capable, wealthier states are less likely to lose control over the negotiations and cede power to international bureaucrats.[33] Transitional and unstable states may tend to delegate greater power to IOs because international legal bureaucrats can exploit openings created by those states' lack of resources and internal disorganization to capture control over designing IOs and negotiating state accession.

Building on this logic, I propose that IC design negotiation delegations from transitional states, compared to delegations from established democracies, will be more likely to push for imbuing the court with wide-reaching authority. This is because legal bureaucrats have greater opportunity to capture control over delegations from transitional states whose political advisers lack the resources, organizational capacity, or political will to fully participate in negotiations. Legal bureaucrats who participate in founding an IC, by virtue of their professional backgrounds and expertise in international law, are likely more inclined than state executives and political advisers to favor creating an IC with broad legal authority.[34] Thus, I anticipate that the written mandates of international courts whose founding membership consists primarily of transitional states will be relatively more expansive compared to the written mandates of courts whose founding membership consists primarily of established democracies.

The predominant regime types within a court's founding membership will also condition that court's exercise of its authority by influencing how judges navigate their relationships with governments. Established democracies that already largely respect human rights will be less inclined to sacrifice sovereignty to an IC because they have less to gain from joining. In this context, IC judges will need to tread carefully and demonstrate respect for domestic sovereignty in order to gain legitimacy. Member state regime type will also impact judges' relationships with domestic institutions by influencing the types of cases that judges confront in the early years of the court. A court whose membership consists primarily of established democracies is likely to face cases involving isolated instances of human rights shortcomings rather than systemic abuses. These conditions are more likely to foster trust in domestic judiciaries among IC judges, guiding the IC toward a deferential interpretation of its authority. Because of the unique signaling incentives that membership in an IC affords transitional regimes, judges within ICs whose membership consists of mostly transitional regimes may not have to behave as deferentially toward national institutions in the early years of the court. Such courts are also likely to face markedly different caseloads compared to ICs whose members are mostly established democracies. Recent systemic (and potentially ongoing) human rights abuses in transitional regimes will lead IC judges to be less inclined to trust domestic judiciaries and more inclined to interpret the IC's power expansively. These dynamics will push the court toward a more interventionist interpretation of its authority.

Introduction to the Regional Courts

To offer some context for the following chapters, the paragraphs below will review some basic background information on each of the three regional human rights courts. The establishment, history, organizational structure, and rules of procedure of each court will be discussed in greater detail later on.

The European Court of Human Rights

The ECtHR is housed within the Council of Europe (CoE), a political organization founded in 1949 to advance the cause of European unity following the devastating intra-continental conflicts of the first half of the twentieth century. As the judicial arm of the CoE, the ECtHR is charged with enforcing the European Convention on Human Rights. The Convention was adopted in 1950 and has been amended and supplemented with additional protocols several times throughout the European Court's history. The ECtHR is the oldest regional human rights court in the world, and the busiest by far. Located in Strasbourg, France, the Court has issued over twenty-four thousand judgments in its history. Accession to the ECtHR has been compulsory for CoE membership since 1998. The Court today possesses jurisdiction over forty-six member states.

The original version of the European Convention that was adopted in 1950 established a two-tier framework for settling human rights disputes. First, the Convention established a Commission of Human Rights made up of an equal number of Commissioners to that of member states. The Commission could receive petitions alleging breaches of Convention obligations from any member government or from individuals or NGOs from states that had accepted the right to individual petition. The Commission assisted petitioners and government representatives in reaching friendly settlements to human rights disputes and issued nonbinding recommendations for states to address established violations of the Convention. In cases where a friendly settlement could not be reached, the Commission could decide to refer the case to the ECtHR.

The ECtHR as it was originally established could only receive cases from the Commission or member governments. The number of judges on the Court was equal to the number of CoE member states, with no two nationals of the same state permitted to serve on the Court. Judges served nine-year terms and could be reelected once.

The Protocol 11 reforms of 1998 eliminated the European Commission as a separate entity from the Court. The Commission's case-processing responsibilities, and many of its personnel, were absorbed into the administrative apparatus of the Court, known as the ECtHR Registry. Concomitant with this restructuring, all CoE member states were required to permit individuals and NGOs to submit petitions directly to the Court. Protocol 11 also reduced ECtHR judge terms from nine years to six years, still permitting judges to be reelected once. Judge terms were again revised by Protocol 14 in 2010, which restored nine-year terms but eliminated the ability for judges to be reelected.

The Inter-American Court of Human Rights

The IACtHR is housed within the Organization of American States (OAS) and headquartered in San José, Costa Rica. The OAS is the world's oldest regional organization, with a spiderweb of subsidiary organizations devoted to wide-ranging mandates encompassing security issues, economic cooperation, human rights, public health, and sustainable development. The IACtHR is responsible for enforcing the American Convention on Human Rights, which was adopted in 1969 and entered into force in 1978. The IACtHR can also adjudicate the compatibility of state practice with all other OAS-sponsored human rights treaties (for example, the Convention of Belem do Pará, the Convention to Abolish the Death Penalty, and the Convention on Enforced Disappearance). However, any case before the Court must involve a legal question concerning at least one of the rights enshrined in the American Convention.

The drafters of the American Convention largely adhered to the Europeans' two-level model when devising procedures for admitting cases to the IACtHR. Petitions alleging violations of the American Convention have to first be submitted to the Inter-American Commission, with no direct individual access to the Court. The Commission investigates admissible petitions and issues opinions on whether respondent states have violated the Convention. In cases where the Commission determines that a violation occurred, it issues nonbinding recommendations for the state to address the violation and attempts to guide the disputing parties to a friendly settlement. According to the original terms of the American Convention, if a friendly settlement is not reached or if the state refuses to implement the Commission's recommendations, the case could be forwarded to the IACtHR at the Commission's discretion (Article 51). This process was later amended in the 2001 reform of the Commission's rules of procedure, which limited the Commission's discretion and established procedures for automatically forwarding cases to the IACtHR. Cases can only be referred to the IACtHR when the relevant state government has acceded to the Court's jurisdiction by depositing a declaration under the American Convention. Depositing that declaration is not required to ratify the Convention or for OAS membership.

The IACtHR is composed of seven judges who serve six-year terms. Judges can be reelected once. No two judges of the same nationality can serve on the Court. The judicial election process functions similarly to that of the ECtHR. State parties who have accepted the jurisdiction of the IACtHR can propose up to three candidates for consideration to fill judicial vacancies. Candidates must be nationals of OAS member states, and at least one of each state's three proposed candidates must be a national of a state other than the proposing state.[35] Judges are elected by absolute majority vote in the OAS General Assembly.

The IACtHR currently possesses jurisdiction over the twenty-four OAS member states (out of thirty-five total member states) that have ratified the American Convention.[36] The IACtHR can only admit cases submitted by individuals and NGOs from the twenty states that have deposited declarations under the American Convention recognizing the right to individual petition. Four states have ratified the American Convention but do not currently recognize the right to individual petition: Dominica, Grenada, Jamaica, and the Dominican Republic.

The African Court on Human and Peoples' Rights

The ACtHPR is charged with enforcing the African Charter on Human and Peoples' Rights as well as all other human rights agreements adopted under the auspices of the African Union (formerly the Organization of African Unity).

The African Charter came into force in 1986, but the ACtHPR was not established until the entry into force of the First Protocol to the Charter in 2004. The ACtHPR officially began operations at temporary headquarters in Addis Ababa, Ethiopia, in November 2006. In August 2007, the Court moved to its permanent headquarters in Arusha, Tanzania, where the Court remains today. The ACtHPR issued its first admissibility decision on a case in 2009 and its first final judgment on the merits of a case in 2013. As the world's newest regional human rights court,[37] the ACtHPR has a much smaller body of case law than its European and Latin American counterparts. However, reflecting on the origins and recent growth of the ACtHPR in comparative context is productive for anticipating how that court will define the boundaries of its authority as its jurisprudence continues to expand.

The African system's case-processing procedures are largely similar to the two-level system in the Americas and the pre-1998 European system. The African Commission on Human and Peoples' Rights can receive petitions alleging breaches of human rights obligations from any member government or from individuals or NGOs. The Commission maintains discretion to refer any case to the ACtHPR in which the Commission believes that a violation has occurred and the respondent government has not complied with the Commission's recommendations. Individuals and NGOs are permitted to bypass the Commission and submit cases directly to the ACtHPR if the relevant respondent government has deposited a declaration under the First Protocol to the African Charter consenting to this competence (Article 5(3)). Depositing this declaration is not required for a state to ratify the Protocol and accede to the ACtHPR.

The ACtHPR's bench consists of eleven judges. All judges must be nationals of African Union (AU) member states, and no two judges can be nationals of the same state. The judicial election process is similar to that of the other two regional courts. State parties to the First Protocol can nominate up to three candidates to fill judicial vacancies on the ACtHPR. At least two of these candidates must be nationals of the proposing state. Unlike the European and American Conventions, the ACtHPR Protocol stipulates that "due consideration shall be given to adequate gender representation" in the judicial nomination process (Article 12).[38] ACtHPR judges are elected by secret ballot by the AU Assembly. The judges serve six-year terms and can be reelected once. Currently, thirty-four AU member states are parties to the Protocol.[39] Only eight state parties to the Protocol also have currently active declarations accepting the competence of the Court to receive case petitions from NGOs and individuals. These states are Burkina Faso, the Gambia, Ghana, Guinea-Bissau, Mali, Malawi, Niger, and Tunisia.

Plan of the Book

Chapter 1 elaborates the theoretical grounding and methodological framework of this project. Chapter 2 describes the founding of each of the three regional human rights courts, with special attention to the political contexts surrounding their establishment and the unique priorities of the actors who were involved in drafting their constitutive documents. Chapter 3 investigates how each court articulated its social purpose through its early judgments on cases involving the right to freedom of expression and personal integrity rights. Chapters 4, 5, and 6 dive into the evolution of each court's jurisprudence over time, assessing the validity of my hypotheses for the conditions under which international courts' interpretations of the reach of their authority *change*. These chapters center in-depth analysis of the evolution of each court's case law with respect to freedom of expression, personal integrity rights violations, and, finally, anti-LGBT discrimination, an area in which international human rights standards have rapidly evolved in recent years. The final chapter discusses the implications of this study's findings for future international legal developments within and beyond human rights.

THEORIZING INTERNATIONAL JUDICIAL AUTHORITY

In 2011, the Inter-American Court ruled that Argentina had violated the freedom of expression of two magazine editors, Jorge Fonteveccia and Hector D'Amico, who had published details of an affair between former Argentine President Carlos Menem and a congresswoman. Argentina's Supreme Court had previously convicted the two men of violating Menem's right to privacy under the American Convention on Human Rights. The IACtHR, however, decided that the published information was of public interest. Thus, in convicting the men, Argentina had violated their right to freedom of expression.[1] This ruling ignited widespread accusations of inappropriate IACtHR meddling in domestic politics.

In 2017, Argentina's Supreme Court struck back at the IACtHR, ruling that the state did not have to comply with the IACtHR's 2011 decision. The Supreme Court's open defiance of the IACtHR sent "shock waves into the field of regional human rights law."[2] While the IACtHR has routinely faced criticism from states contesting the Court's heavy-handed interpretation of its authority,[3] Argentina has stood out among its peers in recent decades as one of the Inter-American system's strongest allies. The Supreme Court justified Argentina's noncompliance with the IACtHR by citing case law from the IACtHR's counterpart across the Atlantic, the European Court of Human Rights. The Supreme Court pointed toward the ECtHR's use of a legal doctrine called the "margin of appreciation," which the ECtHR applies to determine areas in which it defers the implementation of international obligations to the discretion of state governments. Based on its own interpretation of the margin of appreciation, the Supreme Court argued that the IACtHR had overstepped the boundaries of its jurisdiction.

To be clear, legal scholars have argued that the Supreme Court's citation of the ECtHR in this case was a strategic misinterpretation of the margin of apprecia- tion doctrine.[4] However, the Supreme Court ruling demonstrates that domestic judiciaries are picking up on a puzzling disconnect between the IACtHR and ECtHR's interpretations of their respective authorities to intervene in domes- tic affairs. Several scholars have noted the ECtHR's general tendency to grant broader deference to member states relative to the IACtHR when ruling on alleged rights violations and mandating remedies for violations.[5] However, exist- ing scholarship lacks attention to the underlying mechanisms that drive varia- tion across how regional human rights courts interpret the boundaries of their authority. Understanding these mechanisms is crucial for anticipating the con- sequences of inter-court doctrinal disagreement in the increasingly globalized arena of regional human rights litigation.

This chapter will first introduce my argument for where international courts' interpretations of the extent of their authority originate, as well as propose condi- tions under which those interpretations may change. I then describe my research design, including case selection rationale and the indicators I have developed to evaluate deferential and interventionist judicial behavior in international courts. Finally, I contextualize the time periods that constitute focal points for my analy- sis of the historical evolution of each court's case law.

Theory

The geopolitical context in which an international court is founded has profound and abiding influence on how judges interpret the contours of that court's mis- sion and the scope of its authority. In particular, the levels of democratization and regime stability among a court's founding member states fundamentally condi- tion how judges define the sources of that court's legitimacy. There are two cen- tral mechanisms through which these factors impact enduring interpretations of judicial authority. First, regime type and stability can drive the level of influence of legal bureaucrats relative to political advisers in the institutional design pro- cess, with implications for the delegation of authority to the court. Second, lev- els of democratization and political stability among a court's founding member states impact the types of human rights issues that judges confront in the early years of the court. These early cases are crucial for establishing precedent, with long-term influence on how judges and lawyers working within the court inter- pret the reach of the court's jurisdiction. Based on the court's formal mandate (as written into its constitutive documents) and the primary challenges confronted by a court in its early years of operation, court officials will self-define their legitimacy as more or less tied to cooperation with member governments and respect for state consent to jurisdiction. Court officials will reference this legitimation narrative to define the appropriate exercise of court authority, directing the court's involvement in domestic affairs.

An expansive literature analyzes how legitimacy empowers international organizations to wield political authority. An IO is "legitimate" when its exercise of authority is perceived by member states as inherently justified rather than imposed through persuasion or force.[6] Legitimacy in IOs is often understood as grounded in state consent.[7] States consider an IO to be legitimate because they have previously consented to delegate specific powers to that organization, including, in the case of international courts, the power to resolve legal disputes. Codified rules governing an IC's procedures provide mutually agreeable guidelines directing the court's exercise of its authority. But these rules often leave substantial room for interpretation, and ICs vary considerably in their prioritization of state consent when interpreting the reach of their mandates. For example, the IACtHR has been criticized for insufficiently considering state consent in its evolutive interpretation of the American Convention.[8] Helfer and Alter find that "expansive" judicial lawmaking in ICs—lawmaking that extends the court's "jurisdiction or review powers beyond the boundaries imposed by states"—does not automatically provoke a court's constituents to challenge its legitimacy.[9] In other words, the powers formally delegated to an IC do not fully exhaust that court's legitimate authority. Rather, courts may develop de facto authority, meaning that member states feel obligated to comply with the court's decisions and take purposeful action to do so.[10]

Existing scholarship largely assumes that legitimacy is conferred by a court's constituents, namely states and citizens. Little is known about how actors working *within* ICs interpret the sources of their court's legitimacy. This interpretive process is fundamentally guided by an IC's sense of mission to adhere to certain normative principles, what John Ruggie referred to as "social purpose." Ruggie proposed that international regimes fuse power and social purpose to project political authority.[11] Building on this idea, I argue that the geopolitical contexts in which ICs are founded permanently condition their normative commitments, creating a court's social purpose. Judges and lawyers within ICs reference these normative commitments to identify the sources of their institution's legitimacy. This process shapes how judges and lawyers interpret the extent of their authority, establishing a durable framework that guides when and how the IC will intervene in domestic politics.

ICs, like all international organizations, are founded by states to advance those states' collective goals and preferences. ICs are unique, however, in that their legitimacy as judicial institutions intrinsically hinges on independence from political actors. This paradox creates openings for ICs to variably prioritize adherence to state consent when delineating appropriate deference to national authorities. International court judges do not merely apply law as it is written, but evaluate the compatibility of state behavior with the law through the lens of the court's mission to uphold certain normative principles. These principles—in other words, the court's founding social purpose—drive judges' interpretations of the legitimate boundaries of their court's authority. By prying open the black box of the state and examining the dynamics of negotiations to found international courts, we can see that the ability of legal bureaucrats to exert influence in those negotiations varies across states and has important implications for the level of authority ultimately delegated to the IC. Furthermore, the types of cases an IC hears in its early years impact the level of deference that international judges are willing to afford to domestic authorities. As a result, somewhat counterintuitively, the ICs that are founded in the most inhospitable environments for human rights end up asserting broader authority over governments.

Changing Interpretations of IC Authority: Three Hypotheses

The types of governments that constitute an IC's founding membership and the nature of the cases faced by judges in the early years of the court are crucial factors that condition how a court interprets its authority. While the following analysis demonstrates that ICs' founding interpretations of their authority are generally durable, these interpretations are by no means "locked in" throughout the life of a court.

Bureaucracies are not generally known for their dynamism. Institutionalized norms and routinized adherence to established rules and procedures foster bureaucratic tendencies to maintain the status quo. This resistance to change may be particularly acute in ICs. Stringent legal procedures and doctrines foster entrenched organizational cultures within court systems. International judges often value adherence to widely shared legal norms as markers of their professional legitimacy.[12] Even so, factors such as the legalization of new norms, exterior political influence, the rotation of judges serving on a court, and the accession and withdrawal of member states can prompt changes in how a court interprets its social purpose.

I hypothesize three conditions under which regional courts' founding interpretations of their authority can shift along the deferential-interventionist continuum. First, if a regional court has a "deferential" interpretation of its authority, we should expect the court to respond to member state backlash by further constraining its interpretation of its authority to align with vocalized state preferences. This expectation is due to deferential courts' prioritization of state consent in determining the legitimate exercise of their judicial authority. We should not expect an "interventionist" court to be similarly responsive to state backlash. Interventionist courts rely on internally conceived normative interpretations of their authority that are independent from state consent. Consequently, interventionist courts will be less likely to scale back their mandate in response to state opposition. "Backlash" here is conceptualized as a sustained, government-led challenge to a court's "structural, adjudicative, and moral authority," borrowing from Courtney Hillebrecht. In other words, isolated instances of states critiquing a court's rulings do not reach the threshold to be considered "backlash," nor do "wholesale rejections of the liberal democratic order."[13] Rather, in order for a circumstance to be considered "backlash," it must involve targeted state action aimed at undermining the functionality and authority of the court in question.

Second, as inter-court interaction increases between deferential and interventionist courts, a given court might be more receptive to emulating another court's interpretation of its authority within areas of case law in which that other court has more experience. This hypothesis is based on the observation that the regional human rights courts are increasingly seeking to collaborate with one another and reach greater convergence in legal understandings across the three systems. Increasing similarities in the types of cases brought before regional courts are crucial catalysts of inter-court dialogue. Sandholtz and Feldman find that the IACtHR and ECtHR have turned toward each other's case laws when faced with issues with which one court has more experience than the other. The IACtHR has been particularly likely to cite the ECtHR in cases involving civil rights issues (for example, rights to privacy, freedom of religion, and freedom of expression). While these issues have long featured in the ECtHR's case law, they are relatively new to the IACtHR, whose early case law was largely monopolized by personal integrity rights violations. Similarly, the ECtHR began to cite the IACtHR more frequently in the late 1990s and 2000s as the ECtHR faced an uptick in personal integrity rights complaints, an area in which the ECtHR lacked jurisprudence. In both courts, cross-court citation gradually expanded to include issue areas for which each court already had established case law.[14] This finding indicates that judges perceive benefits to importing external jurisprudence beyond simply filling gaps in existing case law. According to Erik Voeten, another benefit of "borrowing" jurisprudence from another court is that it legitimizes judges' decisions by signaling that their legal reasoning is shared by peers. This signaling benefit may be particularly useful for "activist" judges who favor an expansive interpretation of their court's authority. Activist ECtHR judges are more likely to cite external sources of law, suggesting that judges who broadly interpret their mandate may find it helpful to lean on jurisprudence from other courts to justify that interpretation.[15] In that vein, former ECtHR Justice Julia Laffranque has noted that inter-court citation can support legitimate and nonarbitrary "judicial creativity."[16]

Finally, changes in the types of rights violations that dominate a court's docket can prompt the court to reinterpret the extent of its authority. For example, if a deferential IC faces a deluge of cases involving grave human rights crimes (such as torture or other personal integrity rights violations), judges may lose trust in domestic authorities' will and/or ability to uphold rights protections. Consequently, the IC may adopt a more interventionist interpretation of its authority in an effort to reel in governments who are routinely failing to guarantee their citizens' most fundamental rights. Alternatively, an interventionist IC may at some point observe that most of the cases it is receiving involve relatively less severe rights violations, for example property rights or privacy disputes. Observing that governments are generally exhibiting willful compliance with human rights law, the IC may scale back its interpretation of its authority to allow states greater deference. In this way, fluctuations in the types of rights violations that are prevalent within an IC's membership may induce changes in how the IC interprets its role in securing human rights domestically.

An alternative explanation for variance across regional courts' interpretations of their authority might posit that these interpretations are not derived from a court's founding social purpose but rather from logistical conditions. A given court may have a relatively homogeneous group of member states, primarily receive cases raising similar complaints, and/or have a smaller caseload. As a consequence of these material conditions, that court may be less restrictive about admitting cases, have the time to be closely involved in enforcing compliance with its judgments, and be less willing to grant deference to states that deviate from status quo expectations. A different court may have an overloaded docket, member states with diverse legal systems and geopolitical conditions, and/or routinely hear cases along a vast range of issue areas. For the sake of efficiency, this court may be more restrictive about admitting cases, defer responsibility for enforcing judgments to domestic authorities, and more willingly grant states discretion as to how to implement their human rights obligations. If an IC's interpretation of the extent of its authority is determined by logistical constraints, shifts toward more or less interventionist or deferential behavior will occur around the same time periods in which (1) the IC is facing an overwhelming docket, (2) the IC has admitted new member states, and/or (3) the IC has recently undergone institutional reforms oriented toward making the IC more efficient.

Research Design

I propose that ICs fall under two broad categories in terms of how they interpret the extent of their authority—"deferential" and "interventionist." In order to establish this qualitative differentiation in how courts interpret their authority, we need clear definitions of what "deferential" and "interventionist" courts respectively look like. In very general terms, "deferential" courts predominantly derive their legitimacy from state consent to explicit boundaries of the court's jurisdiction. These courts are hesitant to push for extensions in the court's mandate beyond what states have consented to through ratification of the court's constitutive documents. "Interventionist" courts, on the other hand, base their legitimacy on self-interpreted mandates not directly conferred on those courts by state parties. Interventionist courts seek to expand their mandate even in the absence of explicit state consent to do so.

These definitions are admittedly vague. To more specifically delineate the differences between deferential and interventionist courts, I use a series of indicators to evaluate whether a court employs a deferential or interventionist interpretation of its authority. These indicators are observable at the three main stages of case processing within ICs: (1) the admissibility stage, when a court decides whether it possesses jurisdiction to hear a case that an applicant has submitted; (2) the merits stage, during which the court evaluates the substantive claims made in an admitted case and rules on whether an applicant's rights have been violated; and (3) the remedial stage, when the court determines what reparations or other compensatory actions a state must implement to address an established rights violation. An IC's conceptualization of its own authority can be measured by assessing which cases the court takes on, how the court decides whether a state has violated its human rights obligations, and the characteristics of court-mandated remedial measures. In my measurement of court behavioral indicators across these three phases of case processing, "deferential" and "interventionist" are not necessarily mutually exclusive categories. In theory, a court can simultaneously exhibit deferential characteristics in one stage of case processing and interventionist characteristics in another stage, or even within the same stage.

It is important to note that this typology I have developed is not intended to be used as a hard-and-fast diagnostic tool; rather, my intention is that it serves as a framework for thinking through and evaluating diverse ways in which international judges articulate interpretations of the scope of their court's authority. This framework is designed to be transferable across judicial contexts, and consequently some parsimony in the specification of these indicators and their relative significance has been sacrificed for the sake of generality. For example, I do not weigh indicators observed in one stage of case processing as being more or less important than indicators observed in other stages. With regard to the regional courts specifically, each court approaches case processing differently. For instance, the ECtHR typically issues merits and reparations judgments simultaneously in a given case, while the IACtHR and ACtHPR have often issued separate judgments for these two stages of case processing. In most cases, it is not possible to know how imbricated the process of deliberating and writing judgments was across phases of case processing. In other words, conceptualized as data observations, the three stages of case processing I focus on here are not independent from one another. Consequently it does not make sense to try to attribute greater analytical weight to any particular case-processing stage while doing within-court cross-case comparison, let alone cross-court comparison. Furthermore, it must be emphasized that international law literature is already massively biased toward analyzing the merits stages of cases, where a decision on violation of the law is reached. This project is an attempt to push back against that bias, highlighting how judges consequentially project power in other phases of case processing.

Indicators of "Deferential" vs. "Interventionist" Judicial Behavior

In the case admissibility stage, I evaluate two indicators: whether the court (1) adopts a narrow or flexible interpretation of its temporal jurisdiction, and (2) adopts a narrow or flexible interpretation of its procedural admissibility criteria. A court can be categorized as deferential if it adopts narrow interpretations of its temporal jurisdiction and procedural admissibility criteria. A court can be categorized as interventionist if it adopts flexible interpretations of its temporal jurisdiction and procedural admissibility criteria.

In the merits stage, I evaluate three indicators: whether the court (1) applies a "margin of appreciation" or similar doctrine to grant states discretion to implement their international legal obligations, (2) routinely selects to rule only on the *core* allegations in a petition, rather than all allegations, and (3) allocates the burden of proof to the state as opposed to the applicant. A deferential court will employ a margin of appreciation to grant states discretion to implement human rights obligations, routinely rule only on the core allegations in a petition, and maintain evidentiary standards that allocate the burden of proof to the applicant. An interventionist court will not employ a margin of appreciation doctrine, will rule on all or most of the allegations in a petition, and will routinely adjust evidentiary standards to shift the burden of proof to the state.

In the remedial stage, I evaluate two indicators: whether the court (1) mandates remedial measures that focus on individual victims as opposed to targeting underlying societal conditions, and (2) maintains the authority to abrogate domestic legislation. A deferential court will mandate remedies focused on individual reparative measures and not assert that the court has the authority to abrogate domestic legislation. An interventionist court will routinely mandate remedies that go beyond individual measures to target broader societal conditions and will assert that the court has the authority to abrogate domestic legislation. Additionally, a key indicator as to whether a court's founders intended for the court to be deferential or interventionist is the mechanism by which compliance with court judgments is monitored and enforced. In a deferential court, monitoring and enforcement responsibilities will be delegated to a political body, as is the case in the European system. The Committee of Ministers is responsible for monitoring and enforcing ECtHR judgments, in coordination with judges. An interventionist court will be given singular authority to monitor and enforce compliance with its own judgments, as is the case in the Inter-American and African systems. For more precise specification and examples of each indicator I evaluate in this study, see tables A.1 and A.2 in the appendix.

Case Selection

Because of the breadth of each court's case law, I focus my analysis on cases involving specific rights protections. In order to take into account how the human rights challenges faced by each court have evolved over time, I have collected data from cases involving three types of substantive rights: (1) freedom of expression, an issue that was prevalent in each court's early years but to a much greater extent in the ECtHR; (2) personal integrity rights protections (including the right to life and prohibition of torture), which dominated the Inter-American Court's caseload during its early years but were not routinely confronted by the European Court until much later in that court's life; and (3) protections against anti-LGBT discrimination, an issue that was not a concern of any court early on but later received greater focus as international standards evolved. The primary reason to focus on these particular rights is to capture variation across time, as each of these violation categories is more prevalent within each court's case law during different eras. Second, these three rights violation categories embody very distinct types of rights, with freedom of expression being a tenet of democratic governance, physical integrity rights being essential to life itself, and LGBT rights being both essential for democratic governance and life itself, as well as occupying a unique analytical position as rights that were not codified in any regional courts' constitutive documents but that have gained increasing recognition in international law in recent decades.

Identifying Critical Time Periods for Change (or Staying the Course)

Particularly given contemporary trends toward rising nationalism and increased resistance to international governance, it is important to understand when and why ICs adjust their interpretation of their authority relative to domestic institutions. These adjustments can impact which cases ICs admit, the circumstances in which ICs find states in violation of international law, and the types of obligations that ICs impose on states to address established violations. Shifts in these areas redefine what constitutes state compliance with international law, fundamentally shaping the opportunity structure for citizens pursuing recourse for state-sponsored human rights abuses.

More broadly, evolutions in an IC's interpretation of its authority illuminate complicated and understudied relationships between ICs and their member states. For example, if a group of member states publicly criticizes an IC in response to a ruling on a given case, and we subsequently observe that IC declining to admit, find violations, or mandate extensive remedial measures in similar cases, does this indicate a lack of judicial independence? Or, alternatively, does this indicate that the court is simply adopting a more deferential interpretation of its authority to better align with its strategic objectives for improving domestic human rights practices? Are judges in some ICs more responsive to state preferences (or pressure) than others? How durable are ICs' founding interpretations of their authority? These are all important questions that probe the potential limits and frontiers of international human rights adjudication. To shed light on these questions, we need to ascertain the conditions under which ICs might exhibit more interventionist or deferential behavior toward state governments.

Above, I hypothesized three conditions under which ICs' interpretations of their authority are likely to change: First, if a regional court has a "deferential" interpretation of its authority, we should expect the court to respond to member state backlash by further constraining its interpretation of its authority in order to align with vocalized state preferences. We should not expect a more interventionist court to be similarly responsive to state backlash. Second, as inter-court interaction increases, a court may be more receptive to emulating another court's interpretation of its authority within areas of case law in which that other court has more experience. Third, changes in the types of rights violations that dominate an IC's docket can prompt the court to reinterpret the extent of its authority. Alternatively, it may be the case that interventionist or deferential behaviors in ICs are not primarily driven by some internal sense of social purpose, but rather by practical exigencies related to resource availability and caseload processing concerns.

The following paragraphs aim to establish a framework for testing the validity of these explanations for the conditions under which ICs' interpretations of their authority change. To do so, I identify specific time periods in each court's history during which we might expect these interpretations to change based on the hypotheses summarized above. To evaluate the durability of each court's founding interpretation of its authority, I analyze the development of each court's case law during periods when the court is experiencing the accession of new members as well as periods of member state backlash and/or threats of withdrawal. To determine whether logistical constraints are, alternatively, the primary drivers of shifting interpretations of court authority, I evaluate periods during which each court has faced case-processing backlogs and/or has recently undergone institutional reforms aimed at promoting greater efficiency.

Based on the above criteria, I focus my empirical analysis in chapters 4–6 on the following periods in each court's history: I examine the ECtHR's case law from 1990 to 2003, when the Court admitted a wave of new Eastern European member states and underwent institutional restructuring, and 2010 to 2015, when the Court faced a case backlog crisis, implemented new case-processing reforms, and faced unprecedented member state criticism. I examine the IACtHR's case law from 2002 to 2005, when reforms were implemented that limited the role of the Commission in case processing and increased the role of victim participation in Court hearings, and from 2012 to 2020, when the Court grappled with several withdrawals and attempted withdrawals while simultaneously managing a growing caseload. Finally, I examine the ACtHPR's case law from 2016 to 2022. Usage of the ACtHPR rapidly increased in that time. Meanwhile, four ACtHPR member states withdrew the right of their citizens to petition the Court in the span of less than four years. The following sections discuss each of these pivotal time periods. Courts do not interpret law in a vacuum. It is important to have a sense of how the political environments surrounding each court have evolved over time.

THE EUROPEAN COURT OF HUMAN RIGHTS

In chapters 4–6, I devote particular attention to two periods during the ECtHR's history: first, 1990 to 2003, during which the CoE admitted most of Eastern Europe and Russia, the European Commission of Human Rights was dissolved and subsumed into the ECtHR Registry, and the ECtHR was converted into a full-time, permanent court. Second, 2010 to 2015, during which Protocol 14 streamlined case admissibility procedures and the ECtHR faced vociferous backlash from member states, particularly surrounding the Brighton Declaration.

As is typical for international courts, the ECtHR was slow to get off the ground. In its first decade of existence, the Court issued a mere ten decisions on seven discrete cases. The Court found a violation of the Convention in only three of those cases.[17] This limited use of the ECtHR reflects the founding member states' apprehensive stance toward the Court, the discretionary power of the European Commission of Human Rights,[18] and the noncompulsory nature of the right to individual petition.[19] Unlike the IACtHR, the ECtHR did not possess advisory jurisdiction powers that could help build relationships with national authorities and bolster the Court's public profile. Usage of the ECtHR expanded in the 1970s and 1980s, driven by increasing public awareness of the Court and the admission of Portugal and Spain following their emergence from military dictatorships. Still, the ECtHR issued an average of only 2.6 judgments per year in the 1970s and 17 judgments per year in the 1980s.[20]

The 1990s marked a period of monumental change (and growing pains) for the ECtHR. The Soviet Union's dissolution and the breakup of Yugoslavia gave rise to a flurry of newly independent states eager to join Western international institutions. Between 1990 and 2003, the CoE admitted twenty-two new member states, including most of Eastern Europe and Russia.[21] The institutional hangover from communist governance in the new cohort of CoE members presented unique human rights challenges. The European Commission of Human Rights and ECtHR were suddenly confronted with a deluge of cases from countries with weak judiciaries and very recent histories of authoritarianism. Exacerbated by democratic backsliding in Turkey in the late 1980s through the early 1990s, the European human rights system faced a wave of cases it lacked the resources to handle.

In 1991, the Committee of Ministers (CoM) met to discuss the urgent issue of reducing the system's case backlog.[22] The ministers supported integrating post-Soviet states into the CoE, grasping the opportunity to leverage European human rights institutions to advance the eastward expansion of democracy.[23] It is clear that the ministers were not inclined to disqualify newly independent states from CoE membership based on existing shortcomings in their human rights practices.[24] Rather, the ministers sought to imbue the European system with the capacity to manage the immense challenge of guiding these new members toward compliance with European human rights standards. Subsequent meetings over 1992–1993 considered the option of merging the Commission and Court. This proposal would streamline case processing by eliminating procedural redundancies. The ministers also sought to require all CoE member states to accept the right of individuals to petition the ECtHR.[25]

In 1994, these proposals were adopted in Protocol 11 to the European Convention on Human Rights. The Protocol entered into force in 1998. It was at this point that the ECtHR became a full-time, permanent court. Judge terms were reduced from nine to six years, renewable once. The Court's admissibility criteria

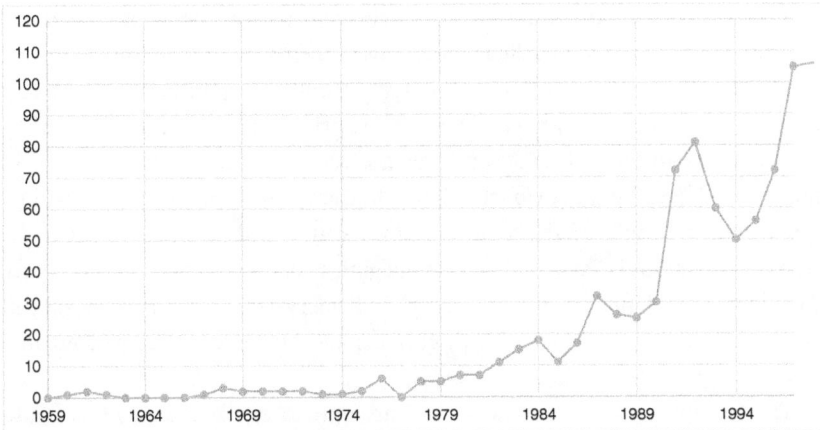

FIGURE 1.1. ECtHR judgments per year, pre–Protocol 11 (Chambers and Grand Chamber)

Note: Chart includes judgments rendered by the Chambers and Grand Chamber only, not three-judge admissibility committees. Inadmissibility decisions that were rendered by these committees are not publicly available. Data are available only for decisions that were ultimately declared admissible. Consequently I have chosen not to include any committee decisions in this chart, as those admissible cases are already accounted for within the Chamber decision data. All data sourced from the HUDOC (Human Rights Documentation) database of the ECtHR.

remained unchanged. The Commission, though technically rendered defunct through the implementation of Protocol 11, did not simply disappear. Rather, it was subsumed into the ECtHR Registry, a permanent administrative apparatus. Many lawyers from the former Commission were transferred directly into positions within the ECtHR Registry. Some of these Commissioners still work within the Registry today.[26]

Protocol 11 marked a transitional phase in the ECtHR's history. The Court had to navigate its new role while herding member states with vastly different judicial systems and levels of democratic experience toward common conceptions of the rule of law. Protocol 11 was ultimately insufficient to alleviate the stressors of the Court's rapid growth. The number of annual judgments issued by the Court continued to grow rapidly. It became clear that additional reforms of the Court's case-processing apparatus were necessary in order to sustain the institution.[27] The November 2000 European Ministerial Conference on Human Rights adopted a resolution recognizing that the European system's effectiveness was in danger.[28] The conference called on the Committee of Ministers to initiate reforms and conduct an "in depth reflection . . . on the various possibilities and options with a view to ensuring the effectiveness of the Court in light of this new situation."[29]

At that time, it was commonly acknowledged that two areas of the Court's caseload posed particular challenges in terms of their sheer volume and demands on the Court's resources. First, a monumental number of applications were being declared inadmissible or otherwise terminated prior to the Court issuing a ruling on the merits. In the early 2000s, this category constituted over 90 percent of all applications.[30] Second, the Court was overburdened with processing individual applications arising from the same "structural cause" within a member state (for example, many individual applications alleging violations of the right to liberty due to systemic deficiencies in a country's judicial system resulting in prolonged pretrial detentions).[31] The CoE's rapidly expanding membership exacerbated case backlogs rooted in these issue areas.

The Committee of Ministers worked urgently to devise reforms that could lighten the Court's caseload without limiting the right to individual petition or compromising the quality of the Court's admissibility decisions. The CoM identified three issue areas of particular consequence for the success of the reform project: (1) "preventing violations at the national level and improving domestic remedies," (2) "optimizing the effectiveness of filtering and subsequent processing of applications," and (3) "improving and accelerating the execution of the Court's judgements."[32] Centering these goals, Protocol 14 "amending the control system of the Convention" was adopted by the CoM and opened for signature in May 2004. The Protocol entered into force in May 2010 following the requisite ratification by all CoE member states.[33]

In January 2004, the Parliamentary Assembly had adopted a resolution advocating for adjustments to judicial term limits and other professional and security arrangements for judges, citing concerns about judicial independence.[34] Protocol 14 addressed these concerns in part by restoring nine-year judge terms and eliminating the ability for judges to be reelected. The introduction of nonrenewable judge terms was explicitly intended to reinforce judges' "independence and impartiality."[35] With the exception of this structural change, the Protocol 14 reforms were primarily procedural. Several changes were implemented to enhance the efficiency of the ECtHR's filtering and processing of applications. For example, Protocol 14 provided that a single judge could declare an application inadmissible.[36] Inadmissibility decisions rendered by single judges are not published on HUDOC, the Court's official database, or made publicly available in any form. Prior to Protocol 14, an inadmissibility decision required the agreement of a committee of a minimum of three judges. Protocol 14 empowered these three-judge committees to rule not only on the admissibility of applications but also on their merits when the application represented a "repetitive case." An application could be categorized as such when the underlying legal question it posed was already the subject of well-established case law.[37]

In addition to altering the process by which cases could be deemed admissible, Protocol 14 added a new admissibility requirement to the Convention. This requirement allows the Court to declare inadmissible any application where it considers that the applicant "has not suffered a significant disadvantage."[38] The introduction of the "significant disadvantage" criterion was intended to accelerate case processing and facilitate the timely issuance of judgments.[39] Because of the unavailability of data on inadmissibility decisions rendered by single judges, it is not clear precisely to what extent the significant disadvantage criterion allowed the Court to lighten its caseload. However, at least one scholarly analysis has found evidence of an increase in the rate of petitions being declared inadmissible following the implementation of the criterion.[40]

Regarding the objective to lighten the Court's caseload by preventing violations and strengthening domestic remedies, Protocol 14 fell decidedly short. During negotiations to draft the Protocol, it was at one point suggested that the Court should be granted competence to issue advisory opinions to clarify interpretation of the Convention and its domestic application. For reasons that are unclear, this proposal was rejected on the grounds that it "might interfere with the contentious jurisdiction of the Court."[41] Protocol 14 did attempt to raise the stakes of noncompliance with Court judgments. The Protocol amended the Convention to allow the Committee of Ministers to bring "infringement" proceedings before the Grand Chamber against any member state that has refused to comply with an ECtHR judgment.[42] In practice, however, this provision has had little impact, owing to lack of utilization. The CoM did not make use of the provision until 2018, when it initiated infringement proceedings against Azerbaijan in the *Khadija Ismayilova* case.[43] To date, the CoM has initiated infringement proceedings in only one other case, that of Osman Kavala, a Turkish political prisoner. In July 2022, the ECtHR ruled that Turkey had failed to comply with a previous judgment ordering the release of Mr. Kavala. As of this writing, Kavala is still imprisoned.

There is evidence that the Protocol 14 reforms helped the ECtHR rein in its unmanageable caseload. The annual number of judgments issued by the Court dropped precipitously after 2010 before leveling out in recent years:

What remains less clear, and what this analysis attempts to investigate, is whether these reforms altered the ECtHR's interpretation of its fundamental social purpose and, in turn, the legitimate reach of the Court's authority. In other words, did the Court's expanding membership and the imperative for efficiency force the ECtHR into a position where judges had to reinterpret the Court's social purpose? Or has the ECtHR's founding interpretation of its mandate remained predominant in judges' exercise of their authority, even as the Court needed to find a way to weed out more cases than ever before? As I analyze the historical

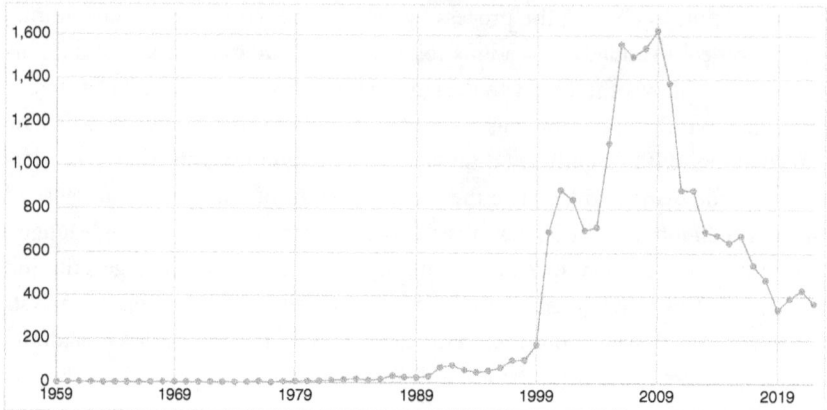

FIGURE 1.2. ECtHR judgments per year (Chambers and Grand Chamber), 1959–2022

evolution of the Court's case law, I investigate whether major reforms have pushed the Court toward more deferential or interventionist behavior.

In order to examine if a deferential IC responds to member state backlash by constraining its exercise of judicial authority, I examine the evolution of the ECtHR's case law around the time of the Brighton Declaration. This declaration was adopted by all CoE member states at a 2012 High Level Conference. Brighton represented an unprecedented level of coordinated pushback against the ECtHR by CoE members. The United Kingdom was a primary instigator. Widespread discontent with certain ECtHR judgments motivated some British politicians, as well as the press, to publicly denounce the power of the "meddling Court" and call for reform.[44] Support for the British agenda spread to other CoE members states, where politicians as well as some national bar associations criticized the ECtHR's alleged overreach into domestic jurisdictions. Bolstering these criticisms were persistent concerns that the ECtHR was still unable to fairly and efficiently process its caseload. The UK took advantage of its 2012 presidency of the Committee of Ministers to capitalize on growing anti-ECtHR sentiment, launching an initiative to "renationalize" some of the Court's power. This initiative, which culminated in the Brighton Declaration, sought to "re-legitimize" the ECtHR by demanding improvements in the quality of both the Court's judgments and its judges.[45]

A central objective of Brighton was to recalibrate the balance of power between the Court and national authorities. Some member states felt that the Court, at that point over a decade into the reform project that began in 1998, had drifted away from its historical commitment that national authorities espoused primary authority for implementing the Convention's guarantees. This challenge to the Court's authority marked a "turning point" where "the reform process shifted from technical tinkering to enhance efficiency, to a full-blown challenge to the very legitimacy and role of the ECtHR in European human rights protection."[46] Brighton called on the Court to lean more heavily on the principle of subsidiarity and the margin of appreciation doctrine. Specifically, the Declaration requested that the margin of appreciation, a previously unwritten doctrine, be formally codified within the Preamble of the European Convention.[47]

This recalibration of power has had observable effects. Mikael Madsen finds that Court judges began to more frequently reference the MOA doctrine following Brighton,[48] with the result of particular deference toward the Court's more senior, liberal democratic member states. This finding, especially in light of Stiansen and Voeten's study providing evidence that ECtHR judges are more inclined to grant deference to liberal democracies who criticize the Court, points to how the regime types represented among an IC's membership might critically influence how that court responds to backlash.[49]

Brighton also pushed several policy recommendations for enhancing the ECtHR's efficiency and legitimacy in the eyes of member states. The Declaration took aim at the quality of the ECtHR's judgments as well as the judges themselves: "The authority and credibility of the court depend in large part on the quality of its judges and the judgements they deliver."[50] To that end, the Declaration advocated for improved guidelines for selecting judges at the national level and called for a reassessment of the judicial election procedure.[51] The Declaration bluntly asserted that "judgements of the court need to be clear and consistent . . . it helps national courts apply the Convention more precisely, and helps potential applicants assess whether they have a well-founded application."[52] The implication here is clearly that member states were frustrated with perceived arbitrary reasoning in the ECtHR's judgments. Brighton represented a push for increased transparency from the ECtHR so that national courts could more effectively enforce the Convention on their own. This would shift the balance of power for enforcing the Convention "back" to the member states. Cementing the role of national courts as the primary enforcers of the Convention would respect the ECtHR's founding commitment to subsidiarity and, ideally, enhance the efficiency of the ECtHR by limiting the number of cases that rose to the level of international adjudication.

Discussion of the ECtHR's case law here focuses on the periods before and after Protocols 11 and 14, as well as the Brighton Declaration. However, other periods of tension are also evaluated, including the recent withdrawal of Russia from the CoE amid President Vladmir Putin's ongoing invasion of Ukraine. Each juncture gives an opportunity to investigate how an IC founded on a deferential interpretation of its authority responds to domestic pushback as well as opportunities for reinvention.

THE INTER-AMERICAN COURT OF HUMAN RIGHTS

To evaluate the conditions under which interpretations of judicial authority evolve in interventionist courts, I focus my analysis of the IACtHR's case law on periods during which the Court (1) underwent procedural reforms that altered its case-processing procedures, (2) faced significant increases in its caseload, and (3) experienced backlash from member states. These periods include the 2001 overhaul of the IACtHR's Rules of Procedure, the rapid post-2017 increase in the Court's annual output, and a handful of incidents that resulted in particular member states withdrawing or threatening to withdraw from the Court's jurisdiction.

The Inter-American system faced a crisis of efficiency in the late 1990s. Lacking clear boundaries between the Inter-American Commission and the IACtHR, cases languished in the processing stages. In 2000 the OAS General Assembly called for reform, emphasizing the need for greater cooperation between the IACtHR and domestic authorities.[53] The Commission and Court responded by adopting new Rules of Procedure that entered into force in 2001. Prior to the new Rules, the Commission's admissibility decision procedures were not formally codified. The Commission also exercised significant discretion regarding whether to forward a case to the IACtHR. The new Rules introduced standardized admissibility procedures and criteria for case forwarding to the IACtHR that limited the discretion of the Commission.[54] The Rules also provided for an increase in victims' participation in hearings before the Court. As a result of these reforms, the IACtHR's workload increased. The dynamics of the Court's public hearings shifted, as victims took a more visible and involved role in presenting their cases to IACtHR judges.[55] In order to assess the impact of these procedural changes on the IACtHR's interpretation of its jurisdiction, I allocate specific focus to the IACtHR's case law between 2002 and 2005 in the following chapters.

The IACtHR's annual rate of judgments has grown considerably in recent years, though it has never approached the ECtHR's numbers. The IACtHR has always been a much smaller court than the ECtHR. The IACtHR has less than half the number of member states (twenty compared to the ECtHR's forty-six), and its budget and staffing numbers are only a small fraction of the ECtHR's in any given year. Still, the IACtHR's output appears to be set in an upward trajectory since 2017. As seen in figure 1.3, the IACtHR released its highest-ever annual number of judgments in 2022.

The IACtHR's workload will likely continue to expand, putting pressure on the chronically underfunded Court. I devote particular attention to the level of deference that the Court has afforded to governments in the post-2017 period.

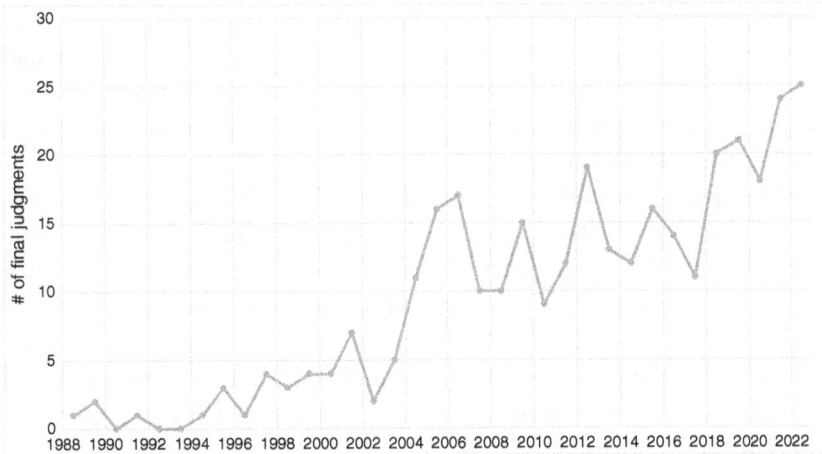

FIGURE 1.3. IACTHR FINAL JUDGMENTS PER YEAR

Note: Graph includes final judgments on contentious cases only. If the merits and reparations in a case were ruled on separately, only the merits judgment is counted to avoid double-counting.

Analysis of this most recent era of the IACtHR's history provides insight into the durability of the Court's founding interpretation of its authority amid rising caseloads.

While episodes of backlash against the ECtHR have historically entailed coordinated efforts among member states, backlash against the IACtHR has occurred on a relatively more state-specific basis. The most severe episodes of backlash against the IACtHR have involved states withdrawing or threatening to withdraw from the Court's jurisdiction. Withdrawal has been a much rarer form of backlash in the ECtHR's experience. Russia periodically threatened to denounce the European Convention throughout the 2010s and was finally expelled from the CoE by means of a March 2022 Parliamentary Assembly vote in response to Russia's invasion of Ukraine. Concomitant to the expulsion proceedings, Russia submitted withdrawal instruments, making it the only state to ever withdraw from the ECtHR. On the other hand, four states have either withdrawn or attempted to withdraw from the IACtHR: Trinidad and Tobago, Peru, the Dominican Republic, and Venezuela.

A state's withdrawal from an IC in response to a particular ruling or set of rulings sends a clear message that the court has overstepped its authority. ICs must constantly balance their judicial mandate with the political reality that rulings against a state may spur withdrawal or otherwise deteriorating relations between the court and member governments. But while withdrawal from an IC in any circumstance indicates a rebuke of that court's legitimacy, we might not expect every instance of withdrawal to prompt a court to rethink the boundaries of its authority. For example, if a state's reason for withdrawal is based on IC rulings that involve issues specific to that state, and these rulings thus do not invoke similar ire from other member states, an IC is unlikely to be sufficiently concerned to reinterpret its mandate.

Of the four instances of withdrawal or attempted withdrawal from the IACtHR, two represent such individualized circumstances: Trinidad and Tobago's 1999 denunciation of the American Convention in response to the IACtHR attempting to restrict the application of the death penalty in that country, and faltering dictator Alberto Fujimori's attempt to withdraw Peru in 1999 following a series of IACtHR rulings that condemned his regime. After Fujimori fled the county in 2000, the transitional democratic regime quickly rejoined the IACtHR and largely cooperated with the Court's handling of cases involving Fujimori-era rights violations.[56]

Two other instances of withdrawal from the IACtHR involve broader concerns regarding the Court infringing on national sovereignty. These episodes provide opportunities to evaluate whether and to what extent member state backlash has driven the Court to reevaluate its interpretation of its authority. First, Venezuela denounced the American Convention and withdrew from the IACtHR in 2012. Venezuela had been a frequent target of scrutiny from the Court throughout Hugo Chávez's regime, which was characterized by systemic violations of Venezuelans' civil and political rights and executive interference in the judiciary. In 2008, the IACtHR determined in *Apitz v. Venezuela* that three Venezuelan judges had been improperly removed from their positions on an appellate court, in violation of the American Convention's right to a fair trial and other due process guarantees. The IACtHR ordered Venezuela to pay reparations to these judges and reinstate them to their positions. The Venezuelan Supreme Court responded to *Apitz* by ruling that the IACtHR's judgment violated domestic constitutional law and sovereignty and thus that it could not be executed. The Supreme Court went so far as to call on Chávez to denounce the American Convention in its ruling. This was an extraordinary step displaying the corruption that had permeated the highest levels of the Venezuelan judiciary.[57]

Venezuelan criticism of the Inter-American human rights system intensified in the years following the *Apitz* ordeal. Launching broader opposition to the OAS, Chávez leveraged arguments that the Commission and Court had overstepped their authority.[58] Following additional IACtHR rulings against Venezuela, including a 2011 case where Venezuela was found to have violated opposition leader Leopoldo López's right to political participation, Venezuela finally denounced the American Convention in 2012. Venezuela withdrew from the OAS entirely in 2017.

A key aspect of this instance of withdrawal is that Venezuelan authorities framed their criticism of the IACtHR as generalized concern about the Court's legitimate authority rather than specific critiques of the Court's reasoning in particular cases. National politicians and judges repeatedly accused the IACtHR of subverting the principle of subsidiarity and positioning itself as a "fourth instance" court in contravention of international legal norms.[59] This condemnation of the IACtHR is evidence of the Court's power in the region as well as, perhaps, the precarity of its interventionism. As Alexandra Huneeus, a scholar of the Inter-American system, has commented, "That Chávez would go to the trouble of formally exiting suggests that the Court and Commission began to have bite. But it also suggests that they misjudged how far they could push states without backlash."[60]

Second, the Dominican Republic's attempted withdrawal from the IACtHR in 2014 directly challenged the legitimacy of the Court. This conflict stemmed from a series of cases involving the Dominican government's discriminatory treatment of Haitian migrants and their Dominican-born children. Tensions between the IACtHR and the Dominican government came to a head after the Court's 2014 ruling on the *Expelled Dominicans and Haitians v. Dominican Republic* case. The Court ruled that the ongoing deportation of Haitian migrants constituted racial profiling and violated due process guarantees. The ruling also condemned a Dominican Constitutional Court decision that had retracted the citizenship of thousands of Dominican-born people of Haitian descent. The IACtHR determined that these actions violated the American Convention's obligation to prevent statelessness.

Just two months after the *Expelled Dominicans and Haitians* ruling, the Dominican Constitutional Court ruled that the state's recognition of the IACtHR's contentious jurisdiction had never received proper congressional approval. Thus, the IACtHR did not possess jurisdiction over the Dominican Republic. Dissenting judges in the Constitutional Court argued that the ruling was a political reaction to *Expelled Dominicans and Haitians*.[61] The Inter-American Commission, the UN Human Rights Committee, the UN Committee on Economic, Social, and Cultural Rights, and the UN Committee on the Rights of the Child all issued statements in response, which ranged from expressing concern to outright condemning the Constitutional Court ruling.[62] Nevertheless, the Dominican president and other high-ranking politicians threw their support behind the ruling and publicly rejected the constitutionality of the instrument of recognition. This development ignited broader criticism of the IACtHR among Dominican authorities, who claimed that the Court and Commission had engaged in illegitimate power-grabbing behavior.

A central element of the Dominicans' criticisms was that the Commission and Court were due to be reformed because they were founded during a bygone era when authoritarianism dominated the region. In this spirit, the Dominican foreign minister called for the Inter-American system to be "revised and redesigned" because "times change."[63] The Dominican government stopped cooperating with the IACtHR and has since declined to send representatives to hearings. The IACtHR, for its part, has issued multiple resolutions maintaining its jurisdiction over the Dominican Republic and continues to process cases against the state. The government has not complied with any IACtHR rulings since 2014. The relationship between the Dominican Republic and the IACtHR thus remains in a strange state of limbo, with Dominican authorities claiming to have withdrawn (or to have never joined the Court in the first place), while the IACtHR continues to claim jurisdiction to rule on cases against the government. This fact alone is evidence that the IACtHR is not inclined to tamp down its interpretation of its authority in the face of political backlash.

The Dominican Republic's (attempted) withdrawal is significant because, even though it stemmed from a specific dispute regarding racial discrimination, it ballooned into a broader conflict challenging the institutional legitimacy of the IACtHR. Dominican authorities' calls for the IACtHR to be "redesigned" in light of the region's modern democratization suggests that while governments might put up with a regional court wielding heavy-handed authority during times of mass state-sponsored violence, continuing to intrude in domestic affairs post-democratization may not be acceptable. Likewise, the IACtHR's insistence on denying the Dominican Republic's withdrawal indicates that a court that becomes accustomed to enjoying a certain level of authority during a time of crisis will not cede that authority easily, even when conditions improve. Evaluating the IACtHR's case law in the period following this contentious interlude provides an opportunity to observe how an interventionist court in an evolving geopolitical landscape responds to accusations of judicial overreach.

I focus on the IACtHR's case law over the 2012–2020 period to get a sense of how these two challenges for the Court (threats of state withdrawal and a rising caseload) may have impacted the IACtHR's interpretation of its authority. One might reasonably expect the dual pressures of a ballooning case backlog and domestic political backlash to push an international court to reevaluate its status quo. Because the IACtHR has faced its largest annual caseloads and the most vociferous state backlash in its history within roughly the same span of years, it is difficult to separate out the impacts of these two challenges on the Court's jurisprudence. One might expect that scaled-back interpretations of an IC's authority stemming from concerns about case overload would manifest most clearly in the admissibility stage. At this stage, the court has the power to weed out cases or specific allegations within cases. Yet if political backlash pushes a court to afford greater deference to governments, this is more likely to be visible in the merits and reparations stages. Observing indicators of deference across the admissibility stage compared to the reparations and merits stages during the 2012–2020 period can help shed light on whether the IACtHR has reinterpreted its mandate due to an increasing caseload and/or member state backlash.

THE AFRICAN COURT ON HUMAN AND PEOPLES' RIGHTS

Although the ACtHPR is young, its judicial output in its first decade has outpaced that of the ECtHR and IACtHR in their respective first decades of operation. The Court has experienced an exponential rise in case output since 2016 and issued its highest-ever annual number of judgments in 2022.

While this growth is encouraging, the Court has faced serious setbacks in recent years. Since 2016, four states (Rwanda, Tanzania, Côte d'Ivoire, and Benin) have withdrawn their declarations permitting individuals and NGOs to submit petitions directly to the Court. These withdrawals are particularly concerning given the small number of states that have accepted the right of individual access to the ACtHPR. Prior to Rwanda's withdrawal in 2016, nine AU member states had submitted declarations permitting individuals and NGOs direct access to the ACtHPR. Three states (the Gambia, Guinea-Bissau, and Niger) have submitted

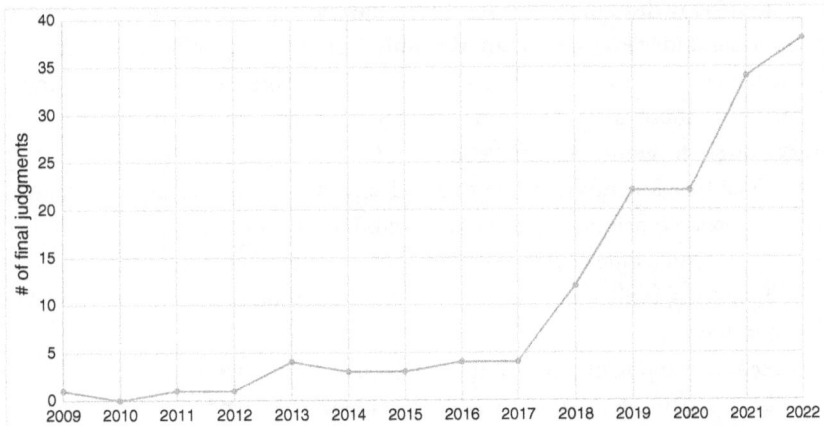

FIGURE 1.4. ACtHPR final judgments per year

Note: This figure includes all decisions on admissibility, merits, and reparations that are considered "final." For example, if the merits judgment in a case occurred in 2017 and the reparations judgment on that same case occurred in 2018, only the judgment in 2018 is included in this graph. This is so that cases that are decided over multiple phases are not double-counted.

such declarations since 2018. Still, even with those accessions, nationals of only eight AU member states have direct access to the Court as of this writing.

Rwanda was the first state to withdraw individual access to the ACtHPR. This withdrawal was a direct response to Court proceedings against Rwanda in a freedom of expression dispute. Freedom of expression was also at the crux of Benin's 2020 withdrawal of individual access to the Court. (Discussion of Rwanda and Benin's withdrawals is reserved for chapter 4 for the sake of properly contextualizing those disputes.) In the years following Rwanda's withdrawal, the ACtHPR has faced a concerning wave of resistance from other member states. In 2019, Tanzania became the second state to withdraw its declaration permitting individuals and NGOs to access the Court. This backlash from Tanzania is particularly alarming because the ACtHPR is headquartered in that country. The Tanzanian withdrawal seems to stem from more generalized discontent with the Court's authority rather than a dispute over particular cases. At the time of the withdrawal, Tanzania, out of all member states, had the highest number of cases filed by individuals and NGOs, as well as judgments issued against it by the ACtHPR. Additionally, the ACtHPR had recently issued a major ruling against Tanzania declaring that mandatory death penalty provisions in the country's penal code violated the right to life and fair trial guarantees.[64] An ACtHPR lawyer I interviewed explicitly identified the deluge of cases against Tanzania as being a critical factor motivating the country's withdrawal, stating that the Tanzanian government was experiencing "litigation fatigue."[65]

Tanzania's withdrawal unfolded within the context of increasing democratic backsliding under President John Magufuli. Notably, Magufuli's administration implemented a series of draconian laws restricting media freedom. The most notorious of these laws, the Media Services Act, gave some state agencies arbitrary powers to grant and revoke licenses for news outlets and journalists.[66] It is possible that Magufuli's desire to avoid scrutiny for increasing state control over the press contributed to Tanzania's withdrawal. Tanzania's minister for foreign affairs, Augustine Mahiga, offered only a vague statement that the declaration permitting individual access to the ACtHPR was "contrary" to Tanzania's Constitution.[67]

Recent developments suggest that Tanzania's dispute with the ACtHPR may have been specific to Magufuli's administration, which ended when the president died in March 2021 (possibly of COVID-19). Current president Samia Suluhu Hassan appears invested in reengaging with the Court. In fact, the new Tanzanian administration seems to be unclear as to whether the country ever actually withdrew from the ACtHPR. Magufuli's administration had deposited a withdrawal instrument with the African Union in November 2019, and the withdrawal officially took effect one year later. However, in May 2021, Tanzania's new foreign minister, Liberata Mulamula, issued a contradictory statement: "We have not withdrawn from the [ACtHPR], that is why Tanzania is still the headquarters of the court. We cannot withdraw and then at the same time still host the court's headquarters." Mulamula elaborated that Tanzania's intention in critiquing the ACtHPR was to encourage citizens to utilize domestic mechanisms of legal recourse: "We have not withdrawn from that court. But what we are saying is that let us start with our courts. If that doesn't work, then we can proceed to the African Court."[68] Given that exhaustion of domestic remedies is already a requirement for citizens to petition the ACtHPR, it is not entirely clear what changes to the Court's standard practice the Tanzanian government would like to see. As of this writing, Tanzania's withdrawal of individual access to the Court remains in place. However, in June 2023, the ACtHPR announced that the government of Tanzania had agreed to contribute public land and nearly US$4 million toward constructing a new permanent headquarters for the Court in Arusha. At least for now, it appears that relations between the ACtHPR and Tanzania are thawing quickly.[69] Two ACtHPR judges I interviewed indicated that there are ongoing discussions between Court officials and high-level government ministers regarding Tanzania potentially reinstating individual access to the Court.[70]

Further limiting the reach of the ACtHPR's jurisdiction, Côte d'Ivoire and Benin announced in 2020 the withdrawals of their declarations permitting individual and NGO access to the Court. Côte d'Ivoire's withdrawal announcement swiftly followed an ACtHPR provisional measures judgment that ordered the government to suspend an arrest warrant for a former rebel leader who was running for president.[71] In a statement to local media outlets, Foreign Minister Ally Coulibaly accused the ACtHPR of rendering a "political decision" in that judgment and implied that the ACtHPR had disrespected the competence of national courts: "We have well-functioning courts. Our justice is impartial. We cannot accept that our jurisdictions are weakened because of this adherence to this protocol of recognition of jurisdiction."[72] The government's withdrawal announcement further emphasized concerns about the ACtHPR overstepping its authority. Sidi Tiemoko Touré, the Ivorian minister of communication, said of the withdrawal decision, "We respect our international commitments, but we also appreciate our sovereignty." He went on to claim that recent ACtHPR decisions were "likely to cause serious disruption to the legal order . . . and undermine the foundations of the rule of law by creating genuine legal insecurity."[73] Côte d'Ivoire's retraction of individual access to the ACtHPR marked a clear signal that the Court had pushed the boundaries of its jurisdiction further than the government deemed legitimate.

For the ACtHPR, still a young institution with a small membership, the stakes are particularly high. The Court is empowered by an expansive written mandate, but implementing that mandate with too heavy a hand could jeopardize the Court's future just as it is getting off the ground. This work's discussion of ACtHPR case law seeks to assess whether and how ACtHPR judges have responded to compounding critiques of judicial overreach in recent years.

Table 1.1. Hypotheses and temporal foci of analysis, summarized

Under what conditions do ICs' founding interpretations of their authority change?

Hypotheses

H1: If a regional court has a "deferential" interpretation of its authority, we should expect the court to respond to member state backlash by further constraining its interpretation of its authority to align with vocalized state preferences. We should not expect an "interventionist" court to be similarly responsive to state backlash.

H2: As inter-court interaction increases between deferential and interventionist courts, a given court might be more receptive to emulating another court's interpretation of its authority within areas of case law in which that other court has more experience.

H3: Changes in the types of rights violations that dominate a court's docket can prompt the court to reinterpret the extent of its authority.

Alternative hypothesis: If an IC's interpretation of the extent of its authority is primarily driven by logistical constraints, rather than founding social purpose, shifts toward more or less interventionist or deferential behavior will occur around the same time periods in which (1) the IC is facing an overwhelming docket, (2) the IC has admitted new member states, and/or (3) the IC has recently undergone institutional reforms oriented toward making it more efficient.

Temporal foci of analysis

ECtHR	• 1990–2003 (new wave of Eastern European accessions and institutional restructuring)
	• 2010–2015 (case backlog crisis, new case-processing reforms, unprecedented member state criticism)
IACtHR	• 2002–2005 (institutional reforms that limited the role of the Commission in case processing and increased the role of victim participation in Court hearings)
	• 2012–2020 (period of withdrawals and attempted withdrawals amid growing caseload)
ACtHPR	• 2016–2022 (rapidly increasing usage of the Court and four withdrawals)

Appendix to Chapter 1

Table A.1. If an IC has a "**deferential**" interpretation of its authority, we should expect to observe the following indicators/behaviors in the admissibility, merits, and remedial stages of case processing:

CASE ADMISSIBILITY STAGE	MERITS STAGE	REMEDIAL STAGE
• Narrow interpretation of *ratione temporis* (temporal jurisdiction) Example: The court decides that ongoing effects of an alleged human rights violation that originated prior to the accused state's accession to the court do not bring that alleged violation into the court's temporal jurisdiction. Consequently, the application alleging this ongoing rights violation is declared inadmissible.	• Applies margin of appreciation doctrine / strongly emphasizes subsidiarity The margin of appreciation doctrine (MOA) is used by international courts to determine the extent to which member states should be granted discretion to implement their international legal obligations as those state deem appropriate within their unique domestic contexts. "Subsidiarity" refers to a legal principle that mandates that disputes should be resolved at the judicial level that is most proximate to where the dispute occurred. MOA example: An IC cites the MOA to support its decision not to rule that an accused state has violated an applicant's rights. The IC argues that because there is not broad consensus across the IC's member states regarding whether the accused state's actions constitute a violation of the rights provision in question, the IC will assume that the state is in compliance with international law. Subsidiarity example: An IC judge cites the principle of subsidiarity to argue that member state governments, and not the IC, should be primarily responsible for deciding how to implement appropriate remedies for established human rights violations.	• Limited reparations mandates focusing on individual measures Example: The court orders a member state government that committed a rights violation to financially compensate the injured party but does not order the government to implement measures of nonrepetition to prevent the state from committing similar violations in the future.

(Continued)

TABLE A.1 Continued

CASE ADMISSIBILITY STAGE	MERITS STAGE	REMEDIAL STAGE
• Strict interpretation of procedural admissibility criteria Example: The court does not make exceptions to the rule that applicants must exhaust domestic remedies for their complaint before petitioning the court, even when applicants allege prohibitive circumstances to applying for domestic remedies.	• Routinely selects to rule only on the core allegations in a petition, not all allegations Example: An applicant alleges that a state violated a long list of rights provisions, but the court elects to rule only on the merits of a few of those alleged violations. • Employs evidentiary standards that allocate the burden of proof to the applicant and resists shifting that burden to the state Maintains that the burden of proof lies with the applicant, in line with standard domestic judicial practice that allocates the burden of proof to plaintiffs. Adheres to this allocation of the burden of proof even in cases of grave human rights violations, for example alleged personal integrity rights violations. A particularly strong example of deferential behavior in this area would be if an applicant alleges a violation whose occurrence can only be substantiated by evidence to which the state has exclusive access, the state refuses to furnish that evidence, and the IC rules against the applicant on the grounds that their claim has not been substantiated.	• Cannot mandate the abrogation of domestic legislation Example: The IC does not have the power to order that states repeal domestic legislation that the IC perceives to contradict the state's international legal obligations. • Enforcement of remedies and assessments of state compliance with judgments are delegated to a political body Example: The IC rules that a violation has occurred, but defers the decision about how to remedy that violation to other domestic or international political actors. In the European system, this political actor is the Committee of Ministers.

Table A.2. If an IC has an "**interventionist**" interpretation of its authority, we should expect to observe the following indicators/behaviors in the admissibility, merits, and remedial stages of case processing:

CASE ADMISSIBILITY STAGE	MERITS STAGE	REMEDIAL STAGE
• Use of *iura novit cura* to add allegations to submitted petitions (Dinah Shelton [2015] calls this the "kitchen sink approach" to constructing a case file). Example: An applicant alleges that the state violated her right to freedom of expression. After examination of the facts contained in the applicant's petition, the case lawyers observe that the applicant's right to family life may have also been violated during the complained-of state action. Consequently, the lawyers add an allegation to the applicant's petition requesting that the court also examine a potential violation of the applicant's right to family life, even though the applicant only alleged a violation of her freedom of expression in her petition.	• Does not apply / rejects application of a margin of appreciation doctrine Example: The IC does not take into account existing member state government consensus regarding the compatibility of a complained-of practice with international law when ruling on whether that practice constitutes a human rights violation.	• Broad reparations mandates focusing on individual as well as societal measures, often requiring action by multiple state actors Example: The court orders a member state government that committed a rights violation to financially compensate the injured party, amend domestic legislation to prevent reoccurrence of the violation, and reopen closed domestic investigations into similar alleged crimes.
• Broad interpretation of *ratione temporis* Example: The court decides that ongoing effects of an alleged human rights violation that originated prior to the accused state's accession to the court bring that alleged violation into the court's temporal jurisdiction. Consequently, the application alleging this ongoing rights violation is declared admissible.	• Use of conventionality control doctrine The conventionality control doctrine is a legal approach applied by ICs that requires domestic judges to keep apprised of developments in the IC's case law and interpret domestic law in accordance with the IC's jurisprudence.	• Can mandate the abrogation of domestic legislation Example: If an IC rules that specific domestic legislation contradicts international law, the IC can consider that law, and its domestic effects, to be null and void.

(Continued)

48   **CHAPTER 1**

TABLE A.2 Continued

CASE ADMISSIBILITY STAGE	MERITS STAGE	REMEDIAL STAGE
	Example: An IC rules that a member state's ban on in vitro fertilization has violated an applicant's right to family life. Applying the conventionality control doctrine, the IC expects all member states to repeal any similar bans on in vitro fertilization to comply with this new development in the IC's case law. If states fail to do so, the IC can find them in violation of the right to family life.	
· Flexible interpretation of procedural admissibility criteria Example: The court routinely makes exceptions to the rule that applicants must exhaust domestic remedies for their complaint before petitioning the court when the applicant alleges prohibitive circumstances to applying for domestic remedies.	· Routinely rules on most/all allegations in a petition Example: An applicant alleges a violation of the prohibition against torture. Case lawyers add allegations that the state also violated the applicant's right to privacy and freedom from ex post facto laws in connection with the alleged torture. The IC rules on the merits of all three of these allegations, even though the torture allegation was the core issue in the case. Another example is the routine use of the legal principle *iura novit curia*, "the court knows the law," to rule on violations that were not initially alleged by the applicant's legal team.	· Court is responsible for assessing state compliance with its own judgments Example: The IC holds compliance hearings after the conclusion of a case to assess the extent to which member states found guilty of violations have complied with the IC's remedial mandates. The IC can respond to noncompliance by ordering additional remedial mandates.

CASE ADMISSIBILITY STAGE	MERITS STAGE	REMEDIAL STAGE
	· Is routinely willing to adjust evidentiary standards to shift the burden of proof to the state Example: If an applicant makes a claim that can only be substantiated by evidence that the applicant does not have access to, the IC will shift the burden of proof to the state to prove that the alleged violations did not occur. In the event that the state refuses to furnish contradictory evidence, the IC will rule in favor of the applicant.	

FOUNDING MOMENTS OF THE REGIONAL HUMAN RIGHTS COURTS

The geopolitical contexts in which international courts are founded fundamentally condition how those courts come to perceive their social purpose. The level of democratization among a court's founding member states, the relative involvement of legal bureaucrats compared to political advisers in designing the court, and the types of substantive issues that emerge in the court's early case law all influence how judges interpret the sources of their court's legitimacy. These interpretations guide when, and to what extent, that court exerts authority over member governments while deciding which cases to admit for litigation, when to find governments in violation of international law, and how governments must address established violations. This chapter investigates the origins of each regional court's interpretation of its authority by examining each court's founding moments. For the purposes of this analysis, that period encompasses the time span from the first proposals for the creation of each court through the selection of the court's first judges.

The European Court of Human Rights: A Court to (Re)build Europe

The Council of Europe (CoE) was founded in 1949 to catalyze European integration.[1] The European Movement, a nongovernmental organization founded in 1947 to promote pan-European solidarity, played a leading role in designing the institutional framework of the CoE. The Movement sought to establish political organizations that could foster shared understandings of identity rooted in liberal democratic ideals, providing an ideological defense against encroachment from the East. In service of that mission, the CoE's first major endeavor was to draft an international convention to define and enforce shared standards for human rights protection among the Council's member states. The resultant treaty, the European Convention on Human Rights, was opened for signature in 1950 and entered into force in 1953.

The road to the Convention was marked by squabbles between state representatives suspicious of international governance and a small but vocal group of legal experts and integrationist visionaries with ambitions for a robust supranational human rights regime. The first draft of what would become the European Convention was written under the auspices of the European Movement by three primary authors: French lawyer and statesman Pierre-Henri Teitgen, British prosecutor Sir David Maxwell-Fyfe, and Belgian politician and legal academic Fernand Dehousse. These authors were assisted by a consultative committee composed primarily of British lawyers, led by John Harcourt Barrington.[2] This group proposed what became known as the European Movement Convention, which enumerated (but refrained from defining) eleven distinct rights protections.[3] The Convention sketched a two-level institutional framework for enforcing those rights, made up of a Commission and a Court of Human Rights. The proposed Commission would monitor domestic adherence to rights guarantees as well as accept complaints by citizens alleging state-sponsored rights violations. These complaints would subsequently be transferred to the Court if a friendly resolution could not be reached.[4]

The drafting committee submitted its proposed Convention to the Consultative Assembly of the CoE in the fall of 1949.[5] Animated by the rhetoric of Teitgen and Maxwell-Fyfe, who were Assembly members at the time, the Assembly directed "Recommendation 38" to the CoE's Committee of Ministers, endorsing the adoption of a European Convention on Human Rights.[6] Upon receipt of the recommendation, the ministers quickly squashed any delusions that a group of idealistic lawyers and functionally powerless Assembly members would dictate binding legal agreements to governments. The Committee, composed of the foreign affairs ministers of each CoE member state, resisted any proposals that could limit governments' authority to handle human rights issues. Public pressure and concern for the CoE's faltering international standing ultimately pushed the ministers to consider the Assembly's recommendations. But the Committee did not accept these recommendations outright and instead insisted on creating its own committee of legal experts to evaluate the potentiality of a European human rights convention.[7] It was during this expert committee's deliberations with government representatives in 1949–1950 that the European Convention as we know it today was created.

Fear of what lurked beyond the other side of the Iron Curtain pervaded government deliberations on drafting the European Convention, which was initially conceived as "a collective insurance policy against the relapse of democracies into dictatorships."[8] Aligned with the European Movement, most architects of the European Convention on Human Rights intended for the document to function primarily as a pact against totalitarianism. But some prominent founding fathers, notably Teitgen, envisioned a more expansive role for the Convention as a constitutional instrument with the potential to evolve into a "European Bill of Rights."[9] Teitgen and his supporters sought to equip the ECtHR with the institutional tools to fulfill that vision, including, importantly, the right of individuals to petition the Court. The right of individual petition was a fiercely contested issue among Convention drafters. Getting states to accept the individual petition mechanism was especially contentious in the 1950s, given the fact that several CoE members still maintained overseas colonies whose residents could potentially drag their colonizers in front of the Court for human rights abuses.[10]

Several governments argued that individual access to the Court was unnecessary, given the high level of existing human rights protections within Europe. Luzius Wildhaber, the first president of the ECtHR after its reformulation as a permanent court in 1998, has noted that during the 1950s and 1960s, "the most frequent justification given [for refusing to accept individual petition] was that the ratification of the Convention was only an act of pan-European solidarity anyway, as the individual state concerned did not in fact need an international control mechanism, because its national courts had long fulfilled the task of protecting human rights."[11] For founding drafters with broader goals of European integration, "pan-European solidarity" was more than a symbolic platitude. Giving individual citizens the right to petition the Court was essential for creating a European identity that would legitimate the broader integration project.[12] At the time, however, most CoE members prioritized state sovereignty. Accepting the jurisdiction of the ECtHR and the right to individual petition was made optional in the final draft of the Convention.

There are three takeaways from the debate over incorporating the right to individual petition that shed light on how the ECtHR developed its social purpose. First, everyone involved recognized the importance of establishing a shared sense of European identity based in liberal democratic values. By enforcing shared human rights guarantees, the ECtHR was designed to serve as an institutional catalyst of European integration. Second, CoE members prioritized deference to state sovereignty in the early years of the organization. Respect for sovereignty has facilitated collective decision-making processes within the CoE that are rooted in compromise and consensus. Third, the founding member states of the CoE felt that their domestic human rights

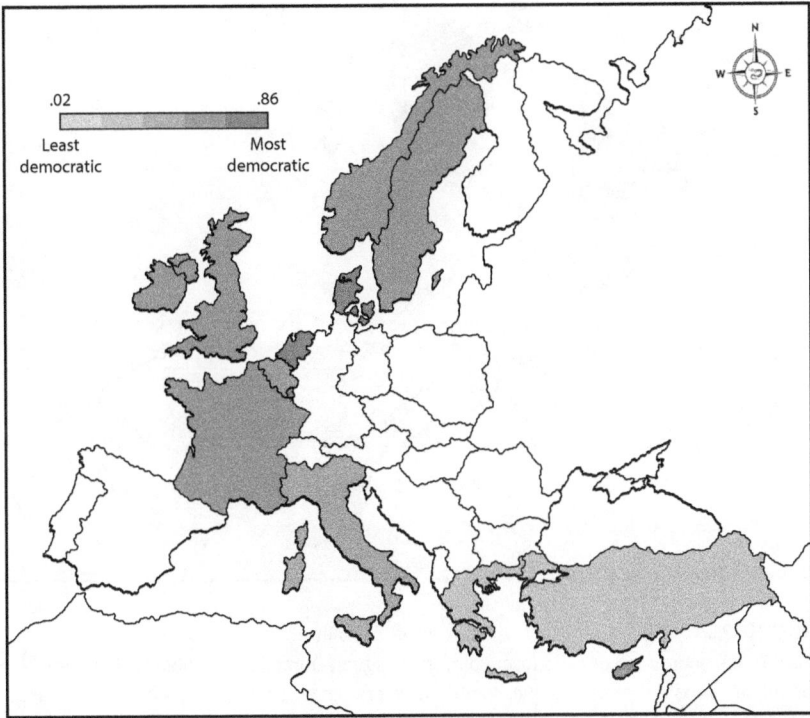

FIGURE 2.1. CoE member states liberal democracy scores, 1949

Note: "Liberal democracy" scores are measured by the Varieties of Democracy (V-Dem) liberal democracy index: (D) (v2x_libdem) (Coppedge et al. 2023). This variable is measured on an interval scale from low to high (0–1).

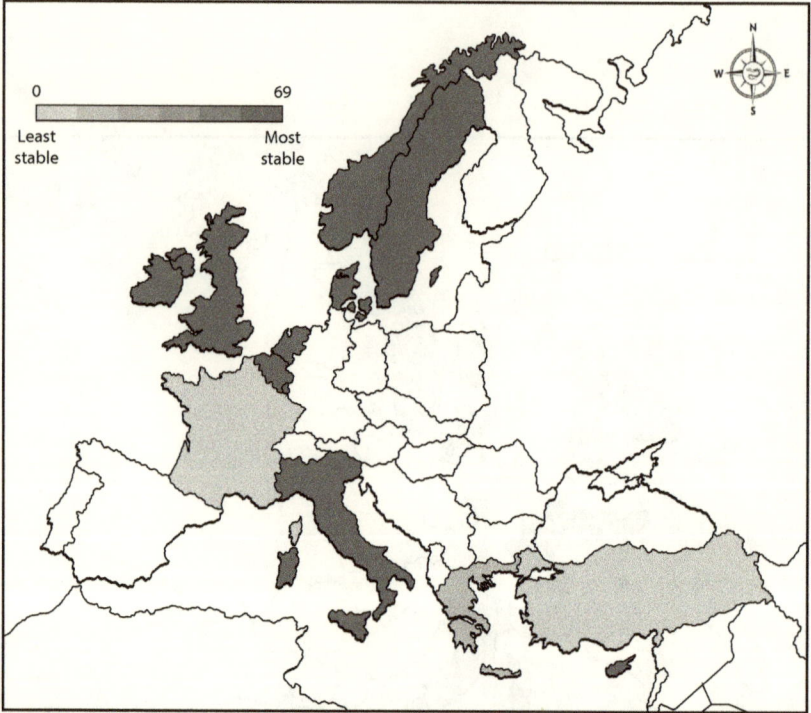

FIGURE 2.2. CoE member states regime stability scores, 1949

Note: These scores are derived from Polity V's "Regime Durability" variable (p_durable). This continuous variable measures the number of years since the most recent regime change. I used this variable to construct "regime stability" scores by counting the number of years between the organization founding year (in this case, the founding of the CoE in 1949) and the next regime change year as recorded in the Polity V "Regime Durability" dataset (Marshall and Gurr 2020). As the dataset ends in 2018, I also ended my count in 2018. The obvious outliers here are France, Greece, and Turkey. France's political stability score is low because of the May 1958 Algeria Crisis, which resulted in the end of the Fourth Republic and transition to the Fifth Republic. Greek democracy was overthrown in a military coup in 1967. Turkey experienced regime change for the first time post–CoE founding in 1960, when a military coup deposed and killed the democratically elected prime minister, Adnan Menderes.

protections were already largely satisfactory. Thus, the ECtHR's founders believed that most human rights issues in Europe would not necessitate supra-national intervention. The Court was conceived as a "safety valve" to deal with isolated human rights problems that might arise within member states, not to be a forum for addressing systemic rights violations.[13] The founders trusted that domestic judicial systems could uphold European rights standards, and anticipated that circumstances necessitating ECtHR litigation would be rare: "Doubts as to whether Europe needed a Court of Human Rights reflected a general view that the authorities in Western Europe had already proved them-selves to be 'the faithful trustees of the rights of man' . . . the chief merit of the Convention, therefore, was as a safety valve for when things went wrong" (Hersch Lauterpacht).[14] The ECtHR was designed to act as a partner to member governments and judiciaries that would respect their sovereignty while remain-ing available as an "insurance policy" to prevent democratic backsliding in dis-crete cases where these institutions failed.[15] The Court's founders espoused a high level of trust in domestic judiciaries and strove to legitimize the Court through demonstrated respect for state consent to jurisdiction. The low num-ber of cases admitted by the Court in its early years and the fact that the Court was not formally made into a permanent body until 1998 reflects this deference to domestic authorities.

This notion that the Court fulfills a subsidiary role relative to member states persists to the present day. Writing in 2018, the ECtHR president at the time, Robert Spano, reinvoked the "safety valve" concept when reflecting on the objec-tives of the Convention: "The Convention directly calls for a system of shared responsibilities and defined roles between the primary system of protection, the States Parties themselves, and the international system of adjudication at Stras-bourg which is subsidiary to primary protection, a safety valve. It is at the out-set for the State Party to decide whether a limitation of a Convention right is necessary in a democratic society, and not just in any democratic society, but specifically its own."[16] Spano's comments demonstrate the enduring legacy of the founders' belief in flexible relationships with state governments as the basis for an effective human rights regime.

The linchpin of this culture of cooperation is the ECtHR's embrace of the "margin of appreciation" (MOA) doctrine. The MOA guides the extent to which the Court will defer to a member state's authority regarding a complained-of practice. When the MOA is wide, "there is an initial presumption in favor of the defendant state; when narrow, a close scrutiny will be made."[17] The width of the margin applied depends on the level of consensus that the Court observes on a given issue among its member governments.[18] This consideration of existing practices when deciding how to apply the MOA reflects the ECtHR's respect for the competence of national judiciaries. These values are rooted in the founders' vision of the ECtHR as a mechanism for fostering a shared European identity: By defining what constitutes consensus among member states, the ECtHR articulates what it means to be "European."

Substantive Jurisdiction of the Court

The *travaux préparatoires* (which detail the conferences at which the Convention was negotiated) indicate that most debate among Convention drafters centered on specification and elaboration of the rights originally proposed by the European Movement. The final Convention draft codified thirteen distinct rights. These rights included ten of the original eleven rights proposed in the European Movement draft.[19] The wording of Article 13 guaranteeing the right to an effective remedy is particularly revealing of the limitations that the Convention's founders sought to impose on the authority of the ECtHR. The drafters first looked to the Universal Declaration of Human Rights (UDHR) for insight as to how to word Article 13. Article 8 of the UDHR states: "Everyone has the right to an effective remedy by the competent *national tribunals* for acts violating the fundamental rights granted to him by the constitution or by law." During negotiations to draft the European Convention, debate arose about whether it was necessary or practically advisable to guarantee citizens the right to an effective remedy before a national tribunal. Codifying such a right would imply that remedies must be *judicial*, in other words, dispensed through national courts rather than political or administrative institutions. While the *travaux* do not offer clear evidence of which delegates objected to adopting the UDHR's wording in Article 13, negotiation records indicate that some faction argued that it was simply not necessary to impel states to provide specific remedies to address rights violations. The form that these remedies should take would be best determined by the states themselves on a case-by-case basis.[20] This opinion reflects the pervasive attitude among drafting delegates that CoE member states already exhibited exemplary respect for human rights. Any potential for international micromanaging thus signified an unnecessary sacrifice of sovereignty. This disposition is reflected in remarks by a British delegate in discussions before the Consultative Assembly in September 1949: "Indeed, the remedies that we have are not remedies which take effect in any particular way. We have no jurisdiction to go into a particular country and rectify any injustices that have been done."[21] While the Consultative Assembly ultimately endorsed defining national tribunals as the source of effective remedies, this wording was altered during deliberations with the Committee of Ministers. The final wording of Article 13 established the right to an effective remedy "before a national authority," without stipulating that said authority be judicial.

Temporal Jurisdiction of the Court

Temporal jurisdiction (*ratione temporis*) refers to the time period during which an alleged action must have occurred in order for a court to be able to consider if that action breached a treaty obligation. Drawing from the Geneva General Act for the Settlement of Disputes, the European Convention drafters unanimously decided that applicants to the Commission of Human Rights must submit their petition within six months of the final domestic decision regarding their complaint.[22] The *travaux* contain no evidence that the drafters discussed the possibility that the Commission or Court would have to consider petitions alleging rights violations that originated prior to state accession.[23] Neither did they consider that ongoing violations across an extended period of time might complicate application of the six-month rule. This is not surprising. The nonretroactivity of treaties was already an established principle of international law in 1950.[24] The concept of "transitional justice" as a mechanism of recourse for human rights atrocities committed by previous regimes had only recently begun to emerge with the Nuremberg and Tokyo Trials of 1946. The Convention's founders did not design the European human rights institutions to impel states to grapple with lingering demons from their pasts.

In investigating the formulation of the ECtHR's temporal jurisdiction, it is helpful to recall that a central intended function of the Court was to foster states' collective commitment to the new European integration project. The European human rights system was designed to be forward-looking, constructing a new regional identity that would pave the way for a more secure and prosperous future following the trauma of the first half of the twentieth century. The ECtHR was designed to create a break with the past, not litigate it.

Remedial Authority

According to Article 50 of the original Convention text (now codified in Article 41 of the contemporary Convention), the ECtHR, upon establishment of a rights violation committed by a member state, is empowered to award "just satisfaction" to the injured party. "Just satisfaction" is a legal term, specific to the ECtHR's practice, which refers to the ability of the Court to award *financial* reparations to applicants. These awards may fall under one or more of three categories: pecuniary damages, nonpecuniary damages, and costs and expenses. The wording of Article 50 is rooted in the Court founders' commitment to subsidiarity—that "if the internal law of the [High Contracting] Party allows only partial reparation to be made for the consequences of this decision or measure, the decision of the Court shall, if necessary, afford just satisfaction to the injured party." Here, the Court is clearly positioned as a last-resort remedial entity, constraining the ability of the Court to take on a more intensive role in remedying human rights violations. Still, modern Court judges have exercised discretion in expanding the scope of Article 41, particularly with regard to developing the pilot judgment procedure, discussed later.

Execution of Judgments

The *travaux* indicate that Convention drafters were not particularly concerned about the potential for state noncompliance with the ECtHR. This disposition further reflects the basis of trust in national authorities that informed the design of the Court. As articulated in a pitch by European Movement delegates to the Committee of Ministers: "The success of the European Court of Human Rights, like that of the International Court of Justice at the Hague, will depend not *so much upon the powers it wields, as upon the moral prestige that it enjoys.* In most cases the pressure of public opinion will be quite sufficient to secure respect for its decisions. Governments will be reluctant to be regarded as violators of their people's liberties and will usually prefer to comply with the judgements of the Court" (my italics).[25] It is clear that the founders of the Convention did not intend to for the Court to amass authority through strong delegated powers, but rather through its constituents' respect for the *idea* that the Court represented: an institutional beacon of liberal democratic values from which Europeans could derive a united source of pride and moral commitment. Perhaps because of confidence that noncompliance would be rare, as well as entrenched resistance to empowering the Court with more authority than strictly necessary, the drafters decided that execution of the ECtHR's judgments would be delegated to the Committee of Ministers. The ECtHR was created not only to fulfill a judicial mandate but to act as a vital piece in a larger institutional puzzle designed to bind the countries of Europe together economically, socially, and culturally, as well as legally. This mission required prioritizing cooperation and consensus. Any authority that could be legitimately wielded had to be rooted in political power emanating from the governments themselves. Consequently, the ministers adopted responsibility for monitoring compliance with Court judgments and deciding what obligations, if any, to impose on noncompliant states.[26]

Election of the ECtHR's First Judicial Bench

ECtHR judges are elected by a majority vote of the Consultative Assembly (which in 1974 was converted to the Parliamentary Assembly). The first election for

ECtHR judges was held on January 21, 1959. The following judges were elected during that session, representing the CoE's sixteen member states at the time:

Lord Arnold McNair, *president of the court*	United Kingdom
René Cassin, *vice president of the court*	France
Frederick Mari Van Asbeck	The Netherlands
Ake Ernst Vilhelm Holmbäck	Sweden
Alfred Verdross	Austria
Georges S. Maridakis	Greece
Henri Rolin	Belgium
Eugène Rodenbourg	Luxembourg
Alf Niels Christian Ross	Denmark
Terje Wold	Norway
Richard McGonigal	Ireland
Giorgio Balladore-Pallieri	Italy
Einar Arnalds	Iceland
Hermann Mosler	Federal Republic of Germany
Kemal Fikret Arik	Turkey

These inaugural judges represented the most accomplished legal professionals in Europe. Several had previous experience in international arbitration: Lord McNair, first president of the ECtHR, previously served as the president of the International Court of Justice. René Cassin, first vice president of the ECtHR, was a former French representative to the League of Nations, cofounder of UNESCO, former president of the UN Commission on Human Rights, and a principal author of the UDHR. Frederik Van Asbeck, Alfred Verdross, Georges Maridakis, Hermann Mosler, and Henri Rolin were all former members of the Hague Permanent Court of Arbitration. Many of the ECtHR's first judges had previously served on their nations' high courts and/or held political positions as legislators or government ministers. Ake Holmbäck was a former member of the Swedish Riksdag and government delegate to the UN Assembly. Henri Rolin was a minister of state and president of the Belgian Senate. Eugène Rodenbourg and Terje Wold served on their countries' Supreme Courts and held high-level political appointments as government ministers. Kemal Arik and Georges Maridakis had represented their governments in several international negotiations and played significant roles in drafting their countries' civil codes. Hermann Mosler represented Germany at the Conference on the Schuman Plan, and Giorgio Balladore-Pallieri advised the formation of Euratom, both crucial processes for the eventual establishment of the European Union.[27] The election of judges with diverse backgrounds in academic, political, and legal institutions speaks to the early professionalism of the Court and a commitment to careful calibration of domestic and international interests.

Summary

The Committee of Ministers guided the Convention drafting process with careful attention to the potential for supranational incursion on national sovereignty. A foundation of trust undergirded relationships between domestic authorities and Convention drafters, as evident in the drafters' belief that the Court would serve as a "safety valve" in isolated circumstances when domestic safeguards failed, not as a forum for litigating systemic abuses. In order to achieve governments' cooperation with the broader European integration project, the Convention's founders knew that they had to tread carefully to avoid backlash. By siphoning petitions through the Commission and delegating the power to enforce Court judgments to the Committee of Ministers, the drafters established buffers to the ECtHR's authority. From its very beginnings, the ECtHR has endeavored to bring states into closer compliance with European human rights standards by fostering collaborative relationships with governments based on deference to national institutions. This mandate, forged in the Court's founding moments, continues to inform the ECtHR's case law today.

The Inter-American Court of Human Rights: Confronting Militarism Through Judicial Creativity

Unlike the CoE, whose founding was inextricably linked to the post–World War II rise of human rights legalization, the groundwork for the Organization of American States (OAS) was established well before the emergence of the international human rights regime. This context is essential for understanding the markedly different relationship that the modern OAS has with the IACtHR compared to the relationship between the CoE and the ECtHR. The OAS's origins can be traced to Latin America's decolonialization struggle. After a wave of independence revolutions swept the region in the 1820s, the new American states sought out regional collaboration as a mechanism to protect themselves from further intervention. Under the direction of Simón Bolivar, then president of Gran Colombia, delegations from several newly independent states convened at the 1826 Congress of Panama to draft the region's first collective security and economic cooperation pacts. While Bolivar's ambitions to establish a military and economic union among the former Spanish colonies ultimately floundered, this meeting laid crucial groundwork for future multilateral cooperation.

Building on the commitments made in Panama, a series of conferences over subsequent decades produced treaties committing Latin American governments to the principles of nonintervention, pan-American solidarity, and collective defense.[28]

The geopolitics of the region shifted in the late 1800s with the emergence of the United States as an international power. US Secretary of State James Blaine proposed that Washington host an inter-American conference to pitch closer economic and diplomatic cooperation between the US and its southern neighbors. This proposal resulted in the First International Conference of American States, held from October 1889 to April 1890. Conference discussions centered on economic issues, including proposals for an American customs union and a common currency.[29] While nothing approximating these ambitious goals came to fruition, the conference marked a pivotal point in inter-American relations. The attending delegations established the International Union of American Republics, an organization dedicated to encouraging commercial interchange within the Western Hemisphere. The International Union became the first institutional predecessor of the modern OAS.

With the onset of World War II, the International Union (which had by this point been renamed the Pan-American Union) refocused on security issues. Harking back to the priorities that initially propelled American multilateralism in the 1800s, the 1933 Convention on Duties and Rights of States reaffirmed the Union's commitment to noninterventionism. The 1930s and early 1940s saw a wave of democratization in Latin America, along with new collective-defense pacts and regional instruments for peaceful settlement of disputes.[30] These developments led to the reconfiguration of the Union as the Organization of American States at the Ninth International Conference of American States in Bogotá in 1948. That conference marked the first time that human rights protections were formally integrated into the inter-American mandate. The American Declaration of the Rights and Duties of Man, adopted alongside the OAS Charter, was the first intergovernmental recognition of detailed human rights provisions in modern history.[31] The American Convention on Human Rights, which created the IACtHR twenty years after the Declaration's adoption, is largely based on the rights framework established in the Declaration.

Latin American diplomats, jurists, and NGOs were at the forefront of campaigns to develop international human rights protections in the post–World War II period. Indeed, Latin American delegations have been credited with successfully persuading reluctant great powers to include human rights language in the draft UN Charter at the 1945 San Francisco Conference.[32] The Inter-American Juridical Committee, a sub-organ of the OAS, provided crucial legal analysis that informed the inclusion of human rights language in the UN Charter, the

American Declaration, and the UDHR. Several Latin American government delegations and legal professionals were predominant contributors to both the American Declaration and the UDHR. Thus, the American Declaration has been recognized as having a "heavy influence" on the UDHR drafting process.[33] While the concept of human rights is often traced back to European Enlightenment roots, it is Latin American diplomats and jurists who were primarily responsible for the incorporation of human rights into the UN's mandate. The UDHR provisions that provided the framework for the modern international human rights regime, including the European human rights system, are directly rooted in Latin American legal innovations.

In 1959, at the Fifth Meeting of Consultation of OAS Ministers of Foreign Affairs in Santiago, Chile, the ministers adopted a resolution directing the Inter-American Council of Jurists (IACJ) to prepare a draft regional human rights treaty. This resolution also directed the jurists to explore the creation of an Inter-American Court, the first such formal proposal for a judicial body within the OAS.[34] The resulting IACJ draft convention incorporated provisions on an expansive range of economic, social, and cultural rights, as well as political and civil rights. The draft treaty's implementation mechanisms were modeled after the European system, with the Inter-American Commission assuming responsibility for accepting individual petitions and guiding parties toward friendly settlements, and an Inter-American Court with the authority to issue legally binding decisions in contentious cases.[35]

The Inter-American Commission commenced operations shortly after the 1959 meeting. The IACJ's draft proposal envisioning a human rights court, however, floundered for years owing to governments' preoccupation with other issues. During the 1960s, the OAS largely devolved into a forum for political clashes between the US's anticommunist crusade and Latin American governments' escalating resentment toward US interference.[36] The OAS was also busy navigating the accession of new member states following decolonization in the Caribbean. Other sources of obstruction were more deliberate. Following a Special Inter-American Conference in 1965 that revived the idea of a regional human rights convention, the OAS Council was charged with considering revisions to the IACJ draft. After several rounds of revisions between the Inter-American Commission and the OAS Council, the Council sent a new draft convention to OAS member governments, requesting their feedback. Two major powers in the region, Argentina and Brazil, responded by calling for the discontinuation of discussion on a regional convention altogether. Eight other states voiced tepid acceptance of continued work on a convention but did not affirmatively support the endeavor. This faction included the US, Chile, Uruguay, and Venezuela, who argued that any potential convention should merely provide regional mechanisms for implementing existing UN Covenants, not construct an independent regional human rights regime.[37]

Out of the OAS's twenty-three member states at the time, only ten governments replied to the OAS's request for feedback by the January 1968 deadline.[38] In the contemporaneous words of renowned American judge and legal historian José Cabranes, this lack of response "would seem to indicate that if the non-responding governments are not in fact opposed to the continued elaboration of a regional convention on human rights, they accord little or no priority to the idea."[39] Here we see some initial indications of deep-seated apathy among OAS governments to the emerging Inter-American human rights system.

Despite member states' prolonged foot-dragging, a conference was convened in San José, Costa Rica, in 1969 to draft the American Convention on Human Rights. It was this Convention that finally established the IACtHR. The fact that the San José conference even occurred is somewhat of a miracle. The year 1969 was marked by widespread instability and repression across Latin America. Exemplifying these challenges, the date of the San José conference had to be pushed from September to November 1969 because of a brief war between El Salvador and Honduras.[40] This conflict killed nearly three thousand civilians before the OAS intervened to broker a ceasefire.[41] During an episode of the drafting conference that provoked applause, the delegates from Honduras and El Salvador voiced support for an article prohibiting war and nationalistic hate.[42] The IACtHR was created against this backdrop of fragile peace and creeping militarism.

In order to convey the unique geopolitical context that surrounded the drafting of the American Convention, it is worthwhile to briefly summarize here the status of the governments who participated in the San José conference. While the states who founded the ECtHR were all functioning electoral democracies, the OAS members who founded the IACtHR represented a much wider range of regime types. Of the OAS's twenty-three member states in 1969, only eight could be considered stable electoral democracies: Barbados, Chile, Costa Rica, the Dominican Republic, Jamaica, Trinidad and Tobago, the US, and Venezuela. Barbados, Jamaica, and Trinidad and Tobago had only just come become democracies in 1962 following their independence from Britain. The Dominican Republic had only been democratic since the conclusion of the 1965–1966 civil war.

Several other member states were governed by democratically elected officials but were experiencing high levels of political violence and human rights abuses in 1969. Among these, Uruguay's democracy was rapidly deteriorating amid civil unrest brought on by economic instability and fighting between the government and the Tupamaros guerrilla movement. Increasing government use of torture was reported during this period, as the US Office of Public Safety began operations in Uruguay to instruct police on torture techniques.[43] The Uruguayan military ultimately seized control over the country in 1973. Mexico, in the middle of the Partido Revolucionario Institucional's seventy-one-year stretch of power, was similarly dominated by militarism. The late 1960s were marked by the "Mexican Dirty War," a low-level conflict between the government, backed by the US, and left-wing student and guerrilla groups. Torture was frequently employed by Mexican state entities during this period.[44]

Colombia had a democratically elected government in 1969 but was five years into a civil war between the government, far-right paramilitaries, organized crime, and leftist guerrillas. Ecuadorian President José María Ibarra was democratically elected in 1968 during a fragile transition from a military junta that had seized power in 1963. However, Ibarra's democratic intentions turned out to be no more sincere than those of his predecessors. Through an *autogolpe* in June 1970, Ibarra dismissed the Congress and Supreme Court, returning Ecuador to dictatorship. In El Salvador, there was some hope for democracy in the late 1960s. An unusually wide range of candidates competed in the 1967 presidential elections, including a leftist candidate who prevailed over a campaign to remove his name from the ballot. However, the military maintained a tight hold on government. Colonel Fidel Sánchez Hernández won the 1967 election, the legitimacy of which was widely contested.[45]

Ten of the states represented at the San José conference were fully authoritarian in 1969. Severe state-sponsored human rights abuses, including politically motivated killings, disappearances, and torture, were pervasive within each of these countries. Haitians suffered the brutal rule of François "Papa Doc" Duvalier. Paraguay was pinned under Alfredo Stroessner, whose thirty-five-year-long reign was the longest dictatorial tenure in modern South American history. Nicaragua was similarly entrenched under the Somoza family military dynasty. The governments of Honduras and Guatemala had been toppled by military coups in 1963, and by 1969 Guatemala was in the thick of a civil war between the government and various leftist rebel groups that persisted through the 1990s. Lieutenant General Juan Carlos Onganía led a military junta governing Argentina following a 1966 coup. Peru and Panama also fell victim to coups in 1968. Brazil's military dictatorship, which had been installed in 1964, was in crisis in the months leading up to the San José conference. From August to October 1969, Brazilian President Artur da Costa e Silva's ultimately fatal bout with cerebral thrombosis created a power vacuum filled by a provisional military junta. Finally, in Bolivia, the civilian government was overthrown in a bloodless coup by General Alfredo Ovando Candia just two months before the San José conference.

Given the prevalence of authoritarianism and the fractious nature of interstate relations within the OAS during the late 1960s, it seems incredible that

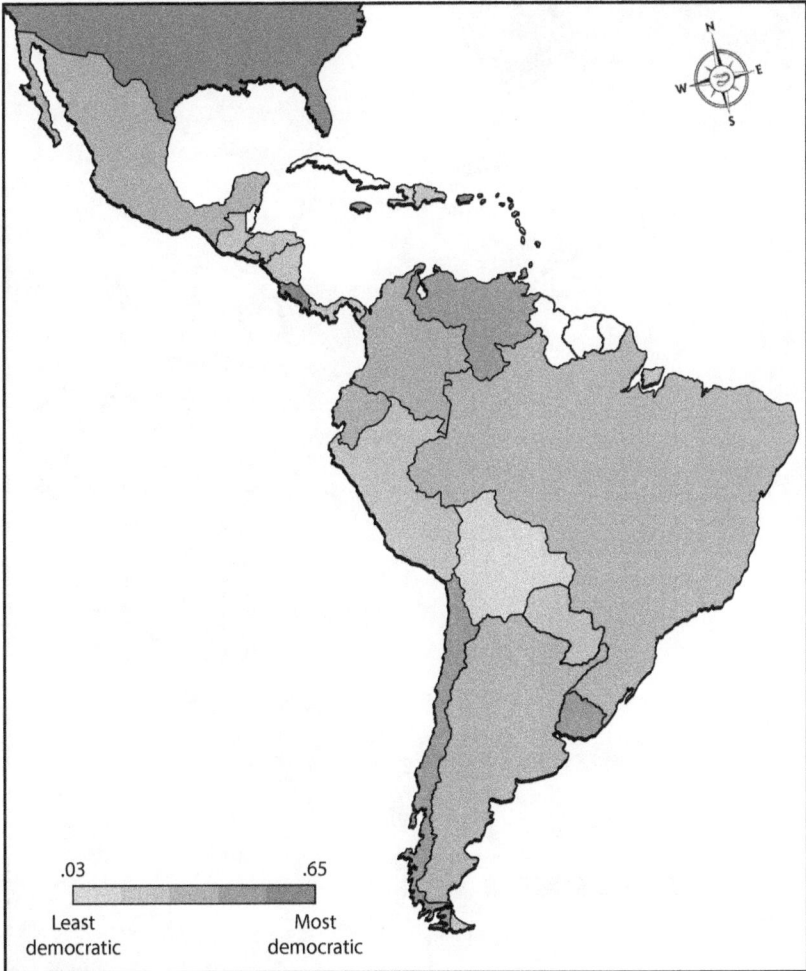

FIGURE 2.3. OAS member states liberal democracy scores, 1969
Source: Coppedge et al. 2023.

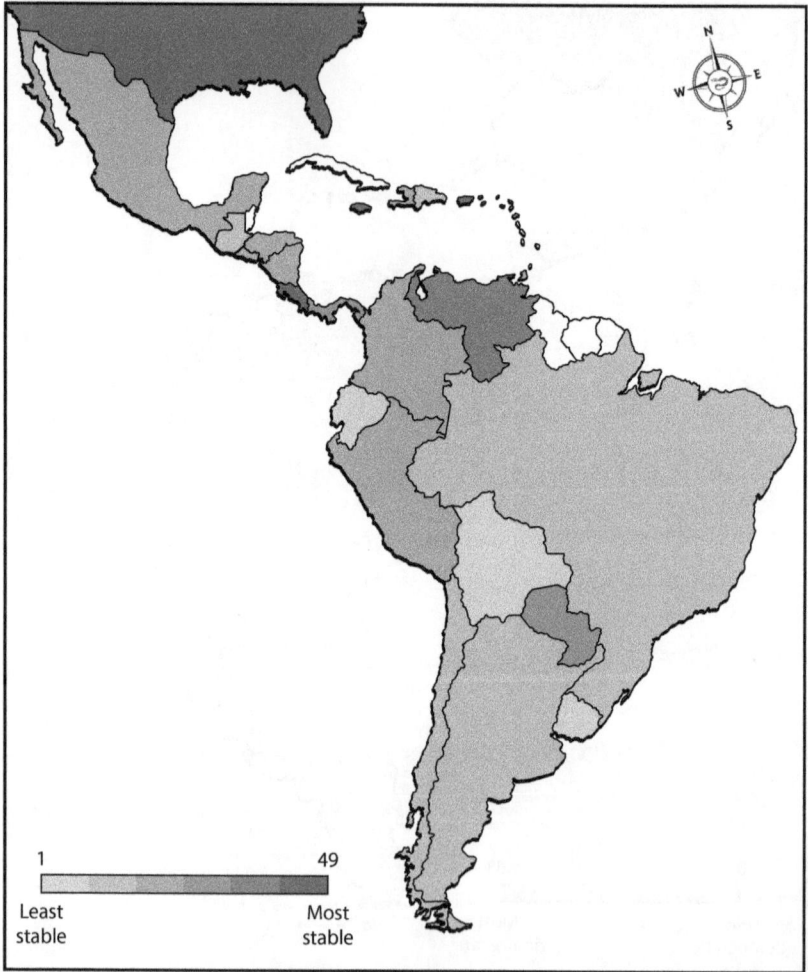

FIGURE 2.4. OAS member states regime stability scores, 1969
Source: Marshall and Gurr 2020.

states adopted a binding human rights convention at San José. Not only that, but they also established an international court that grew to wield an unprecedentedly expansive interpretation of its judicial authority. As it turns out, perhaps the explanation for this puzzling outcome is that governments themselves were not all that involved in developing the project they signed off on. In particular, the most authoritarian governments, which presumably would be the most likely to oppose binding human rights obligations, may have been too preoccupied with beating back domestic opposition to invest much energy into molding the American Convention. Governments do not have unlimited bandwidth. Sporadic involvement in drafting the American Convention among transitional and authoritarian governments might thus be explained by a lack of resources, or, perhaps more simply, a lack of interest. Given the tremendous obstacles to establishing an international human rights court in such an inhospitable political climate, some state leaders may have doubted that the IACtHR would ever actually exist, let alone amass enough power to regulate government conduct. This could have led to complacency at San José, creating an opening for interested actors to design a court with a wide-ranging jurisdiction.

If such an opening existed, who filled it? According to my theory, legal bureaucrats will seek greater influence over negotiations to found an international court in the event that political advisers are insufficiently able or willing to wield control over those negotiations. These legal bureaucrats, because of their expertise and professional interests, will be more likely than political advisers to push for a treaty with a high degree of legalization, including specific binding obligations imposed on states and strong enforcement mechanisms. Consequently, where there is a greater number of legal bureaucrats relative to political advisers present during negotiations to found an IC, we should expect the resulting court to have a broader jurisdiction and greater authority to intervene in domestic affairs. The following section will evaluate that argument, looking to the *travaux préparatoires* of the American Convention for clues as to how the IACtHR developed its unique judicial mandate.

While the *travaux* of the European Convention unfortunately do not provide a full manifest of all negotiation delegations, the *travaux* of the American Convention include a detailed list of participants. This list sheds light on the relative involvement of legal professionals and political appointees at the San José conference.[46] Of the nineteen delegation presidents who attended the conference, at least fourteen were lawyers and/or judges.[47] Several of these individuals had careers centered on participation in international governance and human rights institutions. Argentine delegation president Raúl Quijano's career at the UN Commission on Public International Administration indicates support for international governance, at least in the trade realm. His diplomatic positions under the Onganía dictatorship and Isabel Perón's administration, however, cast doubt on his support for international human rights oversight.[48] Quijano's appointment is thus not surprising from a government that had recently called for the abandonment of the regional convention project. Carlos Abranches, who by 1969 had an established career at the Inter-American Commission and was a well-known human rights advocate, seems a rather more perplexing choice by Brazil's military government, which had joined Argentina in calling for an end to convention development. The delegation presidents from Colombia, Guatemala, and Uruguay were professional legal bureaucrats and academics who dedicated their careers to the development of international law, with Guatemala's Carlos Bauer in particular advocating for deeper international human rights legalization.

The delegation presidents from Costa Rica, Ecuador, El Salvador, Honduras, Mexico, and Nicaragua all held domestic political offices at some point, perhaps indicating a greater proclivity to promoting state interests in the international realm. The choice to appoint Fernando Bustamante to lead the Costa Rican delegation aligns with the interests of President José Trejos Fernández, who was strongly supportive of human rights institutions that could temper the regional trend of democratic backsliding. Juan Vargas's history as a labor rights activist makes him a curious choice for Ecuador's right-wing government on the brink of a relapse into military dictatorship. The appointment of Elisio Cadalso, known for his advancement of women's rights legislation, similarly does not appear to align with the conservative authoritarian agenda of the Honduran government. In Mexico's case, Antonio Baéz's résumé suggests that his political ambitions took a backseat to his professional identity as a jurist, with a particular interest in the human rights of minorities. El Salvador and Nicaragua are the only cases where the delegation presidents' political careers suggest opposition to international human rights legalization in line with domestic executives' interests. Of the delegation presidents with political backgrounds, only Lorenzo Guerrero of Nicaragua was not also a lawyer.

Two delegation presidents, Alejandro Magnet of Chile and Alfredo Simó of the Dominican Republic, personally experienced repression under military dictatorships.[49] Coincidentally, both men are today better known for their contributions to the literary world than their political or diplomatic endeavors. Overall, the majority of delegation presidents at San José were legal bureaucrats whose professional backgrounds suggest, at the very least, an openness to international human rights legalization, if not outright support. Argentina, El Salvador, and Nicaragua are the only cases where delegation presidents' political allegiances, aligned with that of their domestic executives, indicate a proclivity to *oppose* human rights legalization.[50]

It is puzzling that several governments that had horrific human rights records and vocally opposed a regional human rights regime appointed delegates with demonstrated expertise in and support for international human rights institutions. This outcome indicates a lack of strategic deliberation on the part of those governments regarding how to effectively represent their interests at San José. It is possible that these governments sought out delegates with the necessary expertise in international law to participate in the conference, while not fully appreciating that those experts might be more likely to push for higher levels of legalization in the American Convention. Alternatively, perhaps some of these delegates volunteered to go to San José and were granted permission without thorough vetting owing to their governments' preoccupation with domestic crises. Another potential explanation is that these governments did not anticipate the success of the Inter-American human rights regime, and thus simply did not think that the San José conference was worth substantive political investment. Because of the classified status of relevant domestic documents, it is not possible to know for sure how so many proponents of human rights legalization from repressive regimes ended up at San José. But the ideological incongruity between leading Convention drafters and the governments who appointed them indicate that misinformed political strategizing and/or simple lack of government attention occurred somewhere along the line.

The drafters of the American Convention drew upon the European Convention as a model but deliberately did not replicate the European Convention. Drafting delegates argued that Latin America's unique history of human rights development and the contemporary challenges facing the region necessitated a new vision.[51] Shortly after the inception of the Court, founding judge Thomas Buergenthal wrote that "the problems of our Hemisphere are more unique to the Americas than they are universal or European. They can only be solved within the framework of our own legal, cultural, political, and social traditions."[52] The rights enshrined in the American Convention, which imbued the IACtHR with a more expansive jurisdiction than that of any existing international court, reflect the drafters' attention to the distinct geopolitical realities of the region.

Substantive Jurisdiction of the Court

The American Convention protects twenty-three distinct rights, compared to the thirteen rights protected by the original European Convention.[53] The rights codified in the American Convention that were not included in the original European Convention include the right to juridical personality, right to compensation in the case of miscarriage of justice, protection of honor and reputation, right to a name, rights of the child, right to nationality, right to property, freedom of movement and residence, right to participate in government, and the right to judicial protection.[54]

The American Convention includes all thirteen rights guarantees stipulated in the European Convention. The American reformulation of one such right, the right to an effective remedy, has had profound consequences for the IACtHR's interpretation of its authority. The counterpart of the right to an effective remedy within the American Convention is the "right to judicial protection." Recall that the Universal Declaration of Human Rights, heavily influenced by the Inter-American Juridical Committee, codified the right to "effective remedies by competent national tribunals" in the event of state-sponsored human rights violations. Recall as well that the European Convention drafters, after a debate littered with preoccupation about infringement on domestic sovereignty, decided to amend the wording of that provision to instead provide for the right to an "effective remedy before a national authority" in Article 13. The European Convention drafters deliberately did not guarantee the right to an effective *judicial* remedy. Thus, the right to judicial protection adopted in the American Convention exemplifies the drafters' innovation of the European model (or, perhaps more accurately, the San José delegates' refusal to water down emerging Latin American legal norms to align with the Europeans). Article 25 of the American Convention mandates that individuals must have recourse to "a competent court or tribunal." In other words, effective remedies in the American system must be *judicial*, whereas this is not mandated in the European system. The right to judicial protection can be traced to the rights to "justice" and "juridical personality" enumerated in the 1948 American Declaration.

The original proposal for the right to judicial protection, drawing from the Inter-American Juridical Committee draft, guarantees persons the right to "simple, prompt, and effective recourse before judges and competent national tribunals, for protection against acts that violate their fundamental rights recognized by the Constitution or by the law."[55] This provision, modeled from the *recurso de amparo* common in Spanish-speaking legal systems, protects persons from violations of their *constitutional* rights. During negotiations at San José, the Chilean delegation led a motion to amend the wording of the provision to apply not only to national constitutional rights but also to all rights codified within the American Convention itself.[56] This motion, which passed without substantive objections, is critical in that it standardized and broadened the scope of the circumstances in which injured parties could claim a right to judicial protection in international *as well as* domestic litigation. This innovation provided a "broader system of protection" through which the IACtHR could build claims to authority.[57]

Another crucial area in which the American Convention expanded on the European model is that of advisory jurisdiction. The European Convention only granted the ECtHR contentious jurisdiction, meaning the authority to rule on cases involving specific disputes between states or between individuals and state governments. The ECtHR was not originally granted advisory jurisdiction, which allows a court to answer general questions regarding the interpretation of treaties.[58] The American Convention, however, did give the IACtHR the power to issue advisory opinions on interpretation of the American Convention as well as any other OAS-sponsored human right agreements (Article 64). The purpose of advisory opinions in international courts is often to clarify ambiguous areas of law. Advisory opinions can expand an international court's authority by allowing the court to "fill in" any gaps in existing treaties or case law. This process can widen the court's reach into the domestic realm to encompass new issue areas not explicitly codified in the court's constitutive documents. Chapter 3 discusses how the IACtHR's power to issue advisory opinions was crucial for boosting the Court's legitimacy in its early years as it struggled with governments who were antagonistic to human rights legalization.

Temporal Jurisdiction of the Court

On paper, temporal jurisdiction in the Inter-American system is determined much like it is in the European system. The Inter-American Commission can only accept cases in which the alleged violation occurred after the relevant member state ratified the American Convention. This admissibility criterion also applies to the IACtHR, with the added stipulation that the alleged violation must have occurred after the relevant state acceded to the Court (keeping in mind that accession to the Court is not required to ratify the American Convention). Applicants are required to submit petitions to the Commission within six months of the exhaustion of domestic remedies. When a case reaches the IACtHR, the Court conducts its own evaluation of that case's admissibility, which is independent of the Commission's admissibility decision.

In practice, however, the IACtHR has developed a uniquely flexible approach to temporal jurisdiction relative to the ECtHR. This divergence across the two courts is particularly visible in their respective approaches to adjudicating cases involving personal integrity rights violations, as will be discussed in chapters 3 and 5. IACtHR judges have leveraged expansive interpretations of the right to judicial protection to strengthen the Court's authority to admit cases of "continuing violations" that originated prior to states' accessions to the Court, stretching the boundaries of the Court's temporal jurisdiction.

Remedial Authority

Article 63, the central treaty provision establishing the IACtHR's remedial authority, carves out a notably broader path for IACtHR judges to craft reparations orders compared to the corresponding article of the European Convention. Article 63 stipulates that "the Court shall rule that the injured party be ensured the enjoyment of his right or freedom that was violated. It shall also rule, if appropriate, that the consequences of the measure or situation that constituted the breach of such right or freedom be remedied and that fair compensation be paid to the injured party." This provision reflects the founders' commitment to empowering the IACtHR to order a diverse range of remedial mandates, including but not limited to financial reparations.

Execution of Judgments

Unlike the ECtHR, the IACtHR is charged with monitoring and enforcing state compliance with its own judgments. This mandate imbues the IACtHR with exclusive control over the remedial mandates that it can impose on states. The IACtHR has broadly interpreted its authority to issue diverse reparative measures as well as measures of nonrepetition to prevent future reoccurrence of rights violations. The IACtHR's in-house authority to monitor and enforce (or, at least, attempt to enforce) state compliance with judgments has contributed to the Court's innovative approach to legal remedies.

Election of the IACtHR's First Judicial Bench

The American Convention entered into force in 1978 after the requisite eleventh OAS member state deposited its instrument of ratification (Article 74(2)).[59] The following judges were elected by the OAS General Assembly to serve on the IACtHR's founding bench in 1979:

Rodolfo E. Piza Escalante, *president of the court*	Costa Rica
Pedro Nikken, *vice president of the court*	Venezuela
Thomas Buergenthal	United States
Carlos Roberto Reina	Honduras
Huntley Eugene Monroe	Jamaica
Máximo Cisneros Sánchez	Peru
César Ordóñez	Colombia

The IACtHR's first president, Rodolfo Piza Escalante, was an accomplished legal academic who held positions at universities spanning Latin America, the US,

Europe, and Asia prior to his nomination to the Court. He was also a diplomat and ambassador, representing Costa Rica in several international forums, including as a vice president of the UN General Assembly from 1979 to 1980. Escalante went on to serve as the president of Costa Rica's Supreme Court following his time at the IACtHR.[60] Pedro Nikken of Venezuela came from a legal academic background with little experience in international law or governance. After the conclusion of his IACtHR term in 1989, Nikken became a prominent figure in international human rights. He served as an independent expert on the postwar Human Rights Commission for El Salvador, worked to establish a truth commission as UN special envoy to Burundi in 1995, presided over the International Commission of Jurists from 2011 to 2012, and held a number of other high-profile international positions.[61]

Thomas Buergenthal, a US national born in Czechoslovakia, was nominated to the IACtHR's founding bench by the Costa Rican government. Prior to his emigration to the US as a child, Buergenthal was one of the youngest known Holocaust victims to survive the Auschwitz and Sachsenhausen concentration camps. Buergenthal was a professor at the University of Texas Law School in 1979 when he received what he has claimed was an entirely unexpected phone call informing him that the Costa Rican government intended to nominate him for the IACtHR.[62] Buergenthal specialized in the study of international human rights law during his legal education and taught seminars on the topic, but beyond that had no formal experience in international organizations or domestic legal practice.[63] Carlos Roberto Reina was a lawyer with a long history of antiauthoritarian political activism prior to his nomination to the IACtHR. Reina had been imprisoned in 1944 after he publicly criticized dictator Tiburcio Carías Andino. After serving on the IACtHR, Reina was elected president of Honduras in 1993. His administration was notable for its progress in reducing corruption and limiting the role of the military in politics, including the elimination of mandatory military service for Honduran citizens.[64]

Huntley Eugene Monroe was a British-educated lawyer who held numerous positions within the Jamaican government from the 1930s through the 1960s. He served as Jamaica's attorney general from 1964 to 1967 and interrupted his retirement from public service to join the IACtHR. Máximo Cisneros Sánchez was a Peruvian law professor and ambassador. He served as president of the executive committee of the Inter-American Federation of Attorneys and participated in numerous other professional associations for international lawyers. In the early 1970s, Sánchez had fled Peru for a time following a verbal clash with dictator Juan Velasco Alvarado.[65] Finally, César Ordóñez of Colombia was a law professor and social democratic politician famous for his oratory skills. During the early years of the IACtHR, Ordóñez also served as the president of the Free University of Colombia.[66]

From these biographies, there are some clear points of differentiation between the professional backgrounds of the IACtHR's founding judges and those of the ECtHR. Five of the seven founding IACtHR judges came from predominantly academic backgrounds. Remarkably, only one, Monroe, held a domestic judicial position prior to nomination to the Court. Reina and Ordóñez were the only founding judges with political backgrounds, and both had centered human rights concerns in their domestic agendas. Overall, the founding IACtHR judges had significantly less international and domestic legal experience than their ECtHR counterparts. While serving on the ECtHR was the capstone on an already prolific career for many founding ECtHR judges, serving on the IACtHR was instead a launching pad for several jurists who went on to work in other international organizations, domestic courts, politics, and human rights activism. Importantly, two of the founding IACtHR judges, Buergenthal and Reina, had personally experienced human rights violations at the hands of repressive regimes prior to their election to the Court. These experiences undoubtedly informed their judicial philosophies.

As in the European system, the IACtHR's founding judges were charged with drafting the Statute of the Court and the Court's first rules of procedure. Buergenthal's written recollections of this process, which occurred in Costa Rica shortly after the formal constitution of the Court in 1979, illuminate the motivations of the founding judges. These writings also underscore the resource limitations and increasingly hostile political situation that the founding judges faced. The first obstacle that the judges had to overcome was that they had nowhere to do their work. While the Costa Rican government had offered San José as the official seat of the Court, it had not provided any physical Court headquarters, or even office space. As a result, the judges drafted the Statute of the Court in the "bathhouse of the Costa Rican Bar association." As Buergenthal recalled, "Here the voices of children swimming and jumping into the association's pool often drowned out our early drafting efforts, hardly an auspicious beginning for those of us who thought of ourselves as modern-day John Marshalls."[67] The Court was eventually able to move to temporary offices in Costa Rica's Supreme Court building, and, some years later, to a permanent headquarters in San José. The issue of funding has plagued the IACtHR throughout its history, and the early years were no exception. When the OAS General Assembly voted on adopting the IACtHR's first budget, the final count was one vote short of the two-thirds majority needed to fund the Court. (The Nicaraguan delegate, who had previously assured the judges that he would support the budget, later claimed to have "fallen asleep" during the vote.) After the budget adoption failed, the IACtHR had to rely on ad hoc bankrolling from the Costa Rican government to start operations.[68]

Getting the Court off the ground was also complicated by the deteriorating status of democracy in the region. By 1979, Chile, Argentina, and Uruguay had all fallen to military dictatorships. Democracy in the Dominican Republic was on rocky soil. Haiti, Panama, and Brazil were still under the thumbs of unrelenting autocrats. The civil wars in Colombia and Guatemala had intensified, and El Salvador was on the brink of a conflict that would see some of the most egregious human rights abuses in modern history. During the 1979 General Assembly session where state representatives voted to approve the IACtHR's statute, Bolivia, the host country for the session, had three different presidents. In Buergenthal's words, "That left basically only Costa Rica, Venezuela, and Colombia—Peru was just emerging from a leftist dictatorship—among the Latin American countries, in addition to the small Commonwealth Caribbean nations, willing in 1979 to see the Inter-American Commission on Human Rights and Court become effective institutions for the protection of human rights."[69] These developments reflect the precarity of the Court during its early years. Still, the founding judges persevered. According to Buergenthal, "Believing that the draft Statute to be submitted to the OAS General Assembly provided a rare opportunity to enlarge the Court's powers, we drafted it accordingly."[70] The founding IACtHR judges saw themselves as embodying a mission to stifle authoritarianism and protect individuals from their governments against all odds. Accordingly, the judges sought out avenues for expanding their power to intervene in domestic affairs. While the ECtHR was constructed on an assumed faith in national judiciaries, the founders of the IACtHR did not make similar assumptions.

Summary

The selection of delegates to the San José Conference and the selection of founding IACtHR judges were ultimately up to the discretion of state governments. The professional and personal backgrounds of the individuals chosen to fill those roles, however, indicate that perhaps political officials were not allocating sufficient strategic attention to these appointments. The appointments of individuals whose demonstrated goals and values appeared antithetical to those of their governments may be attributed to those governments' lack of material or intellectual resources and/or preoccupation with domestic crises. The result was a cohort of individuals committed to pioneering a robust human rights regime in a region where state-sponsored abuses were tragically common.

Judge Cançado Trindade once attributed the IACtHR's rejection of a margin of appreciation doctrine to democratic deficiencies in the Court's member states.[71] The Inter-American system has long been undergirded by mistrust in the ability of domestic institutions to uphold human rights. While the Court is still working on building this trust, creating a coherent regional identity is a peripheral concern. The *travaux* of the American Convention do not indicate that regional integration was a widely held goal of the drafters.[72] There is little evidence that the OAS has made substantive efforts to instill a shared "American" identity in its member states.[73] These conditions could explain why negotiations to draft the American Convention were not marked by the same, constant anxiety about incursions on state sovereignty that are observable in the *travaux* of the European Convention. The drafters of the American Convention and founding judges of the IACtHR did not have to tread as carefully to placate state interests because, arguably, they had less to lose. The human rights situation in the region was deteriorating rapidly, and the IACtHR's founders saw themselves as the last resort to stall the downward spiral. They may thus have felt liberated to craft an ambitious regime that protected a broad range of rights and supported a Court that would have extensive authority to intervene in domestic affairs.

The African Court on Human and Peoples' Rights: Pioneering a Postcolonial Human Rights Framework

The first proposal for an African human rights court emerged during the 1961 African Conference on the Rule of Law in Lagos, organized by the International Commission of Jurists. The conference was attended by 194 judges, lawyers, and legal scholars from twenty-three African countries and nine other states. The "Law of Lagos," a declaration passed during the conference, implored African governments to adopt a regional treaty on human rights and create a court to enforce that treaty.[74] Conference records indicate support among the attendees for a regional system that would be inspired by, but not replicate, the European and Inter-American human rights systems. Most of the African lawyers who first envisioned a regional human rights system hailed from nations that had only recently achieved independence from European colonizers.[75] These lawyers were acutely aware of the challenges that the continent's colonial legacy posed for creating a regional human rights regime. Proposing that governments abdicate any level of newly won sovereignty to a supranational organization was deeply controversial.[76] Still, the postindependence era was marked by eagerness on the part of African statesmen to join the international legal community on their own terms.

Discussions at the African Conference centered on how to enter this community while navigating the "juxtaposition of an indigenous and a European law of persons."[77] Conference attendees asserted the imperative for African countries to reform their inherited colonial legal systems to incorporate local traditions and achieve representative democracy.[78] Conference attendees did not advocate abandoning those inherited systems as colonial relics. Rather, these lawyers emphasized the philosophical compatibility of so-called Western "rule of law" values with "African ideas of law and justice."[79] Debates focused on how to foster a coherent conceptualization of the rule of law, rooted in individual human rights protections, that could be translated across the diverse legal systems and political structures of African states.[80]

The establishment of the Organization of African Unity (OAU) by thirty-two states in 1963 created an opportunity to implement a regional human rights system under the auspices of that organization. However, OAU governments showed little interest in such a project. Rather, discussions on drafting an African human rights treaty continued to be primarily instigated by the UN, international human rights organizations, and African jurists. At a 1966 UN conference in Dakar primarily attended by African judges, members of ministries of justice, law professors, and international legal advocacy groups, participants proposed creating a two-tier regional system within the OAU mirroring the European Commission and Court of Human Rights.[81] Conference records indicate a consensus among attendees supporting this proposal. However, several participants voiced skepticism about its feasibility, emphasizing that African governments, "so recently freed from the colonial yoke, were particularly jealous of their sovereignty."[82]

This conversation continued at a second conference in Cairo in 1969. Participation at the Cairo conference was more evenly split between African jurists and low-level government diplomats.[83] The idea of an African human rights commission enjoyed broad support, but attendees disagreed regarding the proposed commission's responsibilities. Delegates were unable to come to an agreement on this matter, making discussion of a regional court out of the question. The Cairo conference ended with few concrete results aside from vague pledges to appeal to OAU governments to support a human rights commission.[84] Those appeals fell on deaf ears, and the fledgling regional human rights project stalled for almost a decade.

In response to growing pressure from African and international human rights organizations, stemming in part from unchecked rights abuses in newly independent states, the OAU convened a "meeting of experts" in Dakar in 1979 to compose a preliminary draft of an African human rights treaty.[85] This meeting was primarily attended by African legal experts, with limited participation from government diplomats.[86] The hubris of Europeans purporting to pioneer the concept of global human rights in the 1940s and '50s while still holding African colonies featured prominently among discussions at the Dakar conference. In his address opening the conference, Senegal's President Léopold Sédar Senghor recounted his personal experience with the hypocrisy of the European human rights project. Senghor had been a member of the French parliament when the European Convention on Human Rights was drafted and adopted. He recalled advocating for the automatic application of the Convention to CoE member states' colonized territories, only to be met with rejection by his French colleagues.[87] From the very first words uttered at the Dakar conference, the African human rights treaty was framed as an explicit rejection of the European model that had historically denied the humanity of Africans.

The African Charter on Human and Peoples' Rights is an unprecedented instrument of international law in that it not only codifies "rights" that governments must guarantee, but also "duties" that states have to individuals and that individuals have to their families, communities, and nations. Senghor's speech indicates that this innovation was the result of reflection on how the African human rights system could be grounded in local traditions and philosophies:

> In Europe, human rights are considered as a body of principles and rules placed in the hands of the individual, as a weapon, thus enabling him to defend himself against the group or entity representing it. In Africa, the individual and his rights are wrapped in the protection the family and other communities ensure everyone. . . . Therefore, contrary to what has been done so far in other regions of the world, provision must be made for a system of "Duties of Individuals," adding harmoniously to the rights recognized in them by the society to which they belong and by other men.[88]

The Dakar conference institutionalized a conceptualization of human rights as shared responsibilities, in contrast to a "Western" view of rights as contracted between states and individuals. In doing so, the conference made a seminal contribution to international law, illustrating the possibilities for alternative, postcolonial human rights frameworks.

The African Charter codifies an unprecedentedly broad range of civil and political as well as social, economic, and cultural rights provisions. The Europeans had largely rejected the inclusion of social, economic, and cultural rights in their Convention. These rights featured prominently in the original IAJC draft of the Inter-American Convention but were ultimately watered down substantially to make the agreement more palatable for governments. The drafters of the African Charter thus accomplished what the Americans attempted but could not quite pull off: getting governments to sign an agreement that placed civil, political, social, economic, and cultural rights under a single monitoring and enforcement system. It is this focus on economic, social, and cultural rights that motivated the drafters to include the phrase "Peoples' Rights" in the title of the Charter. Here again, President Senghor's words are illuminative: "We simply meant . . . to show our attachment to economic, social and cultural rights, to collective rights, in general, rights which have a particular importance in our situation of a developing country. . . . Our overall conception of human rights is marked by the right to development."[89]

The draft of the Charter produced during the Dakar conference was finalized at the 1980 OAU ministerial meeting in Banjul, the Gambia, with only minor language amendments.[90] The African Charter on Human and Peoples' Rights was finally adopted by the OAU Assembly in 1981 in Nairobi, Kenya. The Charter established an African Commission on Human and Peoples' Rights with a vague mandate to "promote human rights" but fell short of aspirations for establishing an African human rights court. As no *travaux préparatoires* of the African Charter exist, it is impossible to know the compositions, interests, and contributions of the specific delegations.[91] Without the *travaux*, it is unclear why the court proposal failed. Christof Heyns, a historian of African regional institutions, notes two potential explanations for not establishing a regional court in the original African Charter: first, an "idealistic explanation" rooted in "traditional" African conceptualizations of dispute resolution as best achieved through mediation and conciliation, as opposed to through adversarial legal processes; and second, a perception that, bearing the scars of colonialization, OAU member states were fiercely opposed to subjecting their sovereignty to a supranational court.[92] The African Charter finally came into force in 1986 following the requisite ratification by a simple majority of OAU member states. The African Commission on Human and Peoples' Rights was established shortly thereafter.

Proposals for creating a regional court languished for over a decade after the adoption of the African Charter. Finally, a post-1989 wave of democratization and increasing international attention to human rights concerns in the region contributed to the revival of the court project in the early 1990s. In 1994, the Assembly of the Heads of State and Government of the OAU called for a "Meeting of Experts" to explore the possibility of a regional human rights court once again.[93] The International Commission of Jurists (ICJ) can largely be credited for raising the necessary awareness and political will among OAU governments to green-light further exploration of a regional court. The ICJ, which had written the very first proposal for an African court back in 1961, renewed its efforts in the early 1990s, partnering with the African Commission and various NGOs to build a coalition of actors who could pressure governments to support the court project.[94]

The resultant Meeting of Experts convened in Cape Town in September 1995 to deliberate drafting a protocol to the African Charter that would establish a

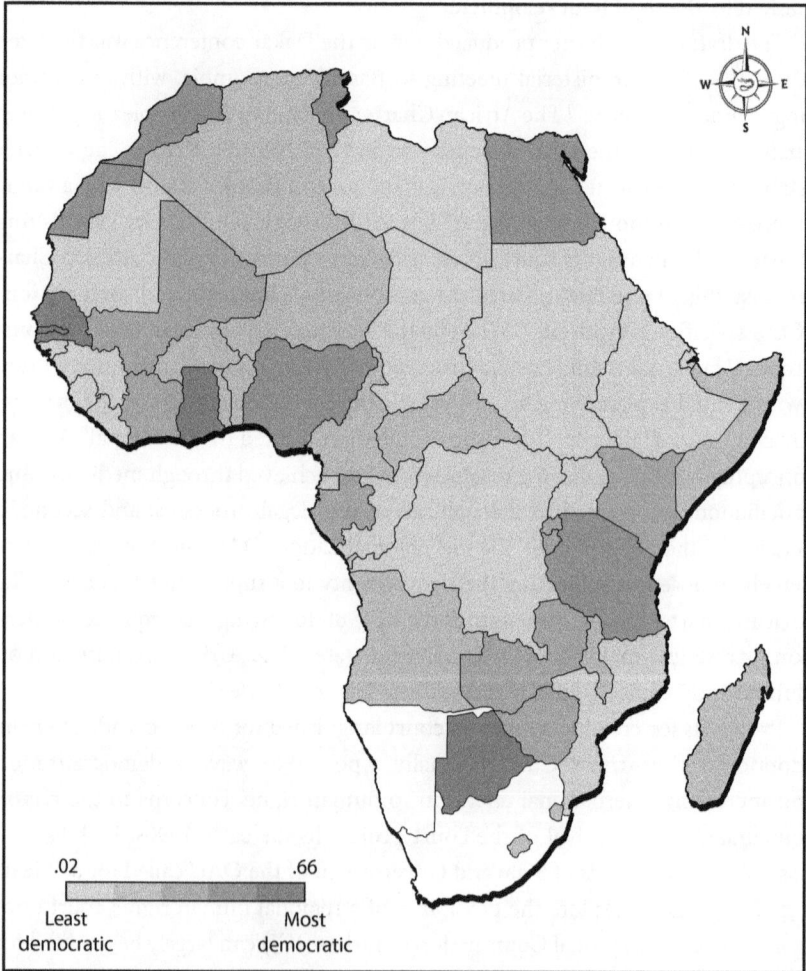

FIGURE 2.5. OAU member states liberal democracy scores, 1980
Source: Coppedge et al. 2023.

The map legend reads:

.02 — .66

Least democratic — Most democratic

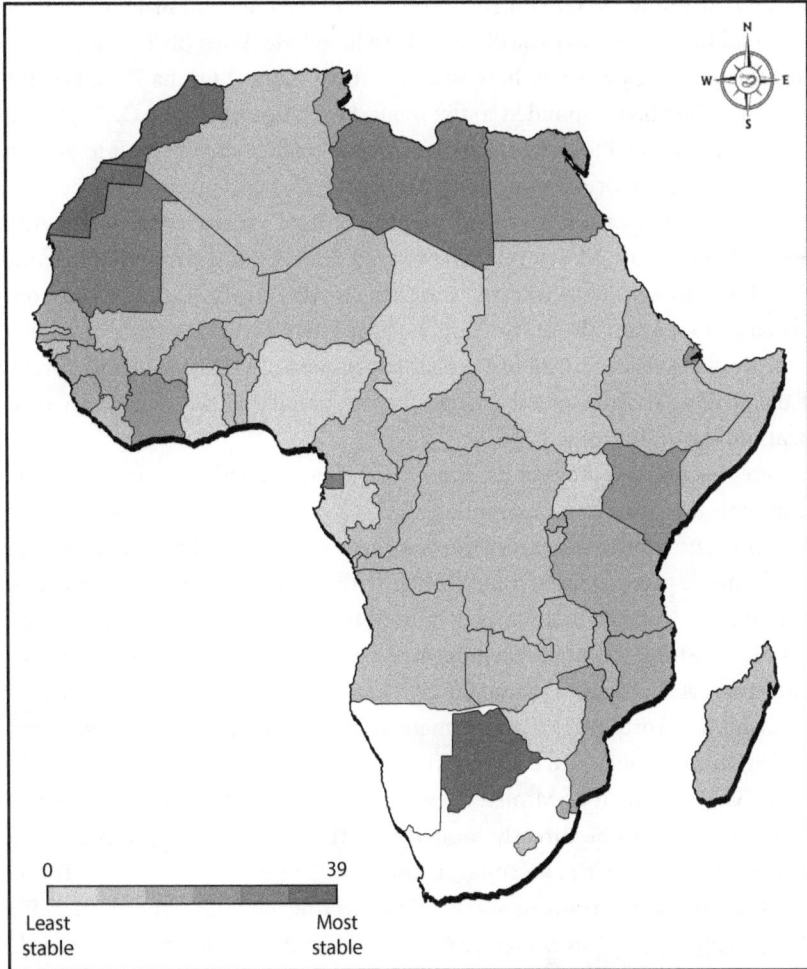

FIGURE 2.6. OAU member states regime stability scores, 1980

Source: Marshall and Gurr 2020.

Note: Polity V data are not available for São Tomé and Principe and the Seychelles. I assigned a regime stability score of 11 for São Tomé and Principe, as eleven years passed between 1980 and the country's first multiparty democratic elections in 1991. I also assigned a regime stability score of 11 for the Seychelles, as eleven years passed between 1980 and the 1991 constitutional reforms creating a multiparty system.

regional court. The Cape Town conference was attended by fifty-six legal experts from twenty-three OAU member states, along with observers from NGOs and various international organizations. The draft protocol adopted at Cape Town was then forwarded to OAU member states with the intention that governments would submit comments to be discussed at a June 1996 Assembly meeting. By the time this meeting occurred, however, only three states (Burkina Faso, Lesotho, and Mauritius) had responded to the request for comments. The OAU Council of Ministers decided to defer the discussion and recirculate the draft to governments in the hope of receiving more feedback. This cycle repeated once more with minimal responses. A second meeting of legal experts convened in April 1997 in Nouakchott, Mauritania. The revised draft resulting from that meeting, named the "Nouakchott Protocol," was then circulated to governments for commentary. Once again, the OAU Council of Ministers decided to defer discussion of the draft because of a lack of government response. At that point, only twenty of the OAU's fifty-four member states had responded to the request for comments on the draft Protocol.[95]

Here we observe echoes of the apathy that characterized government engagement with the American Convention drafting process. Given the proliferation of democratic transitions across the continent in the early 1990s, it is possible that domestic preoccupations and stretched-thin resources precluded sufficient government involvement in the negotiations to establish an African court. Given that the court question had been debated within various OAU organs for over thirty years at that point with no tangible results, perhaps governments did not feel that it was worth investing diplomatic resources to support or oppose a project that seemed unlikely to come to fruition.

The OAU Council of Ministers eventually deduced that government representatives had to be directly looped into the drafting process in order to secure any substantive state engagement with the proposed protocol. To that end, the ministers arranged for a third meeting of legal experts in Addis Ababa, Ethiopia, in December 1997. The Addis Ababa meeting marked the first time since the revival of the court project in 1994 that government diplomats were invited to participate in negotiations on the draft Protocol. Delegates from forty-five of the OAU's fifty-four member states attended the conference, marking an unprecedented level of government participation.[96] Twelve OAU governments submitted prepared commentary on the Nouakchott Protocol for discussion at the conference.[97] The seven governments whose submitted commentary is accessible all vocalized general support for creating the court.[98] Because of the lack of *travaux préparatoires*, it is not possible to know the identities of all the delegates who attended the conference, nor their particular positions. Based on what information is available, however, there does not appear to have been significant pushback against the draft Protocol at Addis Ababa. The conference concluded with delegates conferring a unanimous recommendation to refer the draft Protocol to the OAU Council of Ministers.[99] Shortly thereafter, the Council adopted the draft Protocol without modifications. Finally, in June 1998, the OAU Assembly, "without any discussion," approved the Protocol. The Protocol came into force in January 2004, following its requisite ratification by fifteen member states.[100] At that point, over forty years after the first proposal for an African human rights court, the ACtHPR was finally established.[101]

Substantive Jurisdiction of the Court

Several unique features of the ACtHPR's design contribute to the Court's expansive jurisdiction. First, the jurisdiction of the Court extends to all cases and disputes submitted to it concerning the interpretation and application not only of the African Charter but also *any other relevant human rights instrument* ratified by the state in question.[102] The ACtHPR has leveraged this provision to expand the issue areas in which it can develop jurisprudence. This provision also empowers the Court to incorporate legal interpretations from other human rights systems, including the UN treaty bodies, into its case law. The ACtHPR possesses advisory jurisdiction to issue opinions relating to the Charter or any other human rights instruments at the request of the African Union (AU),[103] any member state, or any African organization recognized by the AU.[104]

The African Charter guarantees the following rights that are not included in either the American or European Conventions:

- The right to work "under equitable and satisfactory conditions," including "equal pay for equal work" (Article 15)
- The right to "enjoy the best attainable state of physical and mental health," which obligates state parties to "take the necessary measures to protect the health of their people and to ensure that they receive medical attention when they are sick" (Article 16)
- The right to an education, which includes a controversial provision that "the promotion and protection of morals and traditional values recognized by the community shall be the duty of the State" (Article 17)
- The right of the "aged and disabled" to "special measures of protection in keeping with their physical or moral needs" (Article 18(4))
- The "right to existence," which encompasses "the unquestionable and inalienable right to self—determination" (Article 20(1))
- The right of all people to "their economic, social and cultural development with due regard to their freedom and identity and in the equal enjoyment

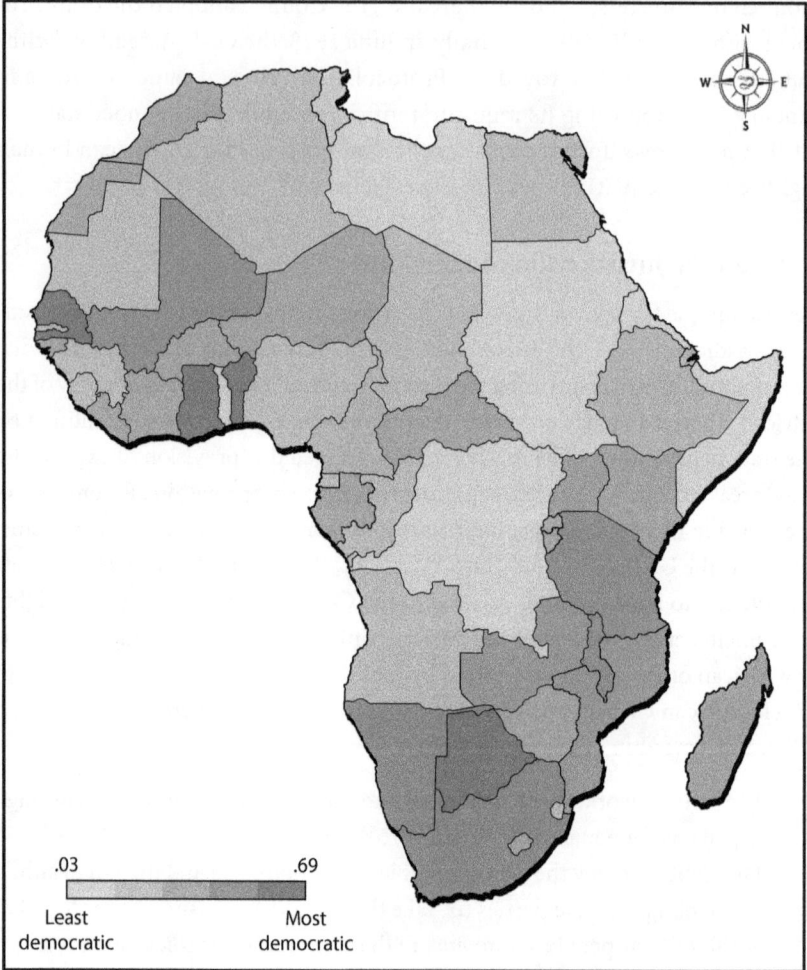

FIGURE 2.7. OAU member states liberal democracy scores, 1998

Source: Coppedge et al. 2023.

Note: Polity V data are not available for São Tomé and Principe and the Seychelles. I assigned a regime stability score of 11 for São Tomé and Principe, as eleven years passed between 1980 and the country's first multiparty democratic elections in 1991. I also assigned a regime stability score of 11 for the Seychelles, as eleven years passed between 1980 and 1991 constitutional reforms creating a multiparty system.

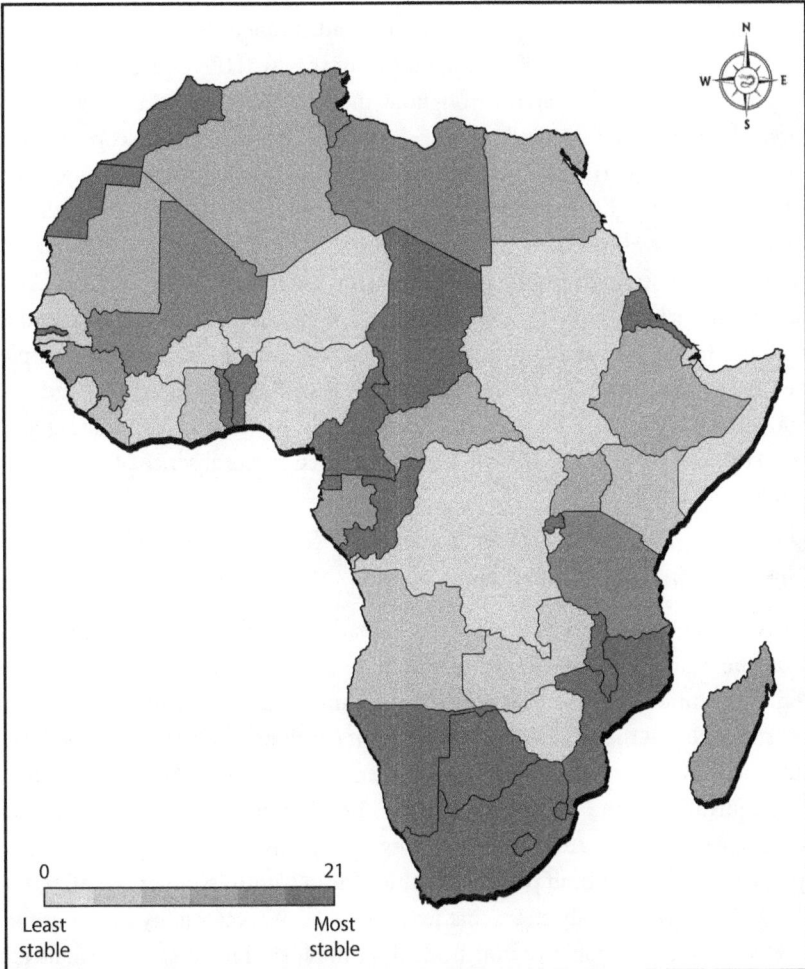

FIGURE 2.8. OAU member states regime stability scores, 1998
Source: Marshall and Gurr 2020.
Note: Polity V data are not available for São Tomé and Principe and the Seychelles. I assigned a regime stability score of 5 for São Tomé and Principe, as five years passed between 1998 and the military coup that deposed President Fradique de Menezes in 2003. I assigned a regime stability score of 21 for the Seychelles, as twenty-one years passed between 1998 and 2018 with consistent democratic elections.

of the common heritage of mankind. States shall have the duty, individu-
ally or collectively, to ensure the exercise of the right to development"
(Article 22)

While the African Charter guarantees a broader range of rights than do the
other regional conventions,[105] the authority of the ACtHPR is arguably diluted
by "clawback clauses" littered throughout the Charter. These clawback clauses
impose limitations on the exercise of specific rights, narrowing the scope of those
rights to what is permissible under domestic law. It is common among international human rights instruments for certain rights, particularly the rights of
association, assembly, and expression, to be subject to limitations for the sake of
national security and/or public safety. However, the clawback clauses in the African Charter permit limitations on a wider range of rights and do not specify that
those limitations can only be applied in emergent circumstances. For example,
the Charter states that "every individual shall have the right to express and dis-
seminate his opinions *within the law*" (my italics), potentially legitimating government censorship of the right to expression even in the absence of emergency
conditions (Article 9(2)).

Temporal Jurisdiction of the Court

The African Charter and its Protocol are remarkable in that they impose no temporal limitations on the ACtHPR's jurisdiction. Unlike in the American and European Conventions, there are no provisions within the African Charter or Protocol
that stipulate that the ACtHPR can only admit petitions in which the alleged violation occurred after the relevant state's accession to the Court. Additionally, there
is no equivalent to the "six-month rule" in the African Charter. Applicants thus
do not have a codified time limit following the exhaustion of domestic remedies
by which they must submit petitions to the African Commission or the ACtHPR.
The African Charter only states that petitions must be received by the Commission "within a reasonable period from the time local remedies are exhausted"
(Article 56(6)), and the Protocol is entirely silent on temporal jurisdiction. It is
puzzling that governments would ratify an agreement that contains no specification of the time period during which they can be held legally accountable.

Remedial Authority

The Protocol to the African Charter contains only a brief (and comparatively
vague) description of the Court's remedial authority, in Article 27(1): "If the
Court finds that there has been a violation of a human or peoples' right, it shall
make appropriate orders to remedy the violation, including the payment of fair

compensation or reparation." Thus, according to the treaty language, the Court maintains the authority to order governments to provide a wide range of monetary and nonmonetary remedies.

Execution of Judgments

The ACtHPR is charged with monitoring state compliance with its own judgments. If a state has not complied with a judgment within the span of time designated by a ruling, the Court's only concrete method of recourse is to report that state's noncompliance to the AU Assembly. It is then up to the Assembly to decide what, if any, enforcement measures might be appropriate (Articles 30–31).

Election of the ACtHPR's First Judicial Bench

The ACtHPR's inaugural judicial bench was elected in January 2006. The bench comprised the following judges:

Gérard Niyungeko, *president of the court*	Burundi
Modibo Tounty Guindo, *vice president of the court*	Mali
El Hadji Guissé	Senegal
Fatsah Ouguergouz	Algeria
Jean Mutsinzi	Rwanda
Bernard Makgabo Ngoepe	South Africa
Kelello Justina Mafoso-Guni	Lesotho
Hamdi Faraj Fanoush	Libya
George W. Kanyeihamba	Uganda
Jean Emile Somda	Burkina Faso
Sophia A. B. Akuffo	Ghana

Gérard Niyungeko had a diverse career in academia, domestic courts, and regional and international organizations prior to his election as the first president of the ACtHPR. From 1992 to 1996 Niyungeko served as the president of the Constitutional Court of Burundi. He held law professorships at universities across Africa and Europe and served as the UNESCO Chair in Education for Peace and Conflict Resolution at the University of Burundi from 1999 to 2003. The ACtHPR's first vice president, Modibo Tounty Guindo, had a twenty-nine-year domestic judicial career before joining the ACtHPR. In his capacity as a designated human rights adviser within the Ministry of Justice, Guindo directed Mali's presentation of its second periodic report before the UN Human Rights Committee.

Six of the ACtHPR's eleven founding judges came from academic backgrounds, where they held professorships in law at universities traversing the globe. Bernard Makgabo Ngoepe had been the chancellor of the University of South Africa since 2000, a position he held until 2016. Ten of the ACtHPR's founding judges had prior experience as domestic judges. Makgabo Ngoepe, Jean Mutsinzi, Kelello Justina Mafoso-Guni, George W. Kanyeihamba, and Sophia A. B. Akuffo had all served as judges on their nations' highest courts. Mafoso-Guni was the first female justice to serve on Lesotho's high court. Mutsinzi had also held various administrative and diplomatic positions within the OAU and served as a judge on the Court of Justice of the Common Market for Eastern and Southern Africa from 2001 to 2003. Kanyeihamba was the only founding judge with a political background, having served in the Ugandan National Legislature. He also held domestic positions as cabinet minister, minister of justice, attorney general, and senior adviser to the president on human rights and international affairs. Jean Emile Somda held numerous governmental and judicial appointments prior to joining the ACtHPR, including minister of public service, president of the Bobo-Dioulasso Court of Appeal, and legal adviser to the minister of justice. Hamdi Faraj Fanoush is a Libyan judge and ambassador who is known for his work conducting training on human rights issues within the Libyan judiciary and promoting other domestic human rights initiatives.

In addition to a legal career in Senegal, El Hadji Guissé served as the secretary-general of the International Organization for the Realization of Cultural, Social, and Economic Rights. He also worked with the UN in various capacities, including as president of the UN Sub-Commission on the Fight Against Discriminatory Practices and the Protection of Minorities, and as president of the Working Group on the Consequences of Activities of Transnational Corporations on Human Rights. Fatsah Ouguergouz, the only inaugural ACtHPR judge without experience in a domestic judiciary, had a prolific career in international adjudication, human rights promotion, and legal education prior to joining the Court. Ouguergouz served as the secretary of the International Court of Justice for twelve years and held various posts within the UN, including as a human rights officer in Rwanda. Following the conclusion of his tenure at the ACtHPR, Ouguergouz was appointed by the UN Human Rights Council to serve as an independent expert on the Situation of Human Rights in Burundi. Ouguergouz has held professorships in universities across Africa, Europe, and North America.[106]

The ACtHPR's founding judges were highly accomplished professors, jurists, and national and international diplomats. Only one judge had held domestic political office. Overall, the founding judges of the ACtHPR were notably more experienced than the founding judges of the IACtHR. Their extensive collective experience in domestic litigation undoubtedly informed how the ACtHPR began to forge relationships with national judiciaries in the Court's early years.

Summary

The story of the ACtHPR's founding is full of fascinating innovations and contradictions. On the one hand, the African Charter and its Protocol are radically progressive documents that extend the scope of the rights protected under the African system well beyond what the architects of the American and European systems ever envisioned. On the other hand, clawback provisions dilute the de jure authority of the Court. The OAU's history reveals a pervasive norm of nonintervention among African governments, stemming from the scars of colonization. Perhaps the more deferential elements of the Charter, as well as the fact that only a handful of governments have permitted their citizens to directly petition the Court, can be traced to this historical suspicion of any encroachment on national sovereignty. Still, this group of governments that scholars are often quick to characterize as resistant to international governance or fixated on "traditional" methods of dispute resolution ultimately created a functioning international court and imposed comparatively few limits on its authority. The ACtHPR is a young court with a relatively underdeveloped case law compared to its European and American counterparts. Still, the ACtHPR's jurisprudence has revealed how the Court's unique mandate has shaped domestic engagement with international law. The following chapters will explore the evolution of each regional court's case law, with particular attention to how judges reference their courts' founding mandates to guide interpretations of the legitimate reach of their authority.

THE COURTS' EARLY YEARS

The unique geopolitical contexts and actors involved in drafting each of the regional courts' constitutive documents drove consequential variation across the substance and scope of those courts' formal mandates. The ECtHR's founding by postwar democracies whose political advisers retained tight control over drafting negotiations resulted in that court's relatively constrained jurisdiction. The IACtHR, on the other hand, was founded amid widespread regime instability and state-sponsored repression. While embattled antidemocratic governments afforded little strategic attention to the court project, legal bureaucrats were able to leverage greater control over the negotiations to draft the American Convention. As a result, the Inter-American system was ultimately empowered with a mandate to protect a broader scope of human rights guarantees. The leadership of African jurists in drafting the African Charter and its Protocol contributed to the ACtHPR's unprecedentedly wide-ranging jurisdiction. However, the Court's mandate is arguably diluted by "clawback" provisions littered throughout the Charter that reflect suspicion of international governance among regimes that had only recently gained independence from their colonizers.

This chapter investigates how the first judges who served on the regional courts interpreted the authority that had been delegated to them. Each court confronted very different types of human rights violations during its early years of operation. Judges calibrated their projection of authority based on the exigencies of their respective political environments. The precedents set in each court's early years are crucial for understanding how these courts navigate their relationships with national authorities today.

An international court's founding interpretation of its authority is guided by the formal mandate set forth in its constitutive documents. But no judge on any court simply applies the law as it written. Law has inherent subjectivities, and it is impossible for those who write laws to anticipate every dispute that might emerge between legal subjects. As judges are charged with interpreting the law, they possess a great deal of agency in molding a court's authority. The judges that constitute a court's founding bench are in a unique position to pioneer their own interpretations of their court's social purpose.

Based on the challenges confronted by a court in its early years, court officials will self-define their legitimacy as more or less tied to cooperation with member governments and respect for state consent to jurisdiction. Court officials will reference this legitimation narrative to define the appropriate exercise of court authority relative to national authority, establishing a durable framework for when and where the court will intervene in domestic affairs. For example, if a regional court faces a high number of cases involving systemic, fundamental rights violations in its early years, indicating widespread disrespect for human rights among member governments, that court will likely feel the need to wield more heavy-handed authority. Judges will legitimize this exercise of authority through internal narratives that emphasize the imperative to keep repressive governments in check. On the other hand, if the cases that a regional court faces in its early years primarily reflect isolated human rights shortcomings, that court might be more willing to trust governments to generally uphold their obligations. The court may not perceive legitimate grounds to adopt a domineering interpretation of its authority and may instead opt for a more deferential approach to resolving disputes.

Case Selection

This chapter investigates the validity of this argument through analysis of each regional court's early case law. Because it is impossible to evaluate the entirety of each court's case law within a project of this length, I focus on three categories of rights: (1) the freedom of expression, which was integral to each court's founding case law; (2) personal integrity rights violations,[1] which dominated the IACtHR's early case law but were not routinely confronted by the ECtHR until the 1990s; and (3) protections against anti-LGBT discrimination, an issue that was not addressed by any court early on but received more attention as international norms evolved. This chapter, which focuses on each court's early years, will only address LGBT rights in the context of the ECtHR (as no relevant cases reached the IACtHR until later on). The ACtHPR is still a young court and has comparatively underdeveloped case law. Accordingly, this chapter will evaluate critical developments in the ACtHPR's early case law with a focus on, but not exclusive attention to, the above rights categories.

Each regional court was founded during a different decade and developed jurisprudence at a different pace. For the purposes of this chapter, I constrain my analysis of each court's "foundational case law" to judgments rendered between 1961 and 1989 for the ECtHR, 1988 to 2001 for the IACtHR, and 2009 to 2016 for the ACtHPR. The ECtHR issued its first merits judgment in 1961, and its jurisprudence grew quite slowly through the mid-1980s. I have chosen 1989 as the cutoff for the ECtHR's foundational period because 1990 marked the first major shift in the Court's membership. The CoE admitted a wave of new Eastern European member states throughout the 1990s. This eastward expansion dramatically shifted the political context in which the ECtHR operated. The IACtHR issued its first merits judgment in 1988. This chapter follows the Court's jurisprudence through 2001, up until the point when the Inter-American system underwent its first round of major procedural reforms. Finally, this chapter evaluates the ACtH-PR's jurisprudence between 2009, the year of the Court's first admissibility decision, and 2016, the year before a sharp uptick in judgments rendered annually. The 2009–2016 period marked a formative era for the Court before the rapid increase in caseload it has experienced since 2016. The following review of case law is not exhaustive. I have elected to discuss particular cases based on their importance for establishing precedent and for assessing each court's exercise of its authority.

Figure 3.1 illustrates variation across the types of rights violations confronted by the ECtHR and IACtHR during each court's foundational period, as well as

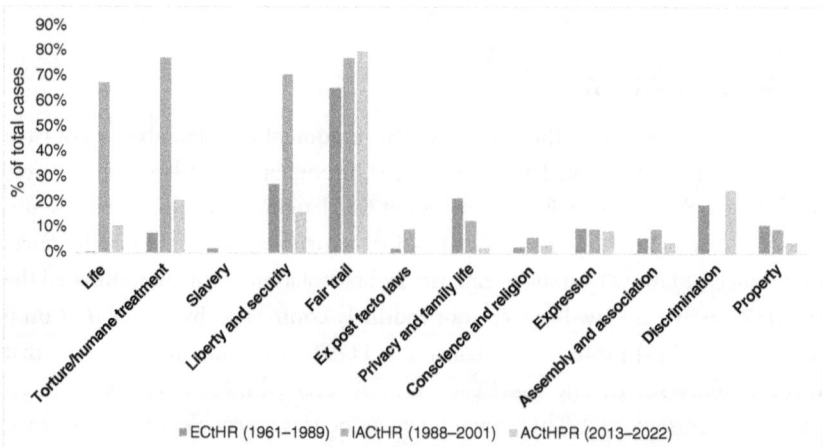

FIGURE 3.1. ECtHR, IACtHR, and ACtHPR early case law

the ACtHPR's jurisprudence from its first merits judgment (2013) through 2022. Each rights violation category is depicted as a percentage of each court's overall case law output, as measured by number of merits judgments. The twelve substantive rights violations on the x-axis are the rights that are shared across the European Convention, American Convention, and African Charter.[2]

These figures illustrate the very different challenges that faced the courts as they sought to gain footing in their respective regions. The fact that 68 percent of IACtHR cases from 1988 to 2001 involved alleged violations of the right to life reflects the severity of the human rights crisis that the Court was tasked with confronting in its early years. Seventy-seven percent of IACtHR cases during that period involved alleged violations of the prohibition of torture / right to humane treatment, further illustrating the abuse wrought by militaristic regimes throughout the region. The ECtHR, meanwhile, only heard one case involving an alleged violation of the right to life between 1961 and 1989, and thirteen cases in which torture or inhumane treatment was alleged (8 percent of total cases during that period). Twenty-eight percent of ECtHR cases heard during this period involved alleged violations of the right to liberty and security, but these cases primarily resulted from isolated instances of prolonged pretrial detention, not systemic state-sponsored violence.[3] While the ACtHPR has encountered personal integrity rights violations less often than the IACtHR in its early years, the ACtHPR has still heard more cases alleging such violations in the past decade than the ECtHR did in its first twenty-eight years in operation. Assessing the case law of the ACtHPR is hindered by the fact that the Court is still so young, but the trajectory of its current output indicates that the ACtHPR is on track to rule on just as many (if not more) cases in its first twenty years as the IACtHR did in its first twenty years.

The European Court of Human Rights

The ECtHR's early case law demonstrated a tendency to broadly interpret the circumstances in which states can legally restrict certain rights guarantees. These circumstances ranged from the need to protect public "morals" to the use of derogation clauses to suspend rights protections during emergencies. The Court's deference to state parties was rooted in general respect for the competence of national authorities. ECtHR judges developed a novel legal doctrine, the "margin of appreciation," to calibrate this deference. Cases involving alleged violations of the right to freedom of expression and anti-LGBT discrimination were particularly important for developing the initial contours of the margin of appreciation. The doctrine's application was closely tied to what the Court saw as regional consensus surrounding given human rights norms, with less deference afforded to states who deviated from that consensus. The early ECtHR lacked experience with personal integrity rights violations, a reflection of the region's general democratic stability. This context likely contributed to the Court's tendency to defer to governments in cases implicating national security, with controversial implications for the Court's handling of cases stemming from the Northern Irish conflict.

Personal Integrity Rights

The prohibition of torture, codified in Article 3 of the European Convention, is among the most fundamental human rights. As a *jus cogens* principle of international law, no derogation from this right is ever permissible, even under conditions of public emergency during which other rights can be validly restricted. Article 3 reads: "No one shall be subjected to torture or to inhuman or degrading treatment or punishment." The ECtHR established an Article 3 violation for the first time in *Ireland v. the United Kingdom* (1978), an example of rare inter-state disputes within the European system. The Irish government called on the Court to determine whether British security forces had engaged in a systematic practice of torturing suspected IRA members in Northern Ireland. The Court was not tasked with ruling on whether specific individuals had been tortured, as the Court can only rule on violations suffered by applicants. When the applicant is a state party, as in this case, that state can only ask the ECtHR to determine whether another state's pattern of behavior has breached the Convention.[4]

At issue in *Ireland* was the question of whether specific interrogation practices employed by British security forces, known as the "five techniques," constituted torture. These techniques included wall-standing in a "stress position," hooding, subjection to noise, sleep deprivation, and deprivation of food and water.[5] In this case, the ECtHR interpreted Article 3 to indicate that a distinction exists between "torture," on the one hand, and "inhuman or degrading treatment or punishment" on the other. This distinction "derives principally from a difference in the intensity of the suffering inflicted." The judgment did not elaborate on what might constitute a minimum level of suffering for an act to be deemed torture. The Court ruled that the "five techniques" qualified as inhuman and degrading treatment and thus violated Article 3. However, despite acknowledging that the techniques caused "intense physical and mental suffering . . . and also led to acute psychiatric disturbances," the Court ruled they "did not occasion suffering of the particular intensity and cruelty implied by the word torture."[6]

The ECtHR's ruling in *Ireland* has been extensively critiqued as an inappropriately narrow application of Article 3.[7] The Court's ruling is especially puzzling because the European Commission had unanimously declared the five techniques to constitute torture in its independent consideration of the *Ireland* case.[8] When the Court was given a rare chance for a redo, it declined. In 2014, the Irish government submitted a "request for revision" of *Ireland* to the ECtHR on the grounds that newly discovered documents contained facts relevant to the severity of the interrogation techniques. The ECtHR dismissed this request, citing that these documents would not have a "decisive influence" on its decision.[9] Even after forty years, the ECtHR's reasoning remained firm.

One way in which international courts can exhibit deference to national authorities is by allowing states to temporarily derogate from their international obligations. Article 15 of the European Convention permits derogations in times of "war or other public emergency." Given the drafters' faith that mass violence in Europe was a thing of the past, it is ironic that the first case ever heard by the ECtHR centered on a simmering civil conflict. Decided on the eve of "the Troubles" in Northern Ireland, *Lawless v. Ireland* (1961) concerned the arbitrary detention of a suspected IRA member. Ireland had submitted a derogation to restrict the right to liberty and security (Article 5) during civil unrest. The ECtHR determined that Ireland applied the derogation appropriately, and no violation was found.[10] This decision instigated a long-term trend in the Court's case law granting state authorities a wide margin to derogate from the Convention in times of civil conflict.[11] Allowing states to derogate implies a level of trust in domestic authorities to restrict rights only to the extent that is required by an acute situation. Outside of a handful of cases stemming from the Northern Ireland conflict, the European system did not routinely confront cases of conflict-era rights abuses until the late 1990s. Consequently, the ECtHR's case law on personal integrity rights remained underdeveloped for decades.

The ECtHR found a violation of Article 3 in only one other case during the 1970s: *Tyrer v. the United Kingdom* (1978). The applicant was a teenager who had been convicted of assault for beating his classmate. The boy was sentenced to three lashes with a birch stick, administered by a policeman. The ECtHR determined that this punishment constituted degrading treatment in violation of Article 3 but did not indicate torture.[12] *Tyrer* and *Ireland* established that a broad span of behavior could constitute degrading treatment—from three birch lashes to prolonged interrogation techniques aimed at inducing physical and mental breakdown. However, it was not until the 1990s that the ECtHR would develop clearer definitions of what actions could be distinctly considered "torture."

States' obligations to refrain from actions that constitute inhuman or degrading treatment were well established in international law by the 1980s. However, the extent to which states have positive obligations to prevent and respond to such treatment inflicted by private citizens on other private citizens was a much murkier legal area. Indeed, the scope of governments' positive obligations to prevent and provide legal remedies for bodily harm committed by non-state actors is still an evolving area within international law today. The ECtHR first grappled with this issue in *X and Y v. the Netherlands*, an incredibly tragic case involving a mentally disabled teenage girl who was raped by an employee's relative at the privately owned care facility where the girl lived. When the girl's father went to the police to file a criminal complaint against the alleged rapist, he was informed that he could not sign the complaint on behalf of his daughter because she was over sixteen years of age. However, the police also determined that the girl was not mentally capable of filing a complaint herself. The public prosecutor's office decided not to pursue criminal proceedings against the alleged rapist on the grounds that no one had legal standing to file a complaint. This decision was upheld by a court of appeals, which found that there was a "gap in the law . . . that could not be filled by means of a broad interpretation to the detriment of [the alleged rapist]."[13]

The case eventually made it to the ECtHR, where the girl's father argued that the "gap in the law" that prevented Dutch parents from launching criminal proceedings against their teenage children's abusers violated the right to private and family life (Article 8), the right to an effective remedy (Article 13), discriminated against the mentally disabled in contravention of Article 14, and constituted inhuman and degrading treatment under Article 3. ECtHR judges unanimously ruled that the lack of legal protection for the applicants violated Article 8, but, having established that violation, the Court "did not have to examine" the complaints under Articles 3, 13, and 14.[14] This judgment is an example of ECtHR judges' tendency to rule only on what they deem to be the core violation(s) in a case petition and not on allegations that are considered to be peripheral or redundant. The judges' decision not to consider whether the applicants' lack of legal recourse for rape constituted inhuman or degrading treatment is revelatory of their stance on states' positive obligations to prevent bodily harm. The ECtHR held the Netherlands accountable for the circumstances that blocked the girl and her father from accessing domestic legal recourse. However, the Court did not find it appropriate to consider whether, by permitting a gap in the law, the state had failed to uphold any positive obligation under Article 3 to prevent and/or respond differently to the assault itself.

The ECtHR first confronted an alleged violation of the right to life (Article 2) in *Soering v. the United Kingdom* (1989), a landmark case that established influential precedent regarding states' human rights obligations to individuals subject to extradition. The applicant, Jens Soering, was a German national who was at the time detained in England pending extradition to the United States to face capital murder charges. Soering had admitted to investigators that he and his girlfriend had murdered his girlfriend's parents in Virginia before fleeing to Europe. Soering argued before the ECtHR that, by sending him to stand trial in a country where he was at risk of receiving the death penalty, the UK would violate Articles 2 and 3 of the European Convention. The ECtHR majority rejected the applicant's claim under Article 2, pointing out that the Convention does not explicitly prohibit capital punishment.[15] Judge De Meyer disputed this conclusion, writing in a separate opinion that "there can be no doubt whatsoever that the applicant's extradition to the United States would violate his right to life." Emphasizing that social tolerance of the death penalty had diminished since the Convention's drafting in 1950, Judge De Meyer argued that extradition to any country where an individual would be susceptible to the death penalty would, in fact, violate Article 2: "Such a punishment is not consistent with the present state of European civilization."[16] ECtHR judges did unanimously rule that, based on prison conditions and average length of pre-execution detention for death row inmates in the US, the UK government would violate Article 3 should it proceed with the Soering's extradition.[17] This case was pivotal in that it broadened the scope of states' responsibilities under the Convention to encompass the consequences of transferring individuals to outside jurisdictions. This decision would have important ramifications for later deportation cases.

The ECtHR did not face any other cases involving potential violations of the right to life until the mid-1990s. Overall, the ECtHR developed very little case law on personal integrity rights violations during its early years. The young ECtHR's lack of cases involving fundamental rights violations illustrates how the types of regimes that constitute an international court's membership influence the court's relationships with member governments. In the absence of systemic rights abuses, ICs can have more confidence in domestic institutions and consequently defer greater authority to those entities to determine how best to implement their international obligations. Perhaps this explains the Court's hesitance to label the UK's treatment of Northern Irish prisoners as torture. The ECtHR found the interrogation techniques to be "degrading" but felt that condemning the UK for practicing torture, with all the loaded connotations of that term, was a bridge too far.

Freedom of Expression

The right to freedom of expression, codified in Article 10 of the European Convention, consistently featured in the ECtHR's early case law. Violation of this right was central to *De Becker v. Belgium* (1962), the second case the ECtHR ever heard. In *De Becker*, the ECtHR was faced with interpreting its temporal jurisdiction in the context of an alleged "continuing violation." A continuing violation entails "the breach of an international obligation by an act of a subject of international law extending in time and causing a duration or continuance in the time of that breach."[18] Unlike for instantaneous actions that take place in a definable moment, it can be tricky to ascertain when an alleged continuing violation starts or ends. This poses a challenge for judges, as the timing of an action implicates its admissibility for judicial consideration. ICs can only admit cases when the complained-of action occurred after the state acceded to the court. In cases alleging continuing violations that originated preaccession, the court must decide whether justification exists for the court to possess temporal jurisdiction over the complaint.

Raymond De Becker was a journalist who had collaborated with the Nazis during the occupation of Belgium. De Becker was condemned to death by a Belgian war crimes tribunal in 1946, but his sentence was later reduced to life imprisonment and the forfeiture of his civil and political rights. Following his conditional release in 1951, De Becker petitioned the European Commission alleging violation of his right to freedom of expression. The case was forwarded to the ECtHR, which admitted the part of De Becker's application that disputed the international legality of the penal code under which he was sentenced. The Court recognized that the ongoing impact of his sentencing had placed De Becker in a "continuing situation."[19] *De Becker* was ultimately struck from the ECtHR's docket after a domestic legislative reform resolved the applicant's complaints. Still, this case set a precedent for acknowledging continuing situations and started to delineate conditions for admitting alleged violations that originated prior to state accession to the Court.

The ECtHR's case law on freedom of expression has been integral in shaping the Court's broader relationships with national authorities. *Engel and Others v. the Netherlands* (1976), the second case in the ECtHR's history to deal with freedom of expression, involved several applicants who were conscripted members of the Dutch military. Two of these applicants had published a journal that their superiors deemed "inconsistent with military discipline." As punishment, they were assigned to a disciplinary unit and banned from publishing articles with similar content. When the applicants continued publishing articles, they were arrested and detained for three months.[20] The ECtHR found no violation of Article 10 in this case. The Court accepted the government's argument that the actions taken were "necessary in a democratic society . . . for the prevention of disorder." This argument draws from acceptable restrictions of the right to freedom of expression outlined in Article 10 (2) of the Convention. The ECtHR elaborated that expression can be restricted not only if the general "public order" is threatened, but also if order is threatened "within the confines of a specific social group" when "disorder in that group can have repercussions on order in society as a whole."[21] Thus, domestic authorities can restrict expression in groups whose activities affect the general public, such as the military (even among conscripted service members).

The applicants in *Engel* had argued that the Convention permits restrictions on expression for the "prevention of disorder" only *in combination* with the "prevention of crime." As the applicants did not incite criminal activity, they argued that their Article 10 rights had indeed been violated. Here, a discrepancy across the Convention's official translations forced ECtHR judges to make an interpretive choice. The French translation of Article 10 (2) states that expression can be restricted for the prevention of disorder *and* crime, while the English translation permits restriction for the prevention of disorder *or* crime. The Court majority found the English version to provide "a surer guide on the point."[22] This decision established crucial precedent widening the circumstances under which states can validly restrict expression. *Engel* was foundational to a strong trend in the ECtHR's jurisprudence of deferring to national authorities in situations implicating public emergency or security concerns, broadly defined.

It was within the context of a freedom of expression dispute in *Handyside v. the United Kingdom* (1976) that the Court first referenced the margin of appreciation doctrine (MOA). This doctrine, while having no textual basis in the original Convention, is a primary instrument through which the Court has historically exercised a deferential interpretation of its authority. The MOA guides the extent to which the Court will defer to a member state regarding a complained-of practice. Judges will apply a wider or narrower MOA depending on the level of consensus the Court observes on a given issue among member governments. This consideration of existing practices when applying the MOA reflects the ECtHR's respect for sovereignty and trust in the competence of national judiciaries. The MOA is rooted in the founders' vision of the ECtHR as a mechanism for fostering a shared European identity: By defining what constitutes consensus among member states, the ECtHR articulates what it means to be "European."

At issue in *Handyside* was the publication of a "reference book" on various topics surrounding sex and sexuality, with an adolescent target audience. British authorities had charged the book's publisher with violating the Obscene Publications Acts. The publisher was convicted and fined, and over a thousand copies of the book were seized and destroyed. The ECtHR found that British officials had acted reasonably under the provision of Article 10(2) that permits expression to be restricted when "necessary in a democratic society . . . for the protection of health or morals."[23] This interpretation upheld the judgment of the domestic court, which had determined that the book could "deprave and corrupt" minors. The domestic court had emphasized concerns regarding the book's lack of discussion of marriage and passages that implied that homosexual relationships could be "something permanent," as well as the author's suggestion that "every school should have at least one contraceptive vending machine."[24]

In *Handyside*, the ECtHR emphasized that "the machinery of protection established by the Convention is subsidiary to the national systems safeguarding human rights," and "it is for the national authorities to make the initial assessment of the reality of the pressing social need implied by the notion of 'necessity' in [Article 10(2)]." Consequently, Article 10(2) "leaves to the Contracting States a margin of appreciation."[25] This marked the first use of the term "margin of appreciation" by the ECtHR. Reiterating the Court's confidence in domestic authorities, the judgment declared that "it is in no way the Court's task to take the place of the competent national courts."[26] Thus, the ECtHR determined that British officials had acted within the MOA, and there had been no breach of the publisher's freedom of expression. The ECtHR again upheld that states can legally seize materials for the sake of "public morals" in *Müller and Others v. Switzerland* (1988), where authorities had confiscated sexually explicit paintings that a group of artists were displaying in a private gallery. The artists were subsequently convicted of publishing obscene materials under the Swiss Criminal Code and fined. The ECtHR majority ruled that neither the artists' conviction nor the confiscation of their paintings violated Article 10.[27]

The ECtHR established a violation of freedom of expression for the first time in *Sunday Times v. the United Kingdom* (1979). At issue was an injunction issued against the *Times* intended to block coverage of the "thalidomide children" scandal. Thalidomide was a sedative drug marketed to pregnant women that was found to have caused severe birth defects in hundreds of children born in Britain in 1961. The *Times* regularly reported on the plight of these children and the drug manufacturer's attempts to evade accountability throughout the late 1960s and early 1970s. In 1972, a British court granted an injunction against the *Times* to block the publication of a forthcoming article that authorities feared could corrupt ongoing settlement negotiations between the drug manufacturer and families of the affected children.

The ECtHR observed that the Convention guarantees "not only the freedom of the press to inform the public but also the right of the public to be properly informed."[28] In light of this, the Court emphasized that "the public interest aspect of the case" must be taken into account.[29] As the thalidomide issue was of public concern, the injunction "did not correspond to a social need sufficiently pressing to outweigh the public interest in freedom of expression."[30] Thus, the UK had violated Article 10. This case contributed to developing the contours of the MOA in freedom of expression cases, namely clarifying that a state's right to determine when social needs justify restriction of expression is not unlimited. The Convention does not permit states to suppress information of significant societal interest, such as public health concerns. It is curious that adolescents' access to sex education, arguably also a public health concern, was not determined to meet this threshold in *Handyside*.

Overall, early ECtHR judges applied a wide margin of appreciation in cases where applicants' expression was restricted for reasons pertaining to public order and morality. The Court even went so far as to permit the confiscation of art and criminal prosecution of artists for violating domestic obscenity laws. However, this deference to governments had limits. ECtHR judges were more inclined to rule against states when restricted information interfered with the right of the public to be informed about matters of widespread societal interest, such as the thalidomide scandal.

Protections Against Anti-LGBT Discrimination

Cases involving marginalized gender identities and sexual orientation discrimination did not emerge within the ECtHR's case law until the 1980s.[31] The first of these cases, *Dudgeon v. the United Kingdom* (1981), concerned now-defunct laws in Northern Ireland that criminalized sex between two men, but not between two women. The applicant in this case, a gay man, argued that these laws not only interfered with his right to private life (Article 8), but discriminated on the basis of gender (in contravention of Article 14). Citing Article 8(2), the government argued that the laws in question qualified as "necessary in a democratic society . . . for the protection of morals."[32] Emphasizing that restrictions of Article 8 must be proportionate to social needs, the Court pointed to changing regional norms regarding homosexuality: "As compared with the era when that legislation was enacted, there is now a better understanding, and in consequence an increased tolerance, of homosexual behaviour to the extent that in the great majority of the member States of the Council of Europe it is no longer considered to be necessary or appropriate to treat homosexual practices of the kind now in question as in themselves a matter to which the sanctions of the criminal law should be applied."[33] The Court also noted that the recent lack of enforcement of laws criminalizing homosexuality in Northern Ireland did not appear to have any detrimental impact on public life: "The authorities [had] refrained in recent years from enforcing the law in respect of private homosexual acts between consenting [adult] males. . . ." There was no evidence to show that this "[had] been injurious to moral standards in Northern Ireland or that there [had] been any public demand for stricter enforcement of the law."[34] The ECtHR found the UK in violation of Article 8 in *Dudgeon* but declined to consider the applicant's second complaint of gender discrimination. Here we observe the court looking to predominant member state practice to determine when to push back against certain states' legislation. Furthermore, the Court indicated sensitivity to "public demand" for the enforcement of law, a clear sign of the Court's attention to social consensus when evaluating whether to defer to national authority.

The ECtHR again confronted the criminalization of homosexuality in *Norris v. Ireland* (1988). The applicant, a prominent gay rights activist, asserted that his physical and mental health were negatively impacted by Irish laws criminalizing homosexuality, as the threat of prosecution induced extreme stress. Again pointing to shifting social norms, the ECtHR established that Ireland's laws criminalizing homosexuality violated Article 8 on the grounds that such laws could not be reasonably interpreted as "necessary in a democratic society . . . for the protection of morals." Given that the case at hand impacted "a most intimate aspect of private life," the Court determined that the government's arguments in favor of criminalizing homosexuality were insufficient to justify such extensive interference in individuals' rights to privacy.

Despite condemning British and Irish laws criminalizing homosexuality in *Dudgeon* and *Norris*, the ECtHR declined to order those states to repeal the laws in question. This decision was typical of the ECtHR's remedial practice, both at that time and through today. While, in accordance with the language of its founding treaty, the Court routinely orders states to pay monetary reparations to victims of rights violations, requiring states to overturn legislation has always been seen as far outside the ECtHR's jurisdiction. The Court has recently begun to mandate nonmonetary remedies in select circumstances, but overturning domestic legislation remains out of the question. Still, the ECtHR's rulings in *Dudgeon* and *Norris* played an integral role in the eventual legalization of homosexuality in Northern Ireland and the Republic of Ireland.[35]

The fight for marriage equality for same-sex couples has represented one of most contested human rights struggles of the past half century. When the ECtHR was founded, no founding member state recognized same-sex marriage or any form of legalized same-sex partnership. Article 12 of the European Convention specifically guarantees the right to marry only to heterosexual couples and asserts the supremacy of domestic authority on this issue: "Men and women of marriageable age have the right to marry and to found a family, according to the national laws governing the exercise of this right." Much has changed since Article 12 was drafted. As of 2024, same-sex marriage is now legal in twenty-two Council of Europe member states,[36] while a further nine states recognize some other form of same-sex partnership (for example, civil unions).[37] The ECtHR has been a central actor in domestic debates surrounding marriage equality across Europe. Investigating how the ECtHR has responded to evolving social norms in this area provides a unique opportunity to assess how the Court interprets appropriate deference to national governments in the context of an issue that the Court's founders likely did not anticipate.

The ECtHR's first experiences adjudicating same-sex marriage rights occurred in cases involving transgender applicants. These cases, in which transgender applicants sought a range of legal protections including the right to marry, established precedent that guided the ECtHR's broader approach to same-sex marriage legalization.[38] It is essential to foreground the issue of transgender rights when analyzing the development of same-sex marriage jurisprudence within the ECtHR. The case of *Rees v. the United Kingdom* (1986) marked the first time in the ECtHR's history that the Court confronted both transgender rights and same-sex marriage. The applicant in this case was a transgender man who argued that the UK government's refusal to amend the sex listed on his birth certificate constituted a violation of his right to private life under Article 8. Additionally, Mr. Rees alleged that this refusal violated his right to marry under Article 12, as UK law prohibiting same-sex marriage dictated that he could not marry a woman so long as his birth certificate listed his sex as "female." With regard to whether states had a positive obligation under Article 8 to give transgender individuals "the option of changing their personal status to fit their newly-gained identity," the ECtHR majority noted that existing state practice on this matter varied considerably: "There is at present little common ground between the Contracting States in this area and that, generally speaking, the law appears to be in a transitional stage. Accordingly, this is an area in which the Contracting Parties enjoy a wide margin of appreciation."[39] The ECtHR ruled that the refusal to amend the applicant's birth certificate did not violate Article 8.[40] While the majority noted changing social norms regarding transgender rights, its decision indicated that the ECtHR was not yet prepared to push those developments forward. The Court's decision contradicted the recommendation of the European Commission, which had unanimously agreed that depriving the applicant of an updated birth certificate violated Article 8 guarantees.[41] The ECtHR's rejection of a unanimous Commission recommendation indicates a strong preference among ECtHR judges to pump the brakes on incursion into domestic authority on this issue. Still, three of the fifteen judges who presided over the case dissented to the majority's finding. These three judges proposed that a middle-ground solution could be reached where the UK could notate changes to the sex listed on transgender individuals' birth certificates while still maintaining the original certificate. For judges to offer proposals for specific domestic policy changes is rare within the ECtHR. This dissenting opinion offered a preliminary indication that ECtHR judges were poised to exert greater authority over transgender rights as social norms continued to evolve.

The applicant's second complaint in *Rees v. the U.K.*, the alleged violation of the right to marry (Article 12), forced the ECtHR to interpret the Convention's disposition toward same-sex marriage for the first time. The Court concluded that there had been no Article 12 violation in this case, offering terse reasoning: "In the Court's opinion, the right to marry guaranteed by Article 12 refers to the traditional marriage between persons of opposite biological sex. This appears also from the wording of the Article which makes it clear that Article 12 is mainly concerned to protect marriage as the basis of the family. Furthermore, Article 12 lays down that the exercise of this right shall be subject to the national laws of the Contracting States."[42] This interpretation of Article 12 in *Rees* was significant for driving future ECtHR case law on LGBT rights. First, it solidified that the Convention's protection of the right to marry did not extend to same-sex couples. Second, the judges defined heterosexual marriage as "the basis of the family," precluding the legal legitimacy of families that fall outside the heteronormative, nuclear family structure. Finally, this interpretation reflected a distinctly originalist approach to interpreting the Convention (in other words, a belief that the text of the Convention should be objectively interpreted as it was written, without attention to contemporary contextual factors).

The *Rees* judgment is puzzling in that the majority judgment at times depicts the Convention as a living instrument whose interpretation should reflect existing social realities, but at other points calls for objective attention to Convention language while eschewing consideration of the contemporary socio-legal climate. While discussing whether Article 8 required states to allow transgender individuals to alter the sex listed on their official identification, the judges in the majority emphasized that the Convention should be "interpreted and applied in light of current circumstances" and left the door open for future revision of the legal status quo "based on scientific and social judgements." When it came to Article 12 and the question of same-sex marriage, however, that rhetoric disappeared. The majority judgment unequivocally quashed the notion that the right to marry applied to same-sex couples, setting a definitive precedent that would prove arduous to wear down. The ongoing fight for transgender rights and marriage equality within the ECtHR will be further discussed in chapter 6, which investigates how the regional courts are interpreting their respective authorities in these rapidly evolving areas of international human rights law.

The Inter-American Court of Human Rights

The IACtHR faced a deluge of cases involving personal integrity rights violations in its early years. In particular, the Court confronted an epidemic of enforced disappearances and extrajudicial executions. Because the ECtHR lacked case law in these areas, the IACtHR was largely flying blind. Given the emergency conditions that early IACtHR judges faced, building collaborative relationships with national authorities was a secondary concern to interrupting systematic rights abuses. Judges sought ways to expand the IACtHR's authority through broad interpretations of the Court's advisory jurisdiction, temporal jurisdiction, and power to issue diverse remedial mandates. The Court also pioneered expanded conceptualizations of who can be considered a "victim" of grave human rights abuses and elaborated interpretations of the burden of proof that favored applicants. Still, the IACtHR was attentive to ECtHR jurisprudence and borrowed from it in areas where the ECtHR already had established case law—for example, in freedom of expression disputes.

Personal Integrity Rights

The IACtHR's early years were marked by widespread state-sponsored violence and civil conflict in Latin America. Personal integrity rights violations unfortunately dominated the Court's docket. These rights as codified in the American Convention include the right to life (Article 4) and the right to humane treatment (Article 5). Article 5 prohibits torture as well as inhuman or degrading treatment.

Unlike in the European system, American states do not automatically accede to the Court's jurisdiction upon ratifying the Convention. However, the Court possesses advisory jurisdiction over all OAS member states that have ratified the Convention. Founding IACtHR judges engaged in creative use of advisory jurisdiction to influence state practice and expand the Court's authority in the early 1980s, even in dealing with states that had not yet acceded to the Court. One example of this is the Court's effort to end summary executions carried out by the Guatemalan government. The Inter-American Commission had declared that these executions violated Article 4 of the Convention, which prohibits the reestablishment of the death penalty in states that have abolished it. Furthermore, Article 4 prohibits states from applying the death penalty to any crimes for which it was not sanctioned under domestic law when the Convention entered into force in that state. Guatemala ratified the American Convention in 1978 and subsequently executed individuals for crimes to which the death penalty was not applicable at that time. Guatemala argued that these executions were legally permissible because of a reservation the state had submitted to Article 4, exempting itself from the prohibition on applying the death penalty to "political offenses or related common crimes."[43]

In response, the Commission requested that the Court issue an advisory opinion on whether governments could impose the death penalty for crimes to which such penalty did not apply when the Convention entered into force. The Guatemalan government objected that this move was an insincere attempt to "disguise" a contentious case targeted against Guatemala as an advisory opinion.[44] Despite these protests, the Court admitted the Commission's request and ruled that reservations to Article 4 do not allow states to extend the death penalty to additional crimes after ratifying the Convention.[45] Following the ruling, Guatemala did stop the executions. This was one of the first instances where the IACtHR successfully stretched the boundaries of its jurisdiction to wield authority over repressive governments. Interestingly, Pope John Paul II had appealed to Guatemalan authorities to end the executions during his visit to Central America the year before the IACtHR ruling, to no avail. Where even the Pope failed, Judge Buergenthal later recalled proudly, "we had succeeded with a mere advisory opinion. It was quite a morale booster for the Court."[46] This statement exemplifies how founding IACtHR judges interpreted the Court's social purpose. Judges were willing to push the prescribed limits of the Court's authority to intervene in abusive practices.

The IACtHR ruled on its first-ever contentious case, *Velásquez-Rodríguez v. Honduras*, in 1988. The case concerned the enforced disappearance of a college student perpetrated by the Honduran Armed Forces. The Court considered whether Honduras had violated the Convention's guarantees under Articles 4 and 5. The judges unanimously interpreted the right to life to impose substantive obligations on states to protect life as well as procedural obligations to investigate violations of that right. These obligations are not extinguished until an investigation is conducted in good faith, and persist through regime changes.[47] Furthermore, enforced disappearances may constitute violations of the right to life even when the victim's death cannot be confirmed (for example, when remains have not been discovered). Disappearances are considered "continuing violations" because they create prolonged uncertainty regarding the whereabouts and fate of victims.[48] Consequently, disappearances trigger procedural obligations to investigate violations of the right to life that can only be discharged through a good-faith investigation and, where possible, punishment of the perpetrators. By establishing a procedural duty to investigate alleged violations of the right to life, the IACtHR set itself up to flexibly interpret its temporal jurisdiction in future enforced disappearance cases.

Unlike ECtHR judges in early cases concerning personal integrity rights violations, the IACtHR, in *Velásquez*, did not attempt to split hairs regarding the difference between torture and inhuman or degrading treatment. While several individuals provided secondhand testimonies that suggested Mr. Velásquez had been tortured and killed by Honduran security forces, no physical evidence or eyewitnesses confirmed this. Velásquez's remains were never found. In the absence of evidence, the Court relied on testimony from over twenty witnesses to determine that Honduran security forces routinely tortured and murdered detainees during the period in which Velásquez was disappeared. This context was sufficient for the Court to rule that Honduras had violated Velásquez's rights to life and humane treatment.[49] This case exemplifies the Court's application of a "dynamic burden of proof" (*carga dinámica de la prueba*) that shifts the burden of proof from the applicant to the respondent state in cases where, because of the nature and context of the alleged violation, it is impossible for the applicant to furnish evidence. Rather, it is incumbent on the state to prove that the allegations against it are unsubstantiated.[50]

Blake v. Guatemala (1998) was the first case in which the IACtHR was called to rule on an enforced disappearance that occurred before the state's accession to the Court. Mr. Blake was an American journalist who had been disappeared by Guatemalan police officers two years before Guatemala accepted the IACtHR's jurisdiction. Relying on the *Velásquez-Rodríguez* precedent, the IACtHR found Blake's disappearance to be a continuing situation that triggered the state's duty to investigate.[51] The Court acknowledged that it could not rule on Guatemala's responsibility for Blake's detention and death. Blake's remains had been discovered in 1992, and evidence established that he was killed in 1985. Unlike enforced disappearance, death is an instantaneous act that occurs within a definable time span. As this death occurred prior to Guatemala's accession, the Court could not evaluate potential violations of Article 4.[52] However, the Court found that it did maintain temporal jurisdiction over the continuing effects of Blake's disappearance, namely the harm incurred by the lack of an official investigation.[53] The Court found Guatemala in violation of Article 5 owing to the mental and emotional trauma suffered by Blake's family. This suffering was exacerbated by Guatemala's refusal to investigate or provide information regarding Blake's fate.[54] Here, the IACtHR took a decisive step toward broadly interpreting its temporal jurisdiction. This move expanded the Court's power to rule on continuing situations that originated prior to state accession. The Court also extended its conceptualization of who can be considered a "victim" of violations of the right to humane treatment. This category includes the loved ones of the dead and disappeared whose mental integrity is violated when a state refuses to investigate an enforced disappearance or extrajudicial killing. Their anguish can in and of itself constitute a continuing situation that expands the Court's temporal jurisdiction.

The IACtHR is notable for its contributions to international jurisprudence establishing that amnesty laws applicable to crimes against humanity violate international law. The Court's first case challenging a domestic amnesty law was *Barrios Altos v. Peru* (2001), concerning the massacre of fifteen civilians at the hands of a government death squad in 1991. For a decade, the military denied its role in the massacre, and the perpetrators were protected from prosecution by dictator Alberto Fujimori's amnesty laws even after Peru returned to democracy. When the case finally reached the IACtHR in 2001, the Court declared Peru in violation of Articles 4 and 5, and furthermore established that Peru's amnesty laws violated the right to judicial protection (Article 25) by precluding victims from seeking legal recourse. The Court ordered Peru to pay reparations to the survivors of the massacre and the victims' families, as well as conduct an official investigation and punish those responsible. In a bold step that underscored the IACtHR's interventionist interpretation of its authority, the Court then declared Peru's amnesty laws to be null and void.[55] The IACtHR's self-interpreted power to unilaterally abrogate domestic legislation, which is rooted in but does not necessarily follow from the wording of Article 63, marks a sharp divergence from the ECtHR's more conservative approach to mandating remedies.

The implications of pioneering regional jurisprudence under conditions of mass state-sponsored violence are plainly visible in the IACtHR's early case law. The Court consistently adopted broad interpretations of its temporal jurisdiction, flexible evidentiary standards for establishing violations in cases against states with track records of human rights abuse, inclusive definitions of victimhood, and an intensive approach to mandating remedies. In doing so, early IACtHR judges exercised an interventionist interpretation of their authority that significantly diverged from the ECtHR's prioritization of deference to governments in its early years. More permissive treaty language in the American Convention relative to the European Convention was necessary, but not sufficient, for arriving at this outcome. The early IACtHR judges' own philosophies about the Court's mission and purpose were critical for establishing enduring interpretations of the Court's authority.

Freedom of Expression

While the IACtHR's early case law was dominated by personal integrity rights violations, cases involving other civil and political rights began to appear before the Court more frequently in the late 1990s and early 2000s. Even so, many of these other rights violations were connected to instances of enforced disappearance, extrajudicial execution, and torture. For example, the IACtHR first confronted an alleged violation of the right to freedom of expression (Article 13) in the aforementioned *Blake v. Guatemala* case. The Inter-American Commission recommended that the Court find an Article 13 violation on the basis that Mr. Blake was targeted by Guatemalan security forces for his work as a journalist.[56] However, unlike the Commission, the Court was constrained in its jurisdiction by the date of Guatemala's accession to the Court. The Court could not evaluate the motivations for Blake's disappearance, which occurred prior to Guatemala's accession, and thus could not establish an Article 13 violation.[57]

"The Last Temptation of Christ" v. Chile, decided in 2001, was only the second case in the IACtHR's history alleging a freedom of expression violation. The applicants, Chilean human rights lawyers, objected to a Supreme Court decision that permitted censorship of a film deemed religiously offensive.[58] The Chilean government stated before the IACtHR its own opposition to the Supreme Court decision. In fact, in response to that decision, the government had proposed a constitutional reform to eliminate cinematographic censorship.[59] Reinforcing the necessity of this reform, the IACtHR found Chile in violation of Article 13 and ordered the state to amend its domestic censorship legislation. The Court referenced ECtHR jurisprudence in Handyside and Sunday Times to underscore the importance of freedom of expression not only for protecting individual speech but also for promoting a well-informed populace that is "the cornerstone of democratic society."[60]

IACtHR judges again leaned on ECtHR precedent in Ivcher-Bronstein v. Peru (2001), which the Court admitted shortly after the fall of the Fujimori dictatorship. The applicant, Mr. Bronstein, was a media channel owner who had immigrated to Peru and become a naturalized citizen. Throughout the late 1990s, a news program produced by Bronstein's channel broadcast investigative journalism critical of the Peruvian Armed Forces. These reports uncovered abuses committed by the military, including torture, assassination, and collaboration with drug traffickers.[61] Following these broadcasts, Bronstein and his family were repeatedly intimidated and threatened by government officials.[62] In 1997, the government issued a "directorial resolution" stripping Bronstein of his nationality. Shortly thereafter, Bronstein was removed as the majority shareholder of his channel in accordance with legislation requiring that media companies be owned by Peruvian citizens.[63]

The IACtHR's judgment on this case discussed ECtHR freedom of expression jurisprudence at length, emphasizing that the ECtHR established a narrow margin for the valid restriction of information pertinent to public interest.[64] Given that Bronstein was targeted for his channel's criticism of the military and deprived of his company as a direct result of his nationality being illegally annulled, the Court established that his freedom of expression had been violated. The Court ordered Peru to pay reparations to Bronstein, restore his ownership of the media channel, and punish those responsible for the rights violations.[65]

Particularly because the IACtHR's case law on freedom of expression was underdeveloped in the early 2000s, it makes sense that judges would look to the ECtHR for guidance in interpreting the substantive qualities of that right. IACtHR judges demonstrated agreement with the precedent set by the ECtHR, especially with regard to the narrow(er) margin for restricting speech regarding matters of public interest. The IACtHR did order more comprehensive remedies for violations of freedom of expression relative to the ECtHR, including ordering domestic prosecutions and legislative reforms. This practice aligns with the IACtHR's generally more invasive approach to mandating remedies for rights violations.

The African Court on Human and Peoples' Rights

While the ACtHPR was officially established in 2006, it did not issue its first decision on the admissibility of a case until December 2009. Its first judgment on the merits of a case was not issued until June 2013. Overall, the ACtHPR's output was low in its early years. This is not unusual. International courts are often slow to get off the ground, as evidenced by the experiences of both the ECtHR and the IACtHR. The number of judgments issued annually by the ACtHPR has risen sharply in recent years, indicating that the Court's capacity to process cases and the public's awareness of the Court are growing. Because the ACtHPR is a relatively new institution that is still coming into its own, we do not have the same benefit of retrospect when it comes to assessing the foundational period of the ACtHPR that we do with the ECtHR and the IACtHR.

The ACtHPR issued its first-ever judgment on the merits of a case in *Tanganyika Law Society, Legal and Human Rights Center, and Rev. Christopher Mtikila v. Tanzania* (2013). This case challenged an amendment to the Tanzanian Constitution that barred independent candidates from seeking political office. The applicants alleged that this amendment violated the African Charter's protections of freedom of association (Article 10) and freedom to participate in governance (Article 13). As the amendment in question had come into effect prior to Tanzania ratifying the Protocol to the Charter (thereby accepting the jurisdiction of the ACtHPR), the government argued that the Court lacked temporal jurisdiction to accept the case. The ACtHPR threw out this argument on two grounds. First, at the time of the alleged violations, Tanzania "had already ratified the Charter and was therefore bound by it."[66] Second, the amendment imposed a "continuing situation" that persisted beyond the dates that Tanzania ratified the Protocol. Therefore the ACtHPR maintained temporal jurisdiction.

Additionally, the Tanzanian government argued that the case was inadmissible because the applicants had failed to exhaust all domestic remedies. The applicants had indeed exhausted all possible challenges to the amendment through the domestic court system. The government, however, argued that the applicants neglected to launch a legislative challenge and thus still had available domestic remedies that would preclude the ACtHPR's jurisdiction. The ACtHPR cited both ECtHR and IACtHR jurisprudence to overrule this objection, establishing that applicants need only exhaust domestic *judicial* remedies, as legislative avenues are often not freely accessible, are not intended to remedy individual disputes, and are subject to repeal.[67] This dialogue indicates the ACtHPR's openness to utilizing ECtHR and IACtHR jurisprudence from its very first case.

The Court found Tanzania in violation of Articles 10 and 13 and ordered the government to take "constitutional, legislative, and all other necessary measures within a reasonable time to remedy the violations."[68] While this mandate stopped short of explicitly ordering Tanzania to repeal the complained-of amendment, it demonstrated the ACtHPR judges' willingness to demand domestic legislative change. This precedent was further expanded in *African Commission v. Libya* (2016), in which the Court ordered Libya to terminate criminal proceedings against the son of the former president, Muammar Gaddhafi.[69] In that case, the ACtHPR moved to directly usurp the power of national courts.

The ACtHPR faced allegations centering on the right to life (Article 4) and freedom of expression (Article 9) for the first time in *Zongo et al. v. Burkina Faso* (2015). The applicants in this case were the families of journalist Norbert Zongo and his younger brother and of two of Zongo's colleagues. The four men had been murdered, allegedly as retaliation for an investigation that Zongo was conducting on political scandals.[70] These murders occurred in 1998, well before Burkina Faso ratified the African Charter or the Protocol. Still, the ACtHPR overruled the state's objection to the Court's temporal jurisdiction on the grounds that national-level legal proceedings pertaining to this case occurred *after* Burkina Faso ratified the Charter and the Protocol. Thus, certain allegations within the *Zongo* case fell within the ACtHPR's temporal jurisdiction. These included alleged violations of the rights to freedom of expression and fair trial. The alleged violations of the right to life, however, remained outside the Court's temporal jurisdiction.[71]

It is worth noting that the continuing effects of the murders on the mental and emotional health of the victims' families are not mentioned in the ACtHPR's judgment in *Zongo*, let alone formulated as justiciable violations of the Charter. This marks a divergence from the standard practice of the IACtHR in cases of state-sponsored killings and could indicate ACtHPR judges' hesitance to adopt similarly flexible interpretations of temporal jurisdiction and legal victimhood. Still, by admitting a case of preaccession political violence, the judges in *Zongo* laid crucial groundwork for the ACtHPR to serve as a legitimate forum for securing state accountability for past rights abuses.

Regarding alleged violations of the right to freedom of expression in *Zongo*, the applicants argued that the murders created an atmosphere of fear and intimidation that impinged on public access to information.[72] The ACtHPR narrowly accepted this argument, ruling 5–4 that Burkina Faso had violated Article 9.[73] Dissenting judges objected that the applicants failed to provide any evidence that there was an "intimidating effect" on journalists resulting from the murders.[74] This ruling suggests that ACtHPR judges may be willing to accept a lower burden of proof on applicants in freedom of expression cases that are connected to particularly egregious circumstances, but this flexibility is limited.

The *Zongo* case also set important precedent regarding the ACtHPR's interpretation of effective remedies for rights violations. The Court established that Burkina Faso had violated the applicants' right to fair trial (Article 7) by denying them the opportunity to "have their cause heard by competent national courts."[75] Interestingly, Article 7 does not explicitly provide for the right to appeal to national judicial institutions in cases of alleged human rights violations. Rather, it establishes "the right to an appeal to competent national organs," without specifying that those organs must be judicial. In this respect, the African Charter's right to fair trial is written more similarly to the European Convention's "right to an effective remedy" (Article 13), which provides for the right to appeal to a "national authority" while also not specifying that that authority must be judicial. In *Zongo*, however, the judges interpreted Article 7 as if it required access to judicial recourse.[76] The ACtHPR's interpretation more closely approximates the American Convention's "right to judicial protection" (Article 25), which requires "effective recourse to a competent court or tribunal." ACtHPR judges unanimously agreed that there had been a violation of Article 7 in *Zongo*, indicating strong support for taking this interpretive liberty to establish the right to be heard by a court.[77] Taking a page from the IACtHR's book, this decision positions the ACtHPR to flexibly interpret its temporal jurisdiction in cases of continuing violations.

ACtHPR judges again looked to ECtHR and IACtHR precedent when evaluating the circumstances in which states can validly restrict the right to freedom of expression. In *Lohé Issa Konaté v. Burkina Faso*, the applicant was a journalist who had been convicted of defamation after publishing articles that accused a state prosecutor of corruption. The Ouagadougou High Court sentenced the applicant to a year in prison and assessed a large fine. Additionally, the magazine that had published the articles was ordered to cease operations for six months.[78] The applicant argued that the provisions of Burkina Faso's penal code relating to defamation and freedom of the press lacked clarity and thus violated international standards pertaining to the rule of law. The ACtHPR considered whether the provisions in question accorded with modern international jurisprudence on freedom of expression, as well as whether the applicant's lengthy prison sentence was proportional to the crime for which he was convicted. On both fronts, judges invoked the jurisprudence of the other regional courts. First, the majority opinion pointed to predominant norms maintaining that the right to freedom of expression can only be restricted (a) to respect the rights and reputation of others, and (b) to safeguard national security, public order, health, or public morality.[79] Second, the judges cited several ECtHR and IACtHR decisions that found that excessive penalties for defamation, including imprisonment and heavy fines, constituted violations of the right to freedom of expression.[80] By this point, both the ECtHR and IACtHR had established that criminal defamation laws should be used only as a "last resort." The IACtHR had outright rejected imprisonment for defamation offenses, considering imprisonment "disproportionate and in violation of freedom of expression."[81]

The ACtHPR majority found Burkina Faso in violation of Article 9 in *Konaté*, signaling the judges' attention to alignment with predominant cross-regional jurisprudence. Further illustrating the ACtHPR's self-interpreted authority to prescribe intensive remedial mandates, the majority ordered Burkina Faso to amend its penal code to repeal custodial sentences for defamation.[82] This broadly interpreted remedial authority, similar to that of the IACtHR, is rooted in, but does not necessarily or inherently result from, founding treaty language. Judicial interpretation is key. For Judges Thompson, Akuffo, Ngoepe, and Tambala, the remedial mandate in *Konaté* did not go far enough. They argued that the ACtHPR had missed an opportunity to eliminate the criminalization of speech of any kind: "Access to civil action, civil sanction, together with specifically defined crimes for safeguarding national security, public peace, and the common interest, should be sufficient. For this Court to hold otherwise would not only be a step backward in the evolution of human rights in Africa, but also out of consonance with the letter and spirit of the Charter, which it is established to uphold."[83] This separate opinion paved the way for a broader interpretation of freedom of expression in Africa, going beyond the jurisprudence of the ECtHR and IACtHR to argue that the African Charter uniquely precludes the criminalization of expression in any form. These four judges went even further by asserting that the majority should have simply declared the relevant provisions of Burkina Faso's penal code to be invalid, rather than asking the government to legislatively amend the provisions.[84] This marked the first time that ACtHPR judges claimed the Court's authority to unilaterally invalidate domestic legislation. This declaration was a daring move for such a young court, clearly following the example of the IACtHR.

The varying types of rights violations faced by each regional court in its early case law significantly shaped how founding judges interpreted their authority. In the absence of widespread fundamental rights abuses, ECtHR judges were generally confident in the competence of national authorities. These conditions favored a deferential interpretation of the Court's authority. This interpretation was most directly expressed through broad application of the margin of appreciation doctrine, flexible applications of rights restriction clauses, and remedial mandates that did not require domestic legal change. The ECtHR was more inclined to denounce state practices that diverged from emerging regional normative consensus, in keeping with the Court's mission to foster shared human rights standards across CoE member states. The IACtHR, in contrast, faced extensive state-sponsored rights abuses in a region plagued by political violence. These atrocities undermined the Court's trust in national authorities and spurred judges to expand the Court's mandate to intervene in domestic affairs. The judges did so by pushing the boundaries of the Court's advisory jurisdiction, broadly interpreting the Court's temporal jurisdiction, adopting flexible evidentiary standards to shift the burden of proof away from applicants, extending legal definitions of victimhood, and mandating intensive remedies—even going so far as to declare the Court's authority to abrogate domestic legislation.

The ACtHPR's early case law reflects somewhat of a "middle ground" interpretation of the Court's authority that is less interventionist than that of the IACtHR but not nearly as deferential as the ECtHR. This could be anticipated given the political dynamics surrounding the drafting of the African Charter and Protocol, which empowered the Court with a broad formal mandate but also promoted judicial restraint through "clawback clauses." ACtHPR judges adopted a flexible interpretation of the Court's temporal jurisdiction, stretching back to state ratification of the African Charter. However, the Court's application of this jurisdiction has been limited by a narrower approach, relative to the IACtHR, to conceptualizing continuing situations connected to violations of the right to life. Likewise, ACtHPR judges have exhibited cautious moderation in evaluating the balance of the burden of proof. Still, the judges have demonstrated a proclivity to judicial activism in their interpretation of state obligations under the right to fair trial as well as remedial mandates that intervene in domestic legal proceedings. The ACtHPR is still developing jurisprudence in key areas that will shape the contours of the Court's authority. The remaining chapters of this work will evaluate the durability of each court's founding interpretation of its authority, with particular attention to how judges navigate institutional reforms and react to member state backlash.

Note on Case Selection

The following chapters dive into three substantive areas within each regional court's case law: (1) freedom of expression, (2) personal integrity rights, and (3) gender identity and sexual orientation discrimination. This review of case law is far from exhaustive. It is impossible to discuss every important case each court has deliberated within a project of this length. Accordingly, I developed various criteria for selecting cases to feature in this analysis. First, I collected every case across the three selected issue areas. Next, I selected particular time periods to focus on according to the historical reasoning outlined earlier (ECtHR: 1990–2003, 2010–2015; IACtHR: 2002–2005, 2012–2020; ACtHPR: 2017–2022). Then I established how often every case that fit within those parameters was subsequently cited by judges within the court that decided that case. I only counted one "cite" per subsequent case. In other words, if Case A was cited once within a later judgment (Case B), I counted one cite. If Case A was cited five times in Case B, I still counted only one cite. I included citations made by judges in separate opinions as well as in majority judgments. For example, if the majority in Case B did not cite Case A in their judgment, but a dissenting judge in Case B cited case A, that citation would still count as a "subsequent cite" for Case A. To account for the three regional courts' varied case-processing structures, all judgments pertaining to a given case (indicated by a shared application number) were treated as one case. For example, I did not differentiate between subsequent citations of the *Janowiec and Others v. Russia* Chamber judgment and the *Janowiec and Others v. Russia* Grand Chamber judgment. Subsequent citations of either judgment simply counted as one citation for *Janowiec and Others v. Russia*. Similarly, if the IACtHR's *Gelman v. Uruguay* case was cited in both the merits judgment and the reparations judgment in a subsequent IACtHR case, I still tallied only one subsequent citation for *Gelman v. Uruguay* in that instance. I used this number of subsequent citations to identify a set of cases that had been particularly influential for setting precedent within each court. In order to facilitate valid comparison across courts, I then reviewed and recorded the basic substantive facts of each case within the frequently cited subset. I used these descriptions to "match" cases with similar underlying circumstances across courts. These matches became the batch of cases that I referenced to write the following chapters.

This case selection process is not perfect. It required me to at times make subjective judgment calls in order to capture variation across time, case output, and regime type while selecting cases with sufficiently similar fact patterns to facilitate cross-court comparison. For example, because of the very different sizes of each court's case law, I could not use a uniform "cutoff" number of subsequent citations to determine whether a case could join the frequently cited subset. Additionally, relying on the number of subsequent citations to identify "important" cases imposes a bias in favor of selecting Grand Chamber judgments in the ECtHR. This potentially risks overlooking important case law developments that unfolded at the Chamber and Committee levels. Still, as the Grand Chamber only rules on cases that pose novel and/or particularly contentious legal interpretive questions, this bias may work in favor of identifying influential cases. In order to mitigate the effect of any potential national peculiarities on this analysis, I tried to select cases involving a wide range of states of varied regime types and membership statuses (e.g., founding member state vs. newer member state). At times, this required me to deflect focus from cases that had higher subsequent citation counts than the cases I ultimately selected.

Given that every case is based on different facts, and therefore the impossibility of perfectly "matching" cases for comparison, I used very broad criteria to identify groups of cases with similar fact patterns. For example, within the collection of cases involving alleged violations of freedom of expression, I grouped together cases that involved "defamation disputes." This matching technique is beneficial in that it helps create a manageable group of cases on which to conduct qualitative analysis. It also enables more direct comparison across cases and across courts. Matching cases in this way, however, does run the risk of neglecting types of cases that are not easily matched. For example, the IACtHR has decided several cases that involved issues of freedom of expression within the context of more severe rights violations, such as enforced disappearances. The ECtHR, in contrast, does not have frequently cited cases involving both freedom of expression and state-sponsored physical violence during the time periods targeted in this analysis. Consequently, some IACtHR cases that involved both personal integrity rights and freedom of expression are not included in the chapter on freedom of expression. Still, given the attention to several categories of case characteristics employed by this matching technique, I am confident that the selection of cases it yielded is sufficiently representative to produce valid analysis.

4

JUDGMENTS ON THE RIGHT TO FREEDOM OF EXPRESSION

In December 2018, the ECtHR issued a pivotal decision establishing that holding news media companies liable for content hyperlinked on their websites violates the European Convention's right to freedom of expression. The applicant in this case was a company called Magyar Jeti Zrt. The company had been found liable in Hungarian courts for "disseminating defamatory statements" in an article it published about an incident of racist harassment against Roma schoolchildren. The statements in question, which implied that the nationalist Jobbik political party incited the harassment, were made by an interviewee in a video produced by a different news company. Magyar Jeti Zrt had posted a hyperlink to that video in their own article, which resulted in Jobbik successfully suing Magyar Jeti Zrt for defamation. The ECtHR found that the Hungarian court's judgment produced a "chilling effect" on the press by discouraging journalists from hyperlinking to external sources, in contravention of the Convention's protections of freedom of expression.[1]

As the drafters of the European Convention were designing the ECtHR in the 1950s, they could not possibly have imagined such a thing as the internet, let alone anticipated the ECtHR's role in deciding when governments could impose restrictions on journalists posting hyperlinked content. As society evolves, international judges are inevitably tasked with applying law to circumstances that are very different from those envisioned by the creators of the law. In these cases, judges have to balance the imperative for consistent legal reasoning with changing social realities. This is a formidable task that may require judges to reinterpret their court's relationship with governments.

International courts are not known to be particularly dynamic. The procedures that guide court operations can only be changed through slow and often arduous reform processes that rely on elusive consensus across member states. Judges must rely on precedent in their decision-making, imposing an inherent bias toward status quo legal interpretations. Even newly appointed judges, who might be expected to impart novel judicial perspectives, may be more inclined to uphold the court's existing norms as a result of their professional socialization.[2] For these reasons, judges' interpretations of the boundaries of their court's authority are likely to be quite durable throughout the life of the institution. Still, these interpretations cannot be assumed to be "locked-in." A court may become more deferential or interventionist over time owing to a variety of factors. I have hypothesized that shifts in each court's membership (which may be accompanied by changes in the types of rights violations faced by a court), state backlash against court decisions, and jurisprudential developments in other human rights courts might push judges to adopt more deferential or interventionist interpretations of the boundaries of their court's jurisdiction.

I expect that courts founded on deferential interpretations of judicial authority, such as the ECtHR, are more likely to be responsive to state backlash. Because deferential courts have historically prioritized respect for state sovereignty, these courts will be more likely to walk back their authority in response to critiques of judicial overreach. In other words, deferential judicial behavior will become entrenched over time. In practice, this self-restriction of authority could take the form of judges adopting narrower interpretations of case admissibility criteria, hesitating to shift the burden of proof to governments, mandating less intensive remedies for violations, or even making statements explicitly urging deference to national authorities. On the other hand, I expect that courts founded on interventionist interpretations of judicial authority, such as the IACtHR, are less likely to be responsive to member state backlash. Interventionist courts are not likely to pull back on their authority, even when former "frequent offender" states demonstrate increased respect for human rights. The logic underlying this expectation is that once courts self-define a given exercise of their authority as legitimate, they will not cede that authority easily. Put more generally, institutions are not inclined to relinquish power, even when the conditions that originally legitimized that power have changed. Indicators that a court is maintaining an interventionist interpretation of its authority include flexibly applying case admissibility criteria in favor of the applicant, frequently shifting the burden of proof to governments, and mandating remedies that significantly interfere in domestic authority, such as annulling criminal convictions or amending legislation.

In addition to state backlash, jurisprudential developments in other human rights courts may provoke a court to adopt more deferential or interventionist behaviors. Through "inter-court borrowing" or "jurisprudential dialogue," judges on one regional court may cite another court's jurisprudence to support a particular legal interpretation.[3] I anticipate that a court will be more receptive to importing jurisprudence from another court within areas of case law in which that other court has more experience. For example, if Court A has little experience ruling on a specific type of rights violation, but Court B already has established case law in that area, Court A might be inclined to cite Court B's jurisprudence within rulings on cases involving that type of violation. Through this process of judicial exchange, deferential courts might develop more interventionist approaches within emerging substantive areas of case law, and interventionist courts might develop more deferential approaches. This chapter evaluates the validity of these proposals through analysis of each court's case law on the right to freedom of expression.

Freedom of expression is a fundamental pillar of democracy that has been integral to the development of each regional court's case law. While each court has adopted a unique interpretation of its authority in this area, there is a high degree of confluence across all three courts' approaches. In particular, IACtHR judges have demonstrated careful attention to European jurisprudence in freedom of expression cases. This may be attributable to the fact that the ECtHR already had a well-established freedom of expression case law by the time that the IACtHR started confronting expression violations in the late 1990s. IACtHR judges naturally looked to their European peers for guidance. Still, the IACtHR has pushed the boundaries of its authority beyond the European example, imposing more intensive remedies for freedom of expression violations and pushing for significant domestic legislative reforms. The IACtHR and ACtHPR have largely shaken off episodes of member state backlash and continued to rule against states that have accused these courts of judicial overreach. The ECtHR, on the other hand, undertook significant revisions of its approach to adjudicating freedom of expression issues after the Brighton Declaration. This inter-court variation provides supportive evidence for the hypothesis that states founded with a deferential interpretation of their authority are more likely to be responsive to state backlash than interventionist courts.

The right to freedom of expression is codified in Article 10 of the European Convention, Article 13 of the American Convention, and Article 9 of the African Charter. Cases involving freedom of expression have featured prominently in each court's case law at varying times. Figure 4.1 displays freedom of expression cases as percentages of total annual judgments across all three courts. The ECtHR has frequently addressed freedom of expression disputes since the 1980s. The IACtHR, on the other hand, did not begin to rule on expression cases until the late 1990s. Despite this late start, the IACtHR has ruled on a particularly high

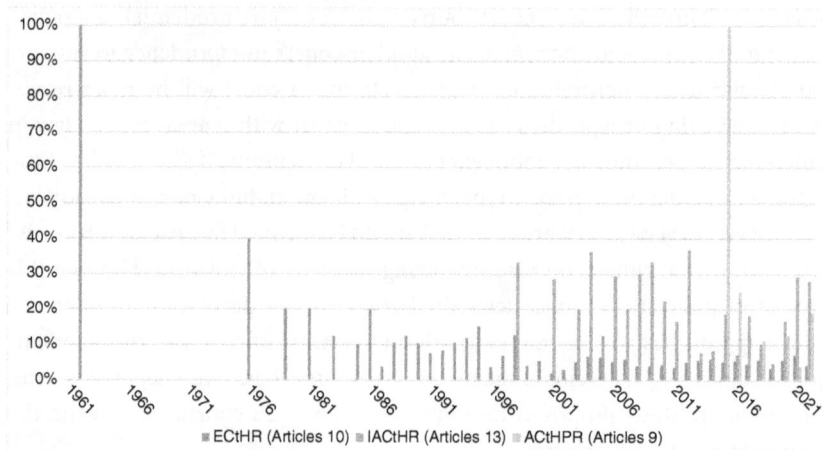

FIGURE 4.1.   Freedom of expression cases as percentage of annual judgments (through 2022)

Note: In order to not count the same case multiple times, only merits judgments are reflected here. For the same purpose, only Chamber and Committee merits judgments are included for the ECtHR, not Grand Chamber judgments. Chart includes cases where a freedom of expression violation was alleged, not necessarily established.

proportion of expression cases. Meaningful comparison with the African court is limited by that court's relatively small body of case law. (For example, even though alleged Article 9 violations featured in 100 percent of ACtHPR cases in 2015, the Court issued only two merits judgments that year.)

This chapter analyses the ECtHR's freedom of expression case law from 1990 through 2003, when the Court admitted a wave of new member states and underwent institutional restructuring, and 2010 through 2015, when the Court faced a case backlog crisis, implemented additional reforms, and faced unprecedented state criticism. I examine the IACtHR's case law from 2002 through 2005, when reforms limited the role of the Commission in case processing and increased victim participation, and from 2012 through 2020, when the Court grappled with several withdrawals and attempted withdrawals amid a growing caseload. Finally, I examine the ACtHPR's case law from 2017 through 2022. Usage of the ACtHPR rapidly increased in that time, as well as incidences of state backlash and withdrawals. Using the matching case selection technique described in the previous chapter, I focus my analysis of the ECtHR and IACtHR's jurisprudence on cases involving defamation allegations. Because the ACtHPR issued only six judgments involving expression during the 2017–2022 period, I address each of these judgments in turn.

The European Court of Human Rights

One of the first major freedom of expression cases the ECtHR faced in the 1990s forced the Court to intervene in domestic debates about publicly invoking Nazism. In *Oberschlick v. Austria* (1991), the applicant had been convicted of defamation for publicly accusing an Austrian politician of promulgating Nazi ideology. The politician, Walter Grabher-Meyer, had suggested that family allowances for Austrian women should be increased "in order to obviate their seeking abortions for financial reasons," while immigrant mothers' allowances should be reduced. Mr. Oberschlick interpreted this statement as an incitement to Nazi ideas, as it implied support for ethnic cleansing through selective abortions. Oberschlick filed a criminal complaint against Grabher-Meyer, which Oberschlick then published in *The Forum*, a magazine where he was editor in chief. In response, Grabher-Meyer pressed defamation charges. Oberschlick was eventually convicted and fined, and the relevant copies of *The Forum* were seized by the state.[4]

The central issue facing the ECtHR was whether Oberschlick's conviction and the seizure of his magazine were "necessary in a democratic society . . . for the protection of the reputation or rights of others" within the scope of Article 10(2). The Austrian government argued that Oberschlick had crossed the line of acceptable critique of a politician by publishing those critiques in the form of a criminal complaint. This format could mislead the public by implying that Grabher-Meyer was the subject of an active criminal investigation. The majority of ECtHR judges rejected this reasoning, maintaining that "a politician is certainly entitled to have his reputation protected . . . but the requirements of that protection have to be weighed against the interests of open discussion."[5] The Court ruled that Austria had violated Oberschlick's freedom of expression and ordered the government to pay financial reparations.[6]

Three dissenting judges, Matscher, Bindschedler-Robert, and Vilhjalmsson, argued that the potentially misleading format of Oberschlick's statement caused it to fall outside the scope of protection provided by Article 10.[7] Furthermore, the dissenters contended, the Austrian court that convicted Oberschlick had correctly upheld its obligation to protect individuals' right to privacy under Article 8 of the Convention. The format of Oberschlick's statement "took it out of the sphere of mere political debate and carried it into the arena of personal attack, thereby impinging on private life."[8] Here, Judge Vilhjalmsson asserted that the majority inappropriately interfered in domestic decisions regarding how to balance competing Convention obligations.

Adjudicating that balance between protecting individuals' reputations and freedom of expression has been a recurring challenge for the ECtHR. As established in the aforementioned *Sunday Times* case in 1979, deciding whether interference in expression is "necessary in a democratic society" requires the ECtHR to determine (1) whether the complained-of interference corresponded to a "pressing social need," (2) whether it was proportionate to the legitimate aim pursued, and (3) whether the reasons given by national authorities to justify it are relevant and sufficient. The ECtHR has repeatedly stressed that national authorities "are left a certain margin of appreciation" to determine what constitutes a "pressing social need" and "legitimate aims" of interference in expression. Still, "this power of appreciation is not, however, unlimited but goes in hand in hand with a European supervision by the Court."[9]

Bladet Tromsø and Stensaas v. Norway (1999) exemplifies the difficulties inherent to interpreting Article 10(2) in defamation cases. The ECtHR was tasked with determining the extent to which media outlets must ensure the veracity of information pertinent to public interest before it is published. *Bladet Tromsø,* a Norwegian newspaper, had published a series of articles based on reporting by Mr. Lindberg, a freelance journalist who reported on seal hunting and later became a government-appointed inspector aboard the *M/S Harmoni,* a hunting vessel. *Bladet Tromsø* reprinted excerpts from Lindberg's reporting that contained allegations of criminal misconduct aboard the *Harmoni,* including animal cruelty.[10] Lindberg, however, had offered little evidence to support his claims. An independent Commission of Inquiry later found that most of Lindberg's allegations either could not be proven or were exaggerated.[11] The crew of the *Harmoni* successfully sued Lindberg and *Bladet Tromsø* for defamation. *Bladet Tromsø* was ordered by pay compensation to the crew members, which formed the basis for the newspaper's complaint before the ECtHR.

The ECtHR Grand Chamber pointed to the fact that Lindberg had produced his report while working as an inspector appointed by the Ministry of Fisheries. Accordingly, the newspaper was not required to undertake independent research to verify Lindberg's statements. The "vital public-watchdog role of the press may be undermined" if the press is required to undertake extensive investigatory procedures on matters of urgent public interest.[12] In finding that Norway violated Article 10, the ECtHR majority determined that the crew members' interest in protecting their reputations was insufficient to outweigh the "vital public interest in ensuring an informed public debate over a matter of local and national as well as international interest."[13]

This decision was met with fervent dissent from judges who argued that it would hamstring national authorities from balancing Convention obligations to protect freedom of expression with protections against defamation. Judges Palm, Fuhrmann, and Baka wrote that the majority had essentially developed "a new test that newspapers can be dispensed from verifying the facts of a story" depending on the nature of the information. Developing these criteria in the context of this case was particularly controversial given that Lindberg's report was never published by the Ministry of Fisheries prior to being picked up by *Bladet Tromsø*. The Ministry had withheld the report precisely due to accuracy concerns. The majority's characterization of the report as "official" was thus tenuous.[14]

The accession of a wave of Eastern European member states in the 1990s brought new judicial perspectives to the ECtHR, as each new member state contributed its own judge. The eastward expansion of the CoE stretched the application of the Convention to states that were still navigating postcommunist transitions to democracy. *Dalban v. Romania* (1999), one of the first major defamation disputes involving a new Eastern European member state, was decided by the Grand Chamber in the same year as *Bladet Tromsø and Stensaas v. Norway*. Comparing the judges' reasoning across these two cases provides an opportunity to evaluate the Court's approach to (somewhat) similar issues within two very different member states. The applicant in *Dalban* was a journalist who reported on fraud at a state-owned agricultural company, allegedly orchestrated by a senator. Romania's Supreme Court had upheld Dalban's conviction for libeling that senator on the grounds that Dalban had "intended to cause prejudice to [the senator] without verifying his information before publishing the articles."[15]

Consistent with the majority's reasoning in *Bladet Tromsø and Stensaas*, the Grand Chamber maintained that journalists cannot be criminally penalized for failing to verify information prior to publication, subject to certain limitations. While journalists are bound to respect the reputations and rights of others, "It would be unacceptable for a journalist to be debarred from expressing critical value judgments unless he or she could prove their truth." The relevance of published information to public interest is a crucial factor that may condition journalists' duty to verify the truth. This interpretation of Article 10 recognizes the barriers that journalists may face to verifying information that the state has an interest in hiding: "The national margin of appreciation is circumscribed by the interest of democratic society in enabling the press to exercise its rightful role of 'public watchdog.'" Furthermore, the Grand Chamber acknowledged that "journalistic freedom also covers possible recourse to a degree of exaggeration, or even provocation."[16] The Grand Chamber was unanimous in its decision that Romania had violated Article 10 by convicting Dalban.

Two judges (Greve and Baka) who had dissented in *Bladet Tromsø and Stensaas* were part of this unanimous decision, despite the fact that they had previously emphasized journalists' duty to establish the truth and cautioned against attributing undue weight to public interest in evaluating states' criminalization of defamation. There could be several explanations for why the Grand Chamber split in *Bladet Tromsø and Stensaas* but was unanimous in *Dalban*. First, the circumstances of the cases were different. Notably, the target of the alleged defamation in *Dalban* was a public figure, whereas *Bladet Tromsø* denounced ordinary seal hunters. The ECtHR has long recognized a distinction between the limitations on expression that are permissible to protect a public figure as opposed to private individuals.[17] Second, while Norway was a founding ECtHR member state and a well-established democracy, Romania had only transitioned to democracy in the past decade following over forty years of communist rule. Judges may be more likely to afford deference to states with long track records of respect for Convention obligations as opposed to new member states still working to bring their domestic institutions in line with European human rights standards.

In the early 2000s, the ECtHR still struggled to establish coherent standards for evaluating acceptable restrictions on expression in defamation cases. The case of *Perna v. Italy* (2001), in which a Chamber judgment that found Italy in violation of Article 10 was later overturned by the Grand Chamber, exemplifies this struggle. The applicant was a journalist who published an article accusing a public prosecutor of corruption. The journalist highlighted the prosecutor's past membership in a militant communist party to imply that the prosecutor was abusing his current office to benefit ideological compatriots. The journalist was convicted of defamation and fined.[18] The ECtHR Chamber rejected the domestic court's argument that the journalist's lack of evidence proving a connection between the prosecutor's politics and his professional decisions caused the article to be defamatory: "The Court observes that a careful distinction needs to be made between facts and value-judgments. The existence of facts can be demonstrated, whereas the truth of value-judgments is not susceptible of proof. . . . Where a judicial officer is an active political militant, his unconditional protection against attacks in the press is scarcely justified by the need to maintain the public confidence which the judiciary needs in order to be able to function properly."[19] The Chamber's distinction between facts and value judgments developed guidance for the conditions under which journalists should be required to furnish proof for potentially defamatory statements. The judges, who ruled unanimously to find Italy in violation of Article 10, again emphasized the concern for public interest that has consistently driven the court's reasoning.

However, the tables turned when Italy appealed the Chamber's ruling to the Grand Chamber. In 2003, the Grand Chamber found that Italy had not, in fact, violated Article 10 in *Perna*. The Grand Chamber rejected the Chamber's assessment that the journalist's accusations against the prosecutor constituted value judgments. Rather, the Grand Chamber considered that the journalist had made specific accusations of misconduct against the prosecutor without furnishing proof. Thus, national courts had correctly applied the Convention when convicting the applicant of defamation.[20] The only dissenting judge in the Grand Chamber, Judge Conforti, had been a member of the Chamber bench that originally established a freedom of expression violation. The fact that the Chamber unanimously found a violation while the Grand Chamber (with the exception of Judge Conforti) unanimously found no violation suggests a lack of consistency across ECtHR judges' legal reasoning.

Based on *Perna*, one might speculate that the Grand Chamber is more likely to express greater deference to member governments compared to Chamber judicial formations. After all, if a state has invested the time and resources to appeal a decision to the Grand Chamber, this indicates substantial domestic dissatisfaction with the court's decision that could potentially put political pressure on the court. However, *Cumpănă and Mazăre v. Romania*, a freedom of expression case decided by the Grand Chamber just months after *Perna*, provides contrary evidence to this conjecture. In *Cumpănă and Mazăre*, it was the Chamber that initially found no violation of Article 10, only to be overturned by the Grand Chamber. The applicants were journalists who were convicted of defamation, sentenced to seven months imprisonment, and banned from working as journalists for one year after publishing an article and a disparaging cartoon of a judge they accused of corruption.[21] The article and accompanying cartoon insinuated that the judge had an extramarital affair. The Chamber maintained that commentary on the judge's personal life caused the journalists' speech to fall outside the protection afforded by Article 10, weighing the need to balance freedom of expression with the right to privacy and family life.[22]

Two judges dissented, arguing that the journalists' accusations of corruption were rooted in credible evidence and thus of public interest: "We are quite aware that, as in libel cases, there is a fine balance to be struck. Reputation and honour are also protected by the Convention, in Article 8 and Article 10 §2. We too are sensitive to that. . . . Overall, however, the balance was tipped slightly too far; in our opinion, there was no 'pressing social need' justifying the lengths to which the Romanian courts went."[23] The Grand Chamber picked up this reasoning, citing both the public interest aspect of the case and the severity of the punitive measures against the applicants in its rejection of the Chamber's ruling: "The criminal sanction and the accompanying prohibitions imposed on [the applicants] by the national courts were manifestly disproportionate in their nature and severity."[24] Essentially, while the Grand Chamber recognized the difficulties of balancing freedom of expression and privacy, the severity of the journalists' punishment constituted a violation.

The ECtHR's defamation case law during the late 1990s and early 2000s was characterized by a few consistencies—for example, less permissive standards for restricting defamatory speech targeted at public officials relative to private individuals. Still, the court struggled to develop clear guidance for member states in applying Article 10. The Grand Chamber's rejection of multiple Chamber decisions is an indication of the murky nature of this area of case law. In all the above cases where the ECtHR established an Article 10 violation, the state was only ordered to pay the applicant financial reparations. The Court did not order states to nullify a conviction or undertake specific domestic policy changes.

The 2010–2015 period was marked by a concerted effort among ECtHR judges to delegate the assessment of evidence to national courts as much as possible. Responding to increasing state criticism of the quality of the Court's decisions, this move was intended to help the Court stay out of the minutiae of domestic adjudication and develop more consistent standards for state behavior. One of the central critiques that states launched at the ECtHR in the 2012 Brighton Declaration was that the Court too often engaged in arbitrary reasoning. This issue, which states acknowledged was in part driven by the Court's overwhelming caseload, "represented a threat to the quality and the consistency of the case law and the authority of the Court."[25] Member states had jointly presented this criticism for the first time at the 2010 Interlaken Conference, where the initial conversations that culminated in the Brighton Declaration took place. The ECtHR was thus aware of states' discontent well in advance of the Brighton Declaration's release.

The case of *Sanoma Uitgevers B.V. v. the Netherlands*, decided by the Grand Chamber just months after the entry into force of Protocol 14 in 2010, illustrates member states' rising frustration in the years leading up to the Brighton Declaration. The applicant in this case was a magazine editor who alleged that the police had violated his freedom of expression by seizing compact disks containing photographs taken for the magazine. The photographs were taken at an illegal street race. The police alleged that one of the race cars was later involved in another crime, and that the photographs on the CDs contained crucial evidence. The magazine editor had refused to turn over the CDs, citing journalistic integrity and the need to maintain the trust of his sources.[26] In 2009, in a 4–3 decision, an ECtHR Chamber found no violation of Article 10 in this case.[27] Although the majority lamented the police's "regrettable lack of moderation" in conducting the seizure, the judges were satisfied that "no reasonable alternative possibility of identifying the vehicle existed at the relevant time."[28]

The Grand Chamber later overturned the Chamber's ruling, declaring that Dutch authorities had indeed violated Article 10. This unanimous decision hinged on the assertion that state law lacked proper procedural safeguards to ensure that the seizure would not reveal identities of the photojournalist's sources.[29] One judge who was a member of the Chamber that initially found no violation flip-flopped and voted to establish a violation in the Grand Chamber.

That judge, Egbert Myjer, was a national of the Netherlands. He explained his position candidly:

> The fact is that I have not found sufficient convincing reason to stick to my guns and vote for no violation. I was originally of the opinion that this was a borderline case in which the circumstances of the case ultimately tipped the scales towards the respondent. I am still of the opinion that this is a borderline case, even after hearing the views of the other members of the Grand Chamber, and I even ask myself whether this case really raises "a serious question affecting the interpretation or application of the Convention . . . or a serious issue of general importance."[30]

Myjer should get credit for his honesty. Still, a judge reaching two different conclusions after examining the same set of facts within different judicial formations raises questions about the rigor of that judge's reasoning. Perhaps of greater concern, Myjer demonstrated rather blunt ambivalence about whether the case even raised "a serious issue." Given this attitude, it is a small wonder that some states had concerns about arbitrary reasoning within the ECtHR around the turn of the 2010 decade.

Kasabova v. Bulgaria, decided one year prior to the Brighton Declaration, demonstrates the ECtHR's shift toward a procedural standard of review that prioritized governments' responsibility to establish legal facts. The applicant was a journalist who had published articles accusing school administrators of accepting bribes from parents in exchange for their children's admission. Domestic courts had convicted the applicant of defamation and imposed a two-year prison sentence. The ECtHR accepted the government's argument regarding the necessity to restrict the applicant's freedom of expression, yet still found that Bulgaria violated Article 10 due to "the potential chilling effect of the proceedings on [the applicant] and other journalists."[31] Given the severity of the penalties imposed by the national courts, the ECtHR majority did not even consider the veracity of the journalist's statements to be particularly relevant to the case: "The Court is prepared to accept that the national courts' finding that the applicant had failed to sufficiently research her article before going to press. . . . However, the Court does not consider it necessary to take a firm stance on that point, because it is in any event of the view that the sanction imposed on the applicant was disproportionate."[32] Unlike in earlier cases, the ECtHR declined to substantively discuss the question of whether restricting the applicant's expression was legally justified. Rather, the Court accepted the government's argument supporting this restriction without engaging in its own evaluation of the facts. This ruling exemplifies a procedural, opposed to substantive, approach to evaluating the compatibility of state behavior with the Convention. Bulgarian judicial authorities were trusted to render a correct decision based on the facts that they discerned. The ECtHR only judged those authorities on the proportionality of the applicant's punishment relative to those facts. The ECtHR's shift toward a procedural standard of review in the early 2010s prioritized the role of national judiciaries in establishing legal facts. This approach further entrenched the ECtHR's deferential interpretation of its authority.

There is evidence to suggest that the Court was aware that states' frustration would peak around spring 2012 and attempted to head off Brighton's criticisms (or at least proactively address them). For example, *Axel Springer AG v. Germany* (2012) demonstrates the Court's responsiveness to critiques of inconsistent reasoning. Discussion of how to balance states' competing obligations under the right to freedom of expression and the right to privacy had been a consistent feature of the Court's case law for decades. Even so, the Court had never before developed clear standards for evaluating the proportionality of restrictions on expression for the sake of respecting privacy. The Court finally did so in *Axel Springer*. This case was decided by the Grand Chamber in February 2012, two months prior to the Brighton Declaration's release. In the judgment, the Court developed the following evaluative criteria for conducting "the balancing exercise" between freedom of expression and privacy: (1) whether the complained-of statements "contribute to a debate of general interest," (2) "how well known is the person concerned and what is the subject of the report," (3) the prior conduct of the person concerned, (4) the method of obtaining the information and its veracity, (5) the content, form, and consequences of the publication, and (6) the severity of the sanction imposed.[33]

Prefacing these criteria, the judgment states that "where the balancing exercise between [freedom of expression and protection of privacy] has been undertaken by the national authorities in conformity with the criteria laid down in the court's case-law, the court would require strong reasons to substitute its view for that of the domestic courts."[34] In other words, having articulated clear standards for balancing Articles 8 and 10 in defamation cases, the ECtHR would only issue a judgment based on whether national authorities had applied that balancing test. The Court would *not* review whether national authorities arrived at a satisfactory result through that test, except in extraordinary cases. The Court's new balancing test thus responded directly to states' call in Brighton for more coherent standards as well as demands for greater deference to national authorities.

The ECtHR has constrained itself to this procedural interpretation of its oversight powers even in cases where domestic courts applied the balancing test to circumstances very different from those in which the test was originally developed. For example, in *Brčko and Others v. Bosnia and Herzegovina* (2015), the

ECtHR found no Article 10 violation when domestic courts ruled that several NGO employees had engaged in defamation by writing a letter that they never disseminated publicly. The employees sent the letter directly to state officials to express concerns regarding a candidate being considered for director of a local public radio station. The candidate had allegedly made ethnically prejudicial comments in the past, which were referenced in the letter. Even though the NGO employees had never intended for the letter to be made public, it was leaked and published in several newspapers. This leak culminated in the employees being forced to pay damages for defamation in a civil suit.[35] When the employees took their case to the ECtHR, a Chamber judgment determined that national courts had taken the appropriate steps to evaluate the balance between freedom of expression and privacy in this case. "Therefore, the Court does not see any serious reason to substitute its own assessment for that of the Constitutional Court."[36] Even though three Chamber judges dissented, primarily citing the fact that the applicants had not purposefully publicized defamatory statements,[37] the Grand Chamber later upheld the Chamber's ruling.

The ECtHR's shift in the 2010s toward a procedural standard of review and development of clearer standards for restricting expression demonstrates the Court's respect for the competence of national judiciaries. This behavior aligns with the expectation that deferential courts are likely to be responsive to state criticism and adjust the exercise of their judicial authority accordingly.

The Inter-American Court of Human Rights

While the ECtHR struggled to establish coherent standards for the burden of proof that rests with journalists when criticizing public figures, the IACtHR's jurisprudence on this issue consolidated relatively more quickly. In *Herrera-Ulloa v. Costa Rica* (2004), the IACtHR was charged with determining whether Costa Rica had violated a journalist's freedom of expression in a defamation case. Mr. Herrera-Ulloa had published articles that partially reproduced information from Belgian media outlets. Those articles connected Félix Przedborski, who at the time was Costa Rica's ambassador to the International Atomic Energy Agency, to an international scandal involving illicit sales of combat helicopters.[38] Herrera-Ulloa was convicted of defamation and fined. Exercising its authority to order provisional measures in pending cases, the IACtHR ordered Costa Rica to refrain from collecting the fine or registering Herrera-Ulloa as a convicted felon until the Court was able to rule on his case.[39]

The government argued that Costa Rica's criminal laws pertaining to defamation "only criminalize malicious conduct" and thus "strike a fair balance between freedom of expression and the right to have one's honor and reputation respected."[40] The government's representatives also maintained that Costa Rican laws did not necessarily require everything published by journalists to be verified as true. They insisted that Mr. Herrera-Ulloa was convicted based on malicious intent rather than an inability to verify the Belgian press's accusations against Przedborski. However, independent lawyers testified before the IACtHR that Costa Rica's defamation laws do require journalists to verify information sourced from foreign media outlets containing "alleged defamatory statements against a Costa Rican public official."[41]

The IACtHR unequivocally rejected the legality of requiring journalists to verify statements critiquing public officials. In a unanimous decision, the judges wrote that the standard of proof required of journalists under Costa Rican law "has a deterrent, chilling and inhibiting effect on all those who practice journalism. This, in turn, obstructs public debate on issues of interest to society."[42] The IACtHR ordered the government to pay Herrera-Ulloa significant financial reparations, as well as nullify his conviction.

Just one month after the *Herrera-Ulloa* judgment, the IACtHR intervened in a delicate freedom of expression dispute rooted in the growing pains of democratization. *Ricardo Canese v. Paraguay* concerned the conviction of Paraguayan presidential candidate Ricardo Canese for slander. Canese had implied that another candidate, Juan Carlos Wasmosy, maintained allegiances to former dictator Alfredo Stroessner. At the time, Wasmosy was the president of CONEMPA, a civil works company with close government ties. Canese publicly stated that Wasmosy "was the Stroessner family's front man in CONEMPA," which prompted CONEMPA members to file a criminal defamation suit against Canese. Canese was sentenced to several months in prison, fined, and prohibited from leaving the country.[43] Canese's prison sentence was stayed, and he was eventually acquitted by Paraguay's Supreme Court while his case was still pending at the IACtHR. Nevertheless, the IACtHR proceeded with the case on the grounds that the Supreme Court had not offered Canese reparations, so the situation had never been sufficiently remedied.[44]

In a unanimous judgment finding Paraguay in violation of Article 13, the IACtHR emphasized that Canese's statements took place in the context of Paraguay's democratization after a thirty-five-year-long dictatorship.[45] The Court cited ECtHR jurisprudence maintaining that any restriction on the speech of political candidates, and particularly opposition candidates, calls for the "closest scrutiny," and that it is "particularly important in the period preceding an election that opinions and information of all kinds are permitted to circulate freely."[46] Furthermore, the IACtHR condemned Canese's prison sentence as disproportionate, claiming that "there was no imperative social interest that justified the punitive measures."[47] The Court ordered Paraguay to pay Canese compensation but stopped short of mandating specific legislative change.

In general, European and Inter-American jurisprudence on freedom of expression in the late 1990s to early 2000s upheld the same basic principles. IACtHR judges took particular note of jurisprudential developments across the pond. In a 2005 case concerning the seizure of a book that called for revised ethical standards within Chile's military intelligence agencies, the IACtHR borrowed directly from the ECtHR's language to declare that the seizure and criminal conviction of the book's author were "disproportionate and unnecessary in a democratic society."[48] The author, a retired naval officer working as a civilian military contractor, was accused of publishing information that constituted a "threat to national security."[49] This is despite the fact that expert reports commissioned by the naval prosecutor concluded that the book "did not breach the secrecy and security of the Chilean Navy."[50] The IACtHR found a freedom of expression violation in this case and ordered Chile to compensate the author and annul his conviction. In a concurring opinion, Judge Sergio García Ramírez noted that the "subject matter in the actions brought before the Inter-American Court coincides with the experience of the European Court of Human Rights," in a clear nod to the attention that American judges afford to European jurisprudence when evaluating freedom of expression disputes.

In the past decade, IACtHR judges have been inclined to take a subsidiary role in evaluating the balance between free expression and protecting individuals' reputations in defamation cases. This interpretation is remarkably similar to the approach employed by the ECtHR. In *Mémoli v. Argentina* (2013) the Court found that Argentina had not violated two citizens' right to freedom of expression when they were convicted of libel for accusing a local company of fraudulently selling burial niches. The IACtHR's decision in this case defied arguments submitted by the Inter-American Commission, which had called on the Court to find Argentina in violation of Article 13.[51] In defense of its position, the Court majority cited several ECtHR cases to emphasize the importance of obtaining balance between protecting individuals' reputations and freedom of expression.[52] Furthermore, the majority echoed the ECtHR's concern with upholding subsidiarity when evaluating national authorities' determination of this balance:

> The Court is not a higher court of a court of appeal to decide disagreements between the parties on some implications of the assessment of evidence.... In strict observance of its subsidiary competence, the Court considers that, in a case such as this one, it must verify whether the State authorities made a reasonable and sufficient weighing up between the two rights in conflict, without necessarily making an autonomous and independent weighing, unless the specific circumstances of the case require this.[53]

Here, the IACtHR seems to embrace a shift toward a procedural standard of judicial review, similar to developments within the ECtHR around the same period. By emphasizing the Court's subsidiary role to national authorities, the majority in *Mémoli* distanced itself from reviewing the substantive conclusions reached by domestic courts. Rather, these judges promoted the idea that the Court should constrain itself to reviewing the procedural compatibility of national judicial proceedings with the state's Convention obligations. In other words, so long as the national courts reasonably considered the balance between expression and privacy with good-faith attention to the Convention, the IACtHR should not attempt to revise the domestic judgment. This push to retrench the subsidiarity of the IACtHR did not go unchallenged. Three dissenting judges, Robles, Vio Grossi, and Mac-Gregor Poisot, ignored the majority's call for greater trust in the judgment of the national courts. Their dissenting opinion included an extensive review of the facts of the case and of the domestic court's reasoning, which the dissenters argued was fundamentally flawed.[54]

The majority in *Mémoli* took care to note that "contrary to other cases decided by this court, in the instant case, the statements for which Messrs. Mémoli were convicted did not involve public figures or officials and did not relate to the functioning of State institutions."[55] Hence, balancing protections of expression and privacy had to be approached differently than in cases involving public figures.[56] This position was reiterated in *Álvarez Ramos v. Venezuela*, decided in 2019. Venezuela's denunciation of the American Convention had entered into force in 2013. However, in accordance with Article 78(2) of the Convention, the IACtHR maintained jurisdiction over cases based in events that occurred prior to the withdrawal date.[57] The applicant, Mr. Álvarez Ramos, had been convicted of defamation in 2005 after writing an op-ed alleging misappropriation of public funds by the Venezuelan National Assembly. Willian Lara, who was then the president of the Assembly, filed a criminal complaint against Álvarez. Álvarez was sentenced to over two years' imprisonment (which was ultimately suspended), prevented from traveling internationally, and temporarily blocked from political participation.[58]

In its unanimous decision finding Venezuela in violation of Article 13, the IACtHR referenced the ECtHR's standards for establishing a "pressing social need" that could justify restriction of expression.[59] The IACtHR could not establish the existence of such a need in this case, emphasizing that government spending is a matter of public interest. Furthermore, the Court declared that any legislation that criminalizes critiquing public officials is incompatible with the American Convention.[60] The Court noted that journalistic conduct can "produce liability in another legal sphere, such as in civil law," but rejected the application of criminal codes to speech criticizing public officials.[61] Still, while the IACtHR ordered Venezuela to expunge Álvarez's conviction, the Court stopped short of explicitly mandating that Venezuela revise its penal code. This decision may be attributable to unresolved questions regarding whether the Court had the power to order such measures given Venezuela's withdrawal.

The evidence discussed above indicates that the IACtHR has, to some extent, taken a turn toward a more procedural standard of review, similar to that promoted by the ECtHR in the 2010s. This development suggests that the ECtHR's example may have induced the IACtHR to ease up on its interventionist approach to reviewing the facts established by domestic authorities (at least in freedom of expression cases). However, not all IACtHR judges have been on board with this trend toward greater deference, as is evident in *Mémoli*'s dissenting opinions. The IACtHR has pushed notably farther than the ECtHR in its development of the idea that criminal punishment for defamation violates international human rights principles. Additionally, the IACtHR has not constrained itself to only ordering financial remedies in cases where states have violated freedom of expression guarantees.

This variation suggests that cross-court convergence in legal standards brought about through inter-jurisprudential dialogue can still produce different outcomes because of each court's divergent circumstances. The IACtHR may afford greater deference on a case-by-case basis (particularly with regard to states such as Argentina that have dramatically improved human rights protections in recent decades), but the Court will not reverse its established authority to push for domestic legislative change and order intensive remedies. One certain conclusion is that the IACtHR has not responded to member state backlash to any extent that is comparable to the ECtHR's post-Brighton reckoning. As seen in *Álvarez Ramos*, the IACtHR did not hesitate to hand down a condemnatory ruling on Venezuela even after that country's withdrawal. Even though the fluid domestic leadership situation in Venezuela might leave the door open for the state's return to the IACtHR, the Court is clearly not inclined to incentivize that return through deferential rulings.

The African Court on Human and Peoples' Rights

The ACtHPR has had a rocky start to its institutional life. The right to freedom of expression was at the center of a dramatic dispute that ultimately provoked Rwanda's withdrawal in 2016. This episode was the first time a state withdrew from the Court and thus the first significant challenge to the ACtHPR's legitimacy by a member state. Rwanda had previously been a strong ally of the Court, as one of only eight states to accept the right of individual citizens and NGOs to petition the ACtHPR directly. This relationship took a sharp turn for the worse after Victoire Ingabire, president of the opposition FDU-Inkingi party, was convicted and imprisoned for the crime of "genocide ideology" in a trial that international human rights organizations criticized as "flawed" and "politically motivated."[62] Ingabire had been arrested after speaking at the Genocide Memorial Center in Kigali. Her speech addressed challenges with reconciliation and ethnic violence, "issues that are rarely discussed openly in Rwanda."[63] A Rwandan court sentenced Ingabire to eight years in prison in 2012. This sentence was later increased to fifteen years following an unsuccessful appeal to the Rwandan Supreme Court in 2013.[64]

While imprisoned, Ingabire launched an application with the ACtHPR, alleging that the Rwandan government had violated her rights to a fair trial, freedom of expression, and equality before the law.[65] Four days before the ACtHPR was scheduled to commence public hearings in Ingabire's case, the Rwandan government sent a terse note to the African Union announcing the country's immediate withdrawal from the provisions of the Protocol to the African Charter permitting individual access to the ACtHPR. Notably, Rwanda did not seek to withdraw from the Protocol entirely. In its announcement, the Rwandan government lamented that "a Genocide convict . . . secured a right to be heard by the Honourable Court, ultimately gaining a platform for re-invention and sanitation, in the guise of defending the human rights of Rwandan citizens." Further illuminating the government's motivations, a Rwandan ambassador commented, "We quickly realised that [the African court] is being abused by the judges on absence of a clear position of the court vis-à-vis genocide convicts and fugitives, and that is why we withdrew."[66] The Rwandan withdrawal was explicitly aimed at obstructing the Ingabire case, placing the ACtHPR in a precarious position on the eve of the first public hearing.

Following its announcement, Rwanda immediately submitted an objection challenging the ACtHPR's jurisdiction to hear Ingabire's case. The case was thrown into a chasm of legal ambiguity by the fact that neither the African Charter nor the Protocol specifies procedures for withdrawal or denunciation of particular provisions. In contrast, the European and Inter-American Conventions elaborate specific timelines between the deposit of a withdrawal or denunciation notice and the entry into force of those instruments (Articles 58 and 78, respectively). The Rwandan government argued that, in the absence of clear direction from the Charter, it fell to the Secretariat of the AU, not the Court, to determine how to implement Rwanda's withdrawal.[67] ACtHPR judges summarily rejected this argument, stating that the Court "is empowered to interpret and apply the Protocol" pursuant to Article 3.[68] Furthermore, the judges cited IACtHR jurisprudence originating from Peru's withdrawal to declare that an advance notice period of one year is necessary before a withdrawal can take effect.[69] ACtHPR judges unanimously upheld the Court's authority to rule on the *Ingabire* case.[70]

However, the ACtHPR's decision to rely on the Inter-American example was not unanimous. In their separate opinion, Judges Gérard Niyungeko and Augustino Ramadhani criticized the majority's lack of reasoning on this front:

> The conventional practice and jurisprudence of the Inter-American human rights system is, like many other, a practice from which we can indeed draw inspiration, but it cannot be applied without prior discussion at the Africa Court. In Europe, the Convention . . . for example, provides for a six month notice period. At the Universal level, the Optional Protocol to the [International Covenant on Civil and Political Rights] for its part provides a three-month notice period. The Court does not explain why it prefers to be guided by the practice in the Inter-American system rather than by the practices in the United Nations system or the European system.[71]

Beyond its general critique of the Court's reasoning in this case, this dissent illustrates some judges' concerns that the ACtHPR was relying too heavily on precedent set by outside institutions rather than developing its own standards.

In its merits judgment in 2017, ACtHPR judges unanimously found that Rwanda had violated Ingabire's right to a fair trial and freedom of expression.[72] While the Court ordered Rwanda to pay significant financial reparations to Ingabire and her family,[73] it stopped short of ordering Ingabire's release from prison. The judges were all in agreement on this issue, emphasizing that the Court "does not have the power to repeal national legislation."[74] Here, the ACtHPR drew a clear line in the sand. However, given the pressure the Court was under amid the withdrawal of one of its key member states, it is remarkable that the Court pushed its authority in *Ingabire* as far as it did. ACtHPR judges self-interpreted new rules that blocked Rwanda's withdrawal from impacting the case. Furthermore, they went on to condemn Rwanda for multiple rights violations even while the government's foot was already hanging out of the door. This episode demonstrates ACtHPR judges' resistance to cede authority, even in the face of unprecedented backlash.[75]

The *Ingabire* case established precedent that impacted the dynamics of another state's fallout with the ACtHPR. Benin's withdrawal of the right of individuals to petition the ACtHPR can be traced to a sensational dispute between President Patrice Talon and Sébastien Ajavon, an opposition politician and livestock mogul known in Benin as the "Chicken King." In 2016, Benin customs authorities discovered eighteen kilograms of cocaine in a container of frozen poultry imported by Ajavon's company. Ajavon was charged with drug trafficking but was later acquitted in a national criminal court. During those proceedings, Ajavon's company's imports into Benin were disrupted, and the signals of two radio stations he owned mysteriously went dark. Following his acquittal, Ajavon submitted a petition to the ACtHPR alleging that the drug-trafficking charges and interferences in his businesses were part of a conspiracy orchestrated against him by President Talon and constituted human rights violations. While the petition was still pending before the ACtHPR, Benin announced the creation of a new court dedicated to economic crimes and terrorism. This special court promptly tried Ajavon for drug trafficking based on the same incident for which he had already been acquitted. Ajavon, who at that point had fled to exile in Paris, was convicted *in absentia* to twenty years in prison.

After an international warrant was issued for his arrest, Ajavon asked the ACtHPR to implement provisional measures postponing the execution of that arrest warrant until the ACtHPR's final ruling on his case.[76] The ACtHPR granted this request and in 2019 ruled that Benin had violated Ajavon's right to a fair trial and equality before the law. The Court ordered Benin to annul Ajavon's conviction by the special court, a move that is indicative of the ACtHPR's increasingly expansive interpretation of its authority to mandate remedies that directly intervene in domestic judicial affairs.[77]

The Chicken King saga was not over, however. Ajavon found himself back at the ACtHPR after President Talon effectively blocked all opposition parties, including Ajavon's Social Liberal Union, from participating in Benin's April 2019 parliamentary elections. This crackdown on political opposition provoked mass protests, which the government suppressed violently. Hundreds of thousands of citizens boycotted the elections out of frustration.[78] Later in 2019, Ajavon filed a petition at the ACtHPR alleging human rights violations stemming from the election violence.[79] In April 2020, the ACtHPR granted a provisional measures request by Ajavon to order Benin to postpone municipal elections scheduled for May 2020 until after the ACtHPR could rule on the case.[80] For Benin, this was the last straw. Ordering a government to suspend scheduled elections is a monumental incursion on sovereignty. Neither the ECtHR nor the IACtHR has ever issued such an order. Eleven days after the ACtHPR's decision, Benin announced it was withdrawing the right of individuals and NGOs to petition the ACtHPR. The government's press release did not mention the Ajavon situation explicitly but called out the ACtHPR as a "source of real legal and judicial insecurity."[81]

Given the *Ingabire* precedent that withdrawals of the right of individual access can only take effect after a year, the ACtHPR was still able to issue a judgment on the merits of Ajavon's case. Exercising its jurisdiction to interpret other human rights agreements beyond just the African Charter, the ACtHPR found Benin in violation of several provisions of the ECOWAS Protocol on Democracy and the International Covenant on Economic, Social, and Cultural Rights (as well as the African Charter). These violations primarily pertained to the state's manipulation of election law, violent repression of protests, and failure to guarantee the independence of national courts.[82] However, the ACtHPR ruled that Benin had not violated Ajavon's right to freedom of expression. This may have been due to the specific allegations lodged by Ajavon. Ajavon only claimed a violation of freedom of expression incurred by the Digital Code, a national law that prohibits racially motivated and xenophobic hate speech. The Court found the Digital Code to constitute an acceptable restriction of expression based on existing norms in international human rights law.[83]

The ACtHPR judgment did not consider whether the right to freedom of expression had been violated in the context of the manipulated election and the state's subsequent crackdown on protesters, even though the Court found multiple other rights violations related to those circumstances. This omission could indicate the Court's resistance to consider violations that are not specifically alleged by the applicant—in other words, resistance to applying the legal principle of *iura novit curia*. Interestingly, Ajavon had alleged a violation of the right to freedom of expression in his first case before the ACtHPR, concerning suspected state interference in his radio companies. The Court, for reasons that are not clear in the judgment, decided not to address that alleged violation. In a separate opinion on that case, Judge Gérard Niyungeko noted that the majority opinion failed to draw clear conclusions on several alleged issues: "In all, these lacunae or shortcomings in the reasoning of the Court on certain issues, in addition to the lack of concordance between the reasoning and the operative part in some areas unfortunately leave a vague impression that the Court was in a haste to produce its judgement, which naturally does not suit the usual serenity of justice."[84] Ajavon's cases are undoubtedly among the most complicated and politically contentious that the ACtHPR has faced. Judge Niyungeko's criticisms, accompanied by the rather glaring lack of attention to freedom of expression concerns in both cases, suggest that the ACtHPR may have found itself overwhelmed. Critiques asserting deficiencies in legal reasoning from within the Court itself are troubling, and may lend credence to the complaints raised within Côte d'Ivoire and Benin's respective withdrawal announcements.[85]

Even amid Benin's pending withdrawal, the ACtHPR continued to employ a heavy-handed approach to ruling on and demanding remedies for human rights violations committed under Talon's regime. In November 2020, the ACtHPR issued a ruling on a case that challenged the international legality of recent amendments to Benin's Constitution. These amendments, which transferred certain legislative powers to the executive, were adopted under irregular procedures that did not comply with domestic law.[86] The applicant argued that the government violated the right to information (a component of freedom of expression under Article 9) by failing to publish the proposed constitutional amendments until after they had already taken legal effect. Publication of new legislation as well as records of legislative debates related to constitutional reform is required under Beninese law.[87]

ACtHPR judges unanimously established that Beninese citizens' right to information had been violated in this case, among several other violations. The ACtHPR ordered the government to repeal multiple laws related to the constitutional reform. Furthermore, the Court stipulated that no further elections could take place in Benin until those laws were repealed.[88] Even after the ACtHPR's prior attempt to intervene in Benin's election schedule provoked the government to withdraw individual access, the ACtHPR continued to assert its authority to delay national elections contingent on compliance with the court's judgments.

The ACtHPR again clashed with Talon's regime in *Houngue Éric Noudehouenou v. Benin* (2022). In this case, a Beninese opposition politician challenged newly implemented legislation that allowed the executive increased influence in the administration of elections, ultimately blocking Mr. Noudehouenou from political participation. As the petition was submitted prior to Benin's withdrawal taking effect, the ACtHPR declared the case admissible. The majority established that Benin had violated Noudehouenou's freedom of expression as codified both in the Charter and Benin's own criminal code, and consequently ordered the government to undertake several legislative and institutional reforms to ensure the independence of the judiciary and free and fair elections.[89] There are indications from Beninese officials that they are open to complying with the ACtHPR's judgments in an effort to patch up relations with the Court, a promising sign that the ACtHPR is amassing greater authority in the region.[90]

The ACtHPR has engaged in a risky strategy by continuing to stretch its authority to order interventionist remedial mandates. One ACtHPR lawyer I interviewed expressed frustration with the Court's attempts to postpone elections and mandate legislative reforms, arguing that more individualized remedial mandates might have been more appropriate in the Benin cases and may have staved off the backlash prompted by the Court's efforts to push for structural domestic reforms. This position was rooted in the lawyer's reflections on the precarious youth of the Court: "We were not yet standing on our own two feet and dropped problematic judgments . . . dropping bombs not even 10 years down the line!"[91] Such critiques notwithstanding, the ACtHPR's freedom of expression case law provides compelling evidence that the Court's judges are committed to expanding their authority even in the face of government backlash.

In general, the development of freedom of expression jurisprudence within the ECtHR and IACtHR has followed remarkably similar trajectories. IACtHR judges have extensively referenced the ECtHR's standards for evaluating state restriction of expression in cases involving defamation. This jurisprudential borrowing was not a two-way street, however. ECtHR judges did not cite IACtHR jurisprudence in any of the cases discussed above. A significant faction of IACtHR judges appears to have taken inspiration from the ECtHR in adopting a more procedural standard of judicial review in expression cases, emphasizing the subsidiary role of the IACtHR relative to domestic authorities. Still, the IACtHR has pushed its interpretation of its authority in this realm beyond the ECtHR's example. Notably, the IACtHR has pioneered jurisprudence in support of the decriminalization of defamation and assumed the authority to unilaterally overturn convictions rendered by domestic courts. However, the IACtHR has repeatedly declined to order the nullification of national legislation in this area, despite assuming the authority to do so in other areas of case law. The IACtHR may simply be more willing to afford governments greater discretion for remedying freedom of expression violations compared to more severe violations (for example, personal integrity rights violations, discussed in the next chapter).

Cross-court convergence in the ECtHR and IACtHR provides evidence that interventionist courts may be willing to adopt more deferential behavior in discrete circumstances. However, persistent divergences across the IACtHR and ECtHR point to the durability of interpretations of authority forged in each court's founding moments. The IACtHR's freedom of expression case law contains little evidence that the Court has adapted its behavior in response to outside criticism and state withdrawals. The ECtHR, in contrast, was clearly shaken by the Brighton Declaration and took concrete steps to address states' criticisms. These steps included developing standardized assessments for balancing freedom of expression and privacy and moving toward a procedural standard of review that limited the Court's role in evaluating evidence. This variation across the ECtHR and IACtHR provides support for the hypothesis that courts founded with a deferential interpretation of their authority are more likely to be responsive to state backlash than are interventionist courts.

The ACtHPR's refusal to capitulate to critiques of judicial overreach is in some ways reminiscent of the early days of the IACtHR. Like founding IACtHR judges, ACtHPR judges are operating within a tumultuous geopolitical context. The ACtHPR's membership includes states with long histories of instability that are still navigating democratic transitions. In this context, international judges may feel emboldened to expand the boundaries of their authority to address the exigencies of the moment and less inclined to cooperate with governments who have records of human rights abuse. Furthermore, younger courts may be willing to roll the dice on more-aggressive incursions into domestic sovereignty in order to bolster the international reputation of the court and garner public support. It remains to be seen how far down this road the ACtHPR can go, particularly as critiques of the quality of the Court's judgments have intensified from actors outside as well as inside the institution.

JUDGMENTS ON PERSONAL INTEGRITY RIGHTS

In 2010, a group of Spanish citizens filed a historic universal jurisdiction lawsuit in an Argentine federal court demanding that the Spanish government investigate and prosecute human rights abuses committed under General Francisco Franco's regime.[1] An amnesty law passed during Spain's democratic transition that blocks the prosecution of Franco-era political crimes has obstructed domestic attempts to obtain justice for decades. That Spanish victims have resorted to courts in Argentina, of all places, is puzzling. Spain pioneered the use of universal jurisdiction starting in the 1990s, when Spanish judges extradited several state officials, including Argentines, who directed human rights abuses during Latin American military dictatorships. The Argentine lawsuit has turned the tables, highlighting Spain's resistance to addressing the same types of atrocities in its own past for which it has condemned former Latin American leaders. The ongoing lawsuit has enabled the exhumation of over one hundred victims of Francoism buried in mass graves across Spain.[2]

Like Spain, Argentina passed amnesties during its 1983 democratic transition that blocked the investigation and prosecution of human rights crimes orchestrated by the former regime. Argentina judicially overturned these laws in 2005 amid a regional trend toward state accountability for past atrocities. This phenomenon, referred to as a "justice cascade," opened the doors for human rights trials and victim reparations across Latin America.[3] The IACtHR has been a critical proponent of the "anti-amnesty norm" that propelled the justice cascade, and has consistently established that member states can be held responsible for serious human rights crimes that occurred prior to their accession to the Court.[4]

The ECtHR has resisted taking a comparably strong stand against amnesties and has historically been more hesitant than the IACtHR to admit cases involving preaccession violations. In recent decades, the ECtHR's increasingly strict case admissibility criteria have limited the scope of the Court's temporal jurisdiction.[5] This has narrowed available legal avenues for Europeans seeking recourse for past crimes. For example, victims of Franco-era violence and their relatives have submitted at least twelve cases to the ECtHR since 2008. All have been dismissed on the grounds that the alleged violations fall outside the ECtHR's temporal jurisdiction.[6] Despite Europe's reputation as a regional citadel of human rights protection, the "justice cascade" never reached Europe.

Cross-court discrepancies in interpreting temporal jurisdiction represent just one example of how regional human rights courts have adopted different approaches to adjudicating state violence. Regional courts have grappled with a wide range of personal integrity (PI) rights violations stemming from such violence, including enforced disappearances, extrajudicial executions, torture, and police brutality. This chapter investigates how the ECtHR and IACtHR's approaches to admitting, ruling on, and ordering remedies in cases implicating PI rights have evolved over time, as well as the ACtHPR's nascent jurisprudence in this area.

Focusing on PI rights cases provides a unique opportunity to investigate the conditions under which regional courts' founding interpretations of their authority change. As PI violations constitute the most fundamental human rights abuses, judges have less legal latitude to grant deference to governments in cases involving alleged PI rights violations relative to other types of cases. Applying the same framework as in the previous chapter, I evaluate whether and how changes in the types of rights violations faced by a court, escalating caseloads, state backlash, and jurisprudential developments in other human rights courts can push judges to adopt more deferential or interventionist interpretations of the boundaries of their authority in PI rights cases.

The following analysis of each court's PI case law yields several findings regarding how each court divergently interprets the boundaries of its authority relative to member governments. There are three main areas of divergence: (1) determining temporal jurisdiction, (2) allocating the burden of proof, and (3) mandating remedies for established PI rights violations. The ECtHR's narrow interpretation of its temporal jurisdiction has become even narrower over time, as the accession of new members has forced the court to deal with an increasing number of violations stemming from past state violence. The ECtHR has historically maintained the evidentiary standard of "proof beyond reasonable doubt," although the Court has demonstrated willingness to relax that standard over the past decade in cases of severe PI rights violations. The ECtHR has also predominately maintained its standard practice of limiting its remedial mandates to financial reparations in PI violation cases. However, beginning with the introduction of the "pilot judgment" procedure in 2004, the Court expanded its authority to mandate nonfinancial remedies in consultation with the Committee of Ministers in a limited number of cases. The IACtHR's flexible interpretation of its temporal jurisdiction, willingness to shift the burden of proof from the applicant to the government, and interventionist approach to mandating remedies have remained largely consistent throughout the Court's history. These practices have persisted even in the face of state backlash and criticisms of judicial overreach. The ACtHPR's jurisprudence on PI rights violations, while still underdeveloped, indicates that the Court is cautiously willing to flexibly interpret its temporal jurisdiction and shift the burden of proof to governments. The ACtHPR has thrown that sense of caution to the wind with regard to remedial mandates, repeatedly ordering specific and intensive domestic policy changes.

The European Convention, American Convention, and African Charter all include strong protections against state interference in individuals' physical and mental well-being. The European Convention's PI rights protections are codified in Articles 2 (right to life) and 3 (prohibition of torture and inhuman/degrading treatment). PI rights are protected by Articles 4 (right to life) and 5 (right to physical, mental, and moral integrity; prohibition of torture and inhuman/degrading treatment) in the American Convention. The African Charter protects PI rights in Articles 4 (right to life) and 5 (respect of human dignity; prohibition of torture and inhumane/degrading treatment). Within international human rights law, the right to life and prohibition of torture are universally recognized as *jus cogens* principles. These principles are non-derogable, meaning that states are never permitted to violate the right to life or participate in torture under any circumstances.

Because of the *jus cogens* status of PI rights, international judges have less latitude to grant deference to governments in cases involving those rights relative to other, derogable rights (for example, protections of expression and assembly, which can be legally suspended in exigent circumstances). Non-derogable rights are often referred to as "core" rights, while derogable rights are "qualified" rights. According to an ECtHR judge, the core–qualified continuum is a key element that drives the Court's application of the margin of appreciation doctrine. ECtHR judges have greater liberty to apply the margin of appreciation to defer to states in cases involving qualified rights as opposed to core rights.[7] Given judges' limited discretion to defer to states in PI rights cases, we would expect to see less cross-court variation in judges' approaches to adjudicating cases involving such rights compared to derogable/qualified rights. Figure 5.1 illustrates the relative historical predominance of cases alleging PI rights violations in each regional court.

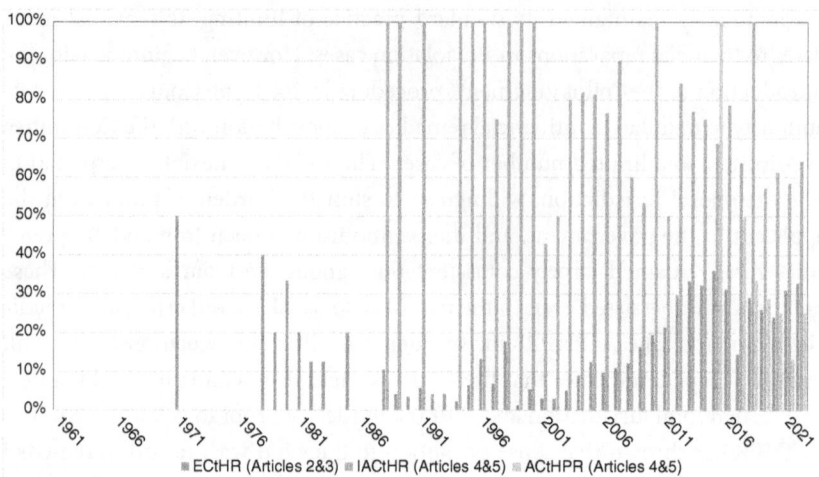

FIGURE 5.1.   Personal integrity rights cases as a percentage of annual judgments (through 2022)

Note: In order to not count the same case multiple times, only merits judgments are reflected in the chart. Only Chamber and Committee merits judgments, and not Grand Chamber judgments, are included for the ECtHR. The chart includes cases where a PI rights violation was alleged, not necessarily established. Early figures for the ECtHR are inflated by the Court's low output in the 1970s–1980s. For example, in 1971, the Court issued only two merits judgments. The ACtHPR's annual percentage figures are similarly inflated because of low case output. For example, in 2015 the Court issued only two merits judgments (both of which involved PI violations).

The European Court of Human Rights

Reflecting the ECtHR's lack of experience with PI cases in its early decades, the Court did not find a member state in violation of the right to life (Article 2) until 1995, thirty-five years after the ECtHR's first judgment. In that 1995 case, *McCann and Others v. the United Kingdom*, judges seized the opportunity to elaborate specific obligations that the right to life imposes on states. Of particular importance, the *McCann* judgment established that Article 2 imposes not only a substantive obligation on states to protect life, but also a procedural obligation to conduct an effective, independent, and transparent investigation when state agents are alleged to have taken a life.[8] The IACtHR had already established independent substantive and procedural obligations under the right to life in the aforementioned *Velásquez-Rodríguez v. Honduras* case (1988); however, ECtHR judges did not cite the IACtHR in *McCann*.

Regarding substantive obligations under Article 2, a central challenge for the ECtHR has been establishing when the burden of proof leans toward the state vs. the applicant in cases of alleged state responsibility for a death. This issue was at the crux of *Kaya v. Turkey* (1998), in which the applicant alleged that her brother had been unlawfully killed by security forces. *Kaya* was crucial for establishing "proof beyond reasonable doubt" as the ECtHR's evidentiary standard in cases of alleged state-sponsored killings. Owing to a lack of cooperation from key witnesses to the applicant's brother's death, the Court ruled that Turkey could not be found to have violated its substantive Article 2 obligations in this case. However, Turkey was found in violation of its procedural obligations for not effectively investigating the killing.[9] The Court reached a similar conclusion in *Tanrikulu v. Turkey* (1999). The applicant alleged that her husband, a Kurdish doctor, was fatally shot by security forces. While the judges in this case acknowledged a broader pattern of state violence against Kurds, they could not establish Turkey's responsibility for the killing "beyond reasonable doubt." Still, the Court found Turkey in violation of Article 2's procedural requirements based on the lack of an investigation.[10]

The ECtHR's jurisprudence on enforced disappearances has developed in large part through cases against Turkey. In *Kurt v. Turkey* (1998), the applicant alleged that her son had been disappeared by state agents following a military attack on their village aimed at rooting out PKK fighters. Four years had passed since her son's disappearance without word of him. The applicant assumed that he had been killed in state custody and submitted that Turkey had violated his right to life as well as the Convention's prohibition on inhuman treatment. Once again citing the lack of proof beyond reasonable doubt, the ECtHR declined to rule on the alleged Article 2 and 3 violations. However, given Turkey's negligence in investigating the son's disappearance, the ECtHR ruled that the applicant herself had suffered a violation of Article 3 due to the "anguish [she] has endured over a prolonged period of time."[11] The *Kurt* ruling expanded the ECtHR's conceptualization of who can be considered a "victim" in cases of PI rights violations and recognized that mental anguish, and not only physical mistreatment, can constitute "inhuman or degrading treatment."

Caraher v. the United Kingdom (2000) offers critical insight into the Court's approach to determining appropriate remedies for Article 2 violations. The applicant in this case was a Northern Irish woman whose husband had been wrongfully shot and killed by British soldiers. Prior to approaching the ECtHR, the applicant had received a monetary settlement from the UK Ministry of Defense through a civil suit. Her motivation for submitting an Article 2 complaint was not to obtain further financial reparations but rather to attempt to secure a judgment mandating that the UK military revise its use-of-force training and investigation procedures to prevent additional civilian deaths. The ECtHR found the applicant's claim to be "manifestly ill-founded" and dismissed it on the grounds that, as she had received a civil settlement, she could "no longer . . . clam to be a victim of a violation of the Convention."[12] The applicant in this case asked the Court to intervene significantly in domestic sovereignty by mandating changes in military protocol. Mandating measures of nonrepetition would defy the Court's standard practice at the time of exclusively mandating financial remedies. It was a step that the Court was not willing to take. Even as the ECtHR faced an increase in Article 2 cases in the late 1990s, judges did not respond to this development by ordering more interventionist remedies.

By the mid-1990s, the ECtHR had found violations of Article 3 (the prohibition of torture and inhuman or degrading treatment) in several cases involving abuse under police custody.[13] In *Yagiz v. Turkey* (1996), in which the applicant claimed to have been beaten while detained at a police station, the ECtHR was faced with delineating the boundaries of its temporal jurisdiction. The Court determined the case to be inadmissible on the grounds that Mrs. Yagiz's alleged mistreatment by police occurred one month prior to Turkey's recognition of the ECtHR's jurisdiction.[14] In doing so, the ECtHR declined to recognize the potential for police brutality to cause continuing physical or mental impairment that might bring elements of events that occurred preaccession into the Court's temporal jurisdiction. The Court's rigid approach to determining admissibility in this case is consistent with its founding predisposition to defer to governments to address past state violence.

The end of the Cold War brought a new frontier for the Council of Europe, as former Soviet states were eager to join Western international institutions. But the European system was ill-prepared to take on the slew of cases that accompanied the accession of new members. During negotiations to draft Protocol 11 in 1991, the Committee of Ministers discussed the urgent issue of reducing the system's case backlog.[15] Notably absent from these discussions was any mention of the need to address ongoing rights violations and past trauma from fallen communist dictatorships. The ministers spoke wistfully of a "pan-European future" and "rallying all the peoples of Europe to the basic values which are our common heritage."[16] They pledged to "promote democratic values and provide training and expertise to those countries in the East which need our help."[17] It is clear that the ministers did not perceive the Council of Europe's mission to include holding new member states accountable for recent human rights atrocities. Rather, the ministers sought to ensure that the ECtHR could handle the task of guiding new member states toward compliance with European human rights standards. Protocol 11, which entered into force in November 1998, marked the largest structural reform in the ECtHR's history. Protocol 11 also represented an opportunity for the Court to reinterpret its authority to intervene in ongoing issues stemming from past violence in new member states.

Regarding alleged rights violations in established member states, Protocol 11 does not appear to have significantly influenced the Court's delineation of its temporal jurisdiction or evidentiary standards in PI cases. In *Göç v. Turkey* (2000), the applicant alleged he had been tortured in police custody. The ECtHR dismissed that claim on the grounds that the applicant had petitioned the Court nearly two years after his release from custody, outside the six-month time limit. The applicant argued that he had attempted to exhaust domestic remedies in compliance with the ECtHR's admissibility requirements but was delayed when domestic prosecutors ignored his complaints. The Court rejected that argument, reiterating its strict temporal admissibility criteria.[18] The Court maintained stringent evidentiary standards in *Labita v. Italy* (2003), another case in which the applicant claimed he had been tortured by police. Acknowledging the inherent power differentials that exist between detainees and state agents, the ECtHR's judgment recognized that "it may prove difficult for prisoners to obtain evidence of ill-treatment by their prison warders. In that connection, it notes that the applicant alleged that the warders at Pianosa applied pressure on the prisoners by threatening reprisals if they were denounced."[19] Still, the Court found no violation of Article 3, citing the lack of positive evidence to prove beyond a reasonable doubt that police had tortured the applicant. The *Göç* and *Labita* judgments are consistent with pre–Protocol 11 jurisprudence, indicating that the Court's dismissal of the Article 3 complaint in *Göç* and its allocation of the burden of proof to the applicant in *Labita* were not products of the reform process. Rather, those judgments reflect the Court's long-established practices of formalistically applying temporal case admissibility criteria and requiring applicants to furnish proof beyond reasonable doubt. Both of these practices are consistent with the ECtHR's deferential interpretation of its authority.

The Court issued a pivotal decision in 2006 developing its approach to determining temporal jurisdiction for conflict-era continuing violations.[20] In this case, *Blečić v. Croatia*, the Court was asked to rule on Croatia's termination of the applicant's tenancy when she left the country in 1991 and was unable to return for several months because of the war.[21] Despite the fact that the final domestic ruling on this case was issued two years after Croatia ratified the European Convention, the ECtHR declared the case inadmissible because the initial violation occurred prior to Croatia's accession.[22] The *Blečić* case marked the first time that the Court grappled with the question of temporal jurisdiction in a civil conflict context following the implementation of Protocol 11 and eastward expansion of CoE membership.

Three years after *Blečić*, the ECtHR's jurisprudence shifted in *Šilih v. Slovenia*, a case involving national authorities' failure to investigate a death caused by medical negligence. The death occurred just over a year prior to Slovenia's accession. The Court considered that the fundamental nature of the right to life merited revised consideration of the temporal jurisdiction standards established in *Blečič*,[23] and ruled that the substantive obligation to uphold the right to life and the procedural obligation to investigate violations of that right could be considered temporally independent obligations.[24] The Grand Chamber judgment in *Šilih* cited several IACtHR cases to support this position.[25]

By ruling that procedural obligations under Article 2 fell within its temporal jurisdiction in *Šilih*,[26] the ECtHR loosened its approach to admitting continuing rights violations. However, the Court added caveats to the *Šilih* decision that would constrain its temporal jurisdiction in future enforced disappearance cases. To admit cases alleging violations of the right to life, a "genuine connection" must exist between the death and the entry into force of the Convention in the relevant state. A genuine connection can be established in one of two circumstances:

(1) When a "significant proportion of the procedural steps required by [Article 2]—which include not only an effective investigation into the death of the person concerned but also the institution of appropriate proceedings for the purpose of determining the cause of the death and holding those responsible to account—will have been or ought to have been carried out after the critical date."

(2) When such a connection can be justified "based on the need to ensure that the guarantees and the underlying values of the Convention are protected."[27]

Interviews with ECtHR Registry lawyers revealed a lack of consensus regarding the interpretation of these criteria. One lawyer commented that the *Šilih* criteria are "vague" and would benefit from further "elaboration."[28] Another interviewee explained that there is no standard metric for determining that a sufficient proportion of the procedural steps has taken place after state accession. Rather, the Court considers the context of a given case.[29]

Continuing rights violations complicate case admissibility decisions even when those violations commenced after state accession. All three regional courts require applicants to submit petitions within six months of the exhaustion of domestic remedies.[30] However, it is not always clear when that period begins and ends. This issue arose in *Varnava and Others v. Turkey*, which concerned the enforced disappearance of nine civilians during the 1974 Turkish invasion of Cyprus. Turkey objected that the ECtHR lacked temporal jurisdiction because the applicants did not petition the Court until 1990. The applicants rebutted by citing an established position in the ECtHR's case law that the six-month time limit starts afresh each day as long as the violation is ongoing.[31] In a decision that extensively cited the IACtHR's jurisprudence on temporal jurisdiction in enforced disappearance cases, the ECtHR admitted the case and ruled that Turkey had continuously violated Article 2 by failing to investigate the disappearances.

However, *Varnava* ultimately narrowed the Court's temporal jurisdiction. The Court specified that the six-month clock starts when the applicant "first became or ought to have become" aware of the infeasibility of a domestic remedy.[32] A defining feature of enforced disappearance is obfuscation by state authorities regarding the whereabouts and fate of the victim(s). The victim(s)' relatives are unlikely to know exactly when there no longer exists a possibility that their loved one(s) will be located. Consequently, they will not know their deadline for seeking international recourse. Within two months after *Varnava*, the ECtHR cited that judgment's specification of the six-month rule to dismiss fifty separate petitions in which applicants alleged that their relatives had been disappeared by the Turkish military.[33]

Gutiérrez Dorado and Dorado Ortiz v. Spain was the first case of a Franco-era enforced disappearance submitted to the ECtHR. This case followed a 2008 decision in Spain's National Criminal Court that effectively foreclosed the possibility of obtaining justice for Franco-era rights abuses through the Spanish court system.[34] The victim's relatives petitioned the ECtHR in 2009, within the six-month limit. They claimed that Spain's amnesty law violates Article 13 of the Convention by blocking any effective remedy for Franco-era disappearances.

The ECtHR declared *Dorado Ortiz* inadmissible. Referencing *Šilih*, the Court first decided it could not find a "genuine connection" between the victim's death and the Convention's entry into force.[35] Second, citing *Varnava*, the ECtHR ruled that the applicants did not exhibit "due diligence" in submitting their petition in a timely manner. This position ignores monumental barriers that Spanish victims faced and still face pursuing domestic recourse for Franco-era rights violations.[36] The developments in Spain's National Criminal Court indicate that investigations into Franco-era disappearances were possible as late as 2008. It is unclear why these proceedings did not constitute a "significant proportion of the procedural steps" after Spain's accession that would activate the Court's jurisdiction. All cases that Spanish victims of Franco-era rights abuses have submitted to the ECtHR since 2008 have been dismissed on temporal jurisdiction grounds.[37]

The ECtHR has accepted temporal jurisdiction over procedural complaints in conflict-era PI cases in which the alleged events occurred just a few years prior to state accession. *Association "21 December 1989" and Others v. Romania* (2011) and *Mocanu and Others v. Romania* (2014) involved applicants who had been injured or whose relatives had been killed during violent crackdowns on antigovernment protesters amid the fall of the communist regime in 1989. The European Convention did not come into force in Romania until 1994. In these cases, the ECtHR ruled that while it could not consider whether Romania had violated its substantive obligations under Articles 2 and 3, the state had violated procedural obligations under those Articles by failing to effectively investigate the applicants' claims.[38]

Subsequent case law suggests the ECtHR is unlikely to admit even procedural complaints under Articles 2 and 3 if the alleged violations occurred more than a few years preaccession. *Janowiec v. Russia* (2013) alleged state failure to investigate a Soviet massacre of Polish prisoners of war in 1940.[39] The Court considered whether the second *Šilih* criterion for establishing a genuine connection might apply here—the need to protect the underlying values of the Convention.[40] Even though the allegations concerned war crimes, the Grand Chamber determined that no genuine connection existed.[41] In 2018, the ECtHR cited lack of temporal jurisdiction to dismiss a case involving the 1948 massacre of twenty-four unarmed civilians by British soldiers in what is now Malaysia.[42] With its stringent application of temporal admissibility criteria even in cases involving war crimes and crimes against humanity, the ECtHR has unequivocally rejected responsibility for securing state accountability for past human rights atrocities. The ECtHR's interpretation of its mandate to hold states accountable for past crimes will likely shrink further in the future. Protocol 15 to the European Convention, which entered into force in 2021, shortened the time that applicants have to submit petitions from six to four months following the exhaustion of domestic remedies.

The Convention's drafters designed the European human rights system not to punish states for their antidemocratic pasts but rather to create a *break* with the past and forge a new future based on a collective commitment to human rights. Creating the Court was, in and of itself, an act of closure. Likewise, the goal of the Court's expansion was not to dredge up new members' pasts but to hold them accountable for their human rights obligations from the moment they joined the club. This required the Court to narrowly interpret its temporal jurisdiction and largely defer to member states to handle transitional justice concerns. As a result, many European victims of continuing violations have been left without options for legal recourse.

The ECtHR's narrow interpretation of its temporal jurisdiction seems to have become more entrenched over time, indicating a durable proclivity to defer to governments to address past state violence. With regard to evidentiary standards in PI cases, however, the Court has gradually become more receptive to shifting the burden of proof from applicants to governments in cases of particularly severe abuses. For example, in *Grinenko v. Ukraine* (2012), in which the applicant claimed to have been tortured while in police custody, the Court acknowledged that detainees are at a distinct disadvantage when it comes to providing evidence of mistreatment at the hands of state agents.[43] Still, the Court ruled that a lack of evidence prevented it from establishing a substantive violation of Article 3. The Court, however, did find Ukraine in violation of its procedural obligations.[44]

The year following the *Grinenko* judgment, ECtHR judges reiterated that alleged PI violations invoke unique imperatives for the Court to shift the burden of proof to the government. In *Askhabova v. Russia* (2013), in which the applicant alleged that her son had been disappeared by state agents, the burden of proof emerged as a key issue: "The Court is sensitive to the subsidiary nature of its role and recognises that it must be cautious in taking on the role of a first-instance tribunal of fact. . . . Nonetheless, where allegations are made under Articles 2 and 3 of the Convention, the Court must apply a particularly thorough scrutiny . . . even if certain domestic proceedings and investigations have already taken place."[45] While careful to emphasize its subsidiary role relative to governments, the Court stipulated that "where the applicant makes out a prima facie case, it is for the Government to provide a satisfactory and convincing explanation of how the events in question occurred. The burden of proof is thus shifted to the Government and if they fail in their arguments, issues will arise under Article 2 and/ or Article 3."[46] The *Askhabova* case marks a distinct shift in approach relative to earlier enforced disappearance cases in which the facts of the case were similarly disputed, for example the aforementioned *Kurt v. Turkey* case. In *Askhabova*, the fact that the applicant's son was last seen detained by police and had not reappeared was enough for the ECtHR to assume that (1) the son had died, and (2) Russia was responsible for that death.[47] The Court thus ruled that Russia had violated both the substantive and procedural requirements of Article 2, in addition to violating Article 3 with respect to the mental suffering endured by the victim's mother.[48]

Although the IACtHR had already established a practice of shifting the burden of proof to governments in PI cases by the 2010s, the ECtHR did not cite the IACtHR at all in the *Grinenko* and *Askhabova* judgments. This does not mean that ECtHR judges have not been influenced by the IACtHR in this area. The ECtHR's relaxation of the "beyond reasonable doubt" requirement in PI cases could reflect judges' receptivity to shifting norms in international human rights law more broadly. The early 2010s coincided with the release of the Brighton Declaration. The ECtHR's reassessment of the burden of proof during this time affords less deference to governments, in contravention of the expectation that the Court would constrict its authority when facing state backlash.

In most cases involving PI violations, the ECtHR has continued to only order states to pay financial reparations to injured parties. In all the cases discussed above in which a violation was established, financial reparations were the only remedies mandated by the Court. However, a new approach to ordering remedies, introduced in 2004, called the "pilot judgement procedure," has expanded the scope of the Court's remedial mandates in certain PI cases. The purpose of pilot judgments is to assist CoE member states in resolving systemic or structural problems that are causing high numbers of cases involving the same underlying issues to arrive at the ECtHR. The procedure was designed to help the ECtHR manage its growing caseload by reducing the number of repetitive cases that are submitted to the Court. There is a trade-off between the authority of the Court and the authority of governments involved in pilot judgments. In such judgments, the Court will identify specific remedial measures that go beyond the scope of individualized financial reparations. These measures are targeted at alleviating the underlying social or legal conditions that give rise to repetitive human rights violations. In exchange for asserting this broader authority, the ECtHR will "freeze" consideration of any related cases against the government in question for a specified period of time. This freeze on proceedings is intended to give the government time to take the necessary measures to comply with the Court's remedial mandate.[49] Under typical circumstances, once a pilot judgment has been issued, the Committee of Ministers engages in talks with the relevant government to discern how to specifically implement the ECtHR's orders and monitor the state's compliance. ECtHR judges are often part of these discussions in an "informal way" through internal conversations with the Execution Department of the Committee, but, according to one ECtHR judge, these conversations are "very casual" and "depend on the direction of the political wind."[50]

The first pilot judgment, *Broniowski v. Poland*, involved applicants whose property was expropriated by the Polish government prior to the Second World War. The postwar government had established a system for compensating individuals deprived of their or their families' property owing to postwar border changes, but this system fell apart because of resource constraints in 1989, two years prior to Poland's accession to the ECtHR. As a result, this unremedied deprivation constituted a continuing violation of the right to property, codified in Article 1 of the first Protocol to the European Convention. Going beyond its standard practice of only ordering financial reparations, the ECtHR, for the first time in its history, ordered that a member state, "through appropriate legal measures and administrative practices, secure the implementation of the property right in question."[51] It is unclear why the Court interpreted its temporal jurisdiction to encompass continuing property rights violations stemming from disputes that occurred in the 1940s, fifty years before Poland joined the ECtHR, but has repeatedly rejected responsibility to adjudicate continuing violations stemming from preaccession enforced disappearances and extrajudicial executions. One might argue that the deprivation of life incurs even greater and longer-lasting harm than the deprivation of property.

The ECtHR has issued only eight pilot judgments in PI rights cases. Seven of these cases involved violations of Article 3 connected to inhumane prison conditions.[52] *Tunikova and Others v. Russia* (2021), a pilot judgment involving PI rights not related to prison conditions, condemned the Russian government for failing to provide protections for victims of gender-based violence.[53] The nonfinancial remedial mandates included in pilot judgments are typically very brief and do not stipulate specific mechanisms for addressing systemic rights issues. For example, in *Varga and Others v. Hungary* (2015), the Court ordered the government to "produce, under the supervision of the Committee of Ministers . . . a time frame in which to make appropriate arrangements and to put in practice preventative and compensatory remedies." In another example, *Neshkov and Others v. Bulgaria* (2015), the Court ordered Bulgaria to "within eighteen months . . . make available a combination of domestic remedies in respect of conditions of detention that have both preventative and compensatory effects." These mandates give governments considerable latitude to decide how to implement domestic reforms. More specific mandates in pilot judgments have ordered the release of prisoners. For example, in *Ilaşcu and Others v. Moldova and Russia* (2004), the Court ordered the respondent states to "take all necessary measures to put an end to the arbitrary detention of the applicants still imprisoned and secure their immediate release."

The *Tunikova* judgment targeting gender-based violence in Russia points to a possible shift in the Court's approach. *Tunikova* features expansive and detailed remedial mandates, a notable development given that the judgment was handed down after Russia's expulsion from the CoE was inevitable following the invasion of Ukraine. In that ruling, the ECtHR ordered Russia to "criminalise and make punishable by appropriate penalties all acts of domestic violence," reform police training procedures regarding recognizing and reporting domestic violence, amend domestic legislation to make restraining orders easier to obtain, "put into place an action plan for changing the public perception of gender-based violence against women," and "design a monitoring mechanism for accurate collection of comprehensive statistics on prevention and punishment of domestic violence and recording of statistical data on domestic violence."[54] Although the IACtHR has repeatedly ordered similar mandates in cases involving similar questions of government responsibility for gender-based violence, ECtHR judges declined to cite any IACtHR jurisprudence in *Tunikova*.[55] While the prospects for compliance with this judgment are abysmal given the state of Russian politics and the country's current estrangement from the CoE, it is still highly significant that ECtHR judges demonstrated willingness to buck historical precedent and expand the scope of pilot judgment remedial mandates in a case specifically challenging impunity for gender-based violence.

The ECtHR has used the pilot judgment procedure to mandate remedies that go beyond individual measures and target broader social conditions that lead to human rights violations. This broadening of the scope of the Court's remedial mandates was not, however, a result of the Court reinterpreting its fundamental social purpose, but rather was borne out of a practical necessity to decrease the number of repetitive cases that were arriving at the Court. The Court has taken care to maintain its deferential exercise of authority even while expanding its remedial mandates by using the pilot judgment procedure in only a small subset of cases, issuing nonspecific mandates that allow states significant discretion to implement the Court's orders, and delegating the enforcement and monitoring of state compliance to the Committee of Ministers, an intergovernmental body.

Throughout the many structural changes and normative evolutions in human rights law that the ECtHR has navigated in the past thirty years, the Court has mostly held firm to its founding disposition to leave the past in the past. A central mission of the Court's founders was to foster states' collective commitment to the new European integration project. The ECtHR was established to create a break with the past, not litigate it. The ECtHR's persistence in employing a narrow interpretation of its temporal jurisdiction has largely been consistent both before and after Protocol 11. That consistency suggests that this practice is a function of the Court's normative mission as opposed to a product of practical exigencies incurred by rising caseloads. In a similarly deferential manner, the Court has historically resisted shifting the burden of proof to governments in PI cases. Still, particularly in the 2010s, the Court loosened evidentiary standards in favor of applicants in cases of severe PI violations such as enforced disappearance and torture. The Court has also broadly interpreted states' procedural obligations under Articles 2 and 3 and expanded definitions of victimhood to encompass the mental anguish endured by victims' relatives. These developments suggest that the political resistance that the Court has faced in the post-Brighton era has not resulted in greater deference to states in this area of case law. Rather, the ECtHR is increasingly willing to subject governments to intense scrutiny in cases of the most serious PI abuses.

The Inter-American Court of Human Rights

Beginning with its first-ever judgment, *Velásquez-Rodríguez v. Honduras*, the IACtHR has established that an observable pattern of state-sponsored PI rights abuses can constitute sufficient evidence to rule against a state even in cases where there exists no physical evidence to support an applicant's claims. The IACtHR's approach to developing evidentiary standards has therefore historically departed from the ECtHR's requirement of "proof beyond reasonable doubt." For example, *Juan Humberto Sánchez v. Honduras* (2003) concerned the alleged kidnapping, torture, and killing of a man by military agents. The state rejected responsibility for these events and submitted evidence that Mr. Sánchez was not kidnapped by the military.[56] The IACtHR emphasized that "a framework of a practice of grave human rights violations promoted or tolerated by the state" must be taken into account when evaluating evidentiary standards. "If it is proven for the specific case that it fits within the pattern of extra-legal executions, it is reasonable to assume and conclude that there is an international responsibility of the State." Therefore, even in the absence of direct evidence of state involvement in Sánchez's death, the IACtHR ruled that Honduras violated his right to life based on the broader context of state involvement in and impunity for PI rights abuses. Furthermore, Honduras had violated Sánchez's family's "mental and moral integrity" by failing to investigate his killing and burying his remains without the family's consent.[57]

The IACtHR shed further light on its approach to delineating evidentiary standards in *19 Merchants v. Colombia* (2004), another enforced disappearance case:

> In the matter of receiving and assessing evidence, the Court has indicated previously that its proceedings are not subject to the same formalities as domestic proceedings. . . . Considering that international courts have the authority to assess and evaluate the evidence according to the rules of sound criticism, *[the Court] has always avoided a rigid determination of the quantum of evidence needed to support a judgment. . . . This criterion is especially true for international human rights courts, which have greater latitude to assess the evidence on the pertinent facts.* [my italics][58]

Here the IACtHR explicitly asserts it authority to shirk the requirement of "proof beyond reasonable doubt" when adjudicating state responsibility. Physical evidence in the *19 Merchants* case was lacking, in part because the bodies of the disappeared victims were never found. Still, the Court found Colombia in violation of Articles 4 and 5 based on circumstantial evidence, witness testimony, the state's negligence in investigating the disappearances, and the broader context of impunity for paramilitary violence in Colombia.

While IACtHR judges have repeatedly emphasized the Court's prerogative to flexibly interpret evidentiary standards, this approach does not always favor applicants. *Norín Catrimán et al. v. Chile* (2014) concerned the detention and conviction of several Mapuche Indigenous activists under Chile's controversial antiterrorism legislation.[59] The applicants alleged that they had been subjected to inhuman treatment during their time in prison. They primarily cited physical deterioration due to the hunger strike they embarked on while jailed and mental decline due to prison conditions. The IACtHR rejected this argument, finding that (1) the state could not be held responsible for the applicants' decision to engage in a hunger strike and (2) that the evidence submitted by the applicants did not indicate that their treatment in prison amounted to a violation of Article 5.[60] This case clarifies the limits of the IACtHR's general tendency to shift the burden of proof to the state in cases of alleged PI rights violations.

The aforementioned *19 Merchants* case exemplifies the IACtHR's interventionist approach to mandating remedies for PI abuses. In addition to ordering that financial reparations be paid to the victims' families, the Court mandated that Colombia

> erect a monument in memory of the victims and, in a public ceremony in the presence of the next of kin of the victims, shall place a plaque with the names of the 19 tradesmen. . . .
>
> . . . organize a public act to acknowledge its international responsibility for the facts of this case and to make amends to the memory of the 19 tradesmen, in the presence of the next of kin of the victims, and in which members of the highest State authorities must take part. . . .
>
> . . . provide, free of charge, through its specialized health institutions, the medical and psychological treatment required by the next of kin of the victims.[61]

The IACtHR's elaboration of specific memorialization acts requiring the participation of high-level state authorities, as well as its mandate that the state provide medical care to the next of kin, marks a sharp divergence from the ECtHR's standard practice of mandating only financial reparations. Even in its pilot judgments, the ECtHR's remedial mandates do not reach anywhere near the level of specificity of the IACtHR's. The IACtHR has consistently adopted a holistic approach to its remedial orders that recognizes the diverse mental and physical needs of victims of state violence.

Beyond remedial mandates targeted at individual victims, the IACtHR has also adopted an interventionist approach to specifying remedies aimed at ensuring the nonrepetition of rights violations. A notable example of this approach is found in *Tibi v. Ecuador* (2004), in which the applicant was arbitrarily detained, denied legal counsel, held without trial for over two years, and repeatedly tortured. The IACtHR ruled that, in addition to financial reparations and a public acknowledgment of wrongdoing, Ecuadorian officials must implement nationwide reforms to intervene in the recurring issue of prisoner mistreatment. The Court outlined the required components of such reforms in great detail:

> The State must establish a training and education program for the staff of the judiciary, the public prosecutor's office, the police and penitentiary staff, including the medical, psychiatric and psychological staff, on the principles and provisions regarding protection of human rights in the treatment of inmates. Design and implementation of the training program must include allocation of specific resources to attain its goals, and it will be conducted with participation by civil society. For this, the State must establish an inter-institutional committee to define and execute the training programs on human rights and treatment of inmates. The State must report to this Court on the establishment and functioning of said committee, within six months.[62]

The IACtHR has consistently maintained and even expanded its authority to order intensive remedial mandates through the present day. For example, in a November 2022 judgment involving an Ecuadorian man shot and killed while in police custody, IACtHR judges ordered the government to pay the victim's family financial reparations, provide them with free psychological and psychiatric care, investigate and prosecute those responsible for the murder, publish the IACtHR's ruling in a national paper and on the government's official website, and perform a public act of acknowledgment of responsibility in accordance with the prior consultation and consent of the victim's family.[63] The IACtHR's detailed enumeration of mandates for reform, as well as its commitment to monitoring the state's compliance with those mandates, exemplifies the Court's wide-reaching interpretation of its authority to intervene in domestic policymaking.

Recent case law indicates that, even as the IACtHR has faced growing critiques of judicial overreach,[64] the Court has declined to soften its approach. For example, even after Venezuela's denunciation of the American Convention in 2013 and withdrawal from the IACtHR, the Court ruled against the state in several cases involving PI rights violations.[65] The Court has mandated a wide range of remedies in those cases, including criminal investigations and prosecutions, provisions for free medical care, public apologies, and nationwide policy reforms in the areas of prison administration and police and military use of force.

The IACtHR has leveraged the right to judicial protection alongside a flexible interpretation of the Court's temporal jurisdiction to admit cases involving pre-accession PI violations. This approach has engendered the IACtHR's pioneering role in developing international jurisprudence prohibiting amnesties for crimes against humanity. For example, the IACtHR admitted *Serrano-Cruz Sisters v. El Salvador*, which concerned the disappearance of two girls perpetrated by the

Salvadoran military thirteen years before El Salvador's accession to the Court. While the IACtHR accepted that it could not rule on alleged violations of the right to life due to the time that had passed between the girls' disappearance and the state's accession to the Court, the Court did retain temporal jurisdiction over the continuing effects of their disappearance post-accession. Accordingly, the IACtHR ruled that El Salvador continuously violated the right to judicial protection (Article 25) by applying an amnesty law to block investigations into the sisters' disappearance. The Court also found that El Salvador violated the prohibition of inhuman treatment (Article 5) with respect to the mental anguish suffered by the girls' family members.[66] In addition to financial reparations and free medical care for the family, the Court ordered that El Salvador establish "a national commission to trace the young people who disappeared during the armed conflict," "organize a public act acknowledging its responsibility for the violations," and identify and prosecute the perpetrators.[67] The *Serrano-Cruz* case was crucial for consolidating a now-entrenched regional norm opposing the application of amnesties to crimes against humanity.

The IACtHR's position that enforced disappearances violate the right to judicial protection marks a stark divergence from the ECtHR's approach to disappearance cases. This maneuver has enabled the IACtHR to be "more generous with temporal jurisdiction in enforced disappearance cases."[68] In general, the IACtHR will interpret its temporal jurisdiction more broadly in cases where the violation in question is permanent (for example, involving a death or disappearance) and requires implementing measures to ensure that the violation is not repeated.[69] This position illustrates the Court's distinct consideration of the gravity of continuing violations when rendering admissibility decisions, as well as the Court's hesitance to assume that regime change is sufficient to preclude the reemergence of past atrocities. Unlike the drafters of the European Convention (and a majority of ECtHR judges through the present day), IACtHR judges have not subscribed to the idea that the creation of the IACtHR or a given state's accession to the Court constitutes a "break" with the past. Rather, the IACtHR sees itself as an agent for securing closure for victims of past atrocities and ensuring that similar abuses are not repeated.

Uruguay and Chile also passed amnesties after their respective transitions back to democracy in 1985 and 1990 that blocked the investigation and prosecution of dictatorship-era human rights violations. In *Gelman v. Uruguay* (2011), the IACtHR condemned the state's amnesty law and ruled that the continuing effects of Ms. Gelman's disappearance brought the case within the Court's jurisdiction, even though Gelman disappeared nine years prior to Uruguay's accession.[70] The IACtHR mandated that Uruguay amend its amnesty law to exclude application to "serious human rights violations."[71] Similarly, the IACtHR found an Article 25 violation and mandated that Chile amend its Pinochet-era amnesty law in *Almonacid-Arellano et al. v. Chile* (2006), a case based on an extralegal execution committed seventeen years before Chile's accession to the Court.[72] The IACtHR has consistently maintained an interventionist approach to admitting and mandating remedies in cases involving PI rights violations committed during civil conflict, even when the violations originated prior to state accession.

Almonacid-Arellano et al. v. Chile is also notable as the first case in which the IACtHR asserted the "conventionality control doctrine" (*la doctrina del control de convencionalidad*).[73] The doctrine obligates national authorities to incorporate the American Convention's norms and principles into domestic legislation, modify legislation to accord with the IACtHR's interpretation of the Convention, and give direct effect to IACtHR rulings. The "intensity" of these obligations varies according to the depth of a given state's legalization of Inter-American human rights principles—hence, like the margin of appreciation in the European system, the conventionality control doctrine upholds the principle of subsidiarity in the Inter-American system.[74] However, while the MOA maintains a certain distance between the ECtHR and the authority of national institutions, conventionality control empowers closer supervision by the IACtHR.[75] The central aim of the conventionality control doctrine is to enhance state compliance with IACtHR rulings. Still, the doctrine has been criticized as an excessive incursion on national sovereignty, supporting the IACtHR's "radically monist approach to the relationship between international and national law."[76] Ariel Dulitzky argues that the conventionality control doctrine is "one of the tools the court uses to define its own identity and role in the hemisphere" and furthermore that the doctrine elevates the American Convention as "no longer a subsidiary treaty but an integral, fundamental, and hierarchically superior norm of the national domestic legal system."[77] Other assessments emphasize that the doctrine supports a multidirectional, not hierarchical, participatory process in which IACtHR and domestic judges can better communicate with one another to determine how best to implement Convention obligations in diverse contexts.[78] In any case, the conventionality control doctrine represents an unprecedented attempt by a regional court to self-legitimize extending its own authority in the domestic realm. That this doctrine emerged within a case in which the IACtHR flexibly interpreted its temporal jurisdiction and ordered the modification of national legislation suggests interventionist intentions on the part of the judges.

Even as the IACtHR's annual caseload has grown throughout the years, the Court has never, on temporal jurisdiction grounds, rejected a petition alleging conflict-era or dictatorship-era PI rights violations.[79] These figures suggest that efficiency concerns cannot, on their own, explain constriction of a court's admissibility criteria. This is not to say that the ECtHR's overwhelming caseload is unrelated to its increasingly narrow interpretation of its temporal jurisdiction. But to pin that interpretation solely on practical exigencies is insufficient. Of course, the IACtHR still faces an overall caseload that is only a small fraction of the ECtHR's in a given year. It is possible that the IACtHR's caseload has not yet reached a critical tipping point for the Court to interpret its temporal jurisdiction more narrowly. The IACtHR also benefits from the Commission as a buffer institution to guide parties toward friendly settlements, deflecting cases from reaching the Court. Nevertheless, the IACtHR has faced cases of grave state-sponsored violence since its inception and consistently interpreted its temporal jurisdiction flexibly in such cases. The Court has done so even in the face of perpetual underfunding and a chronic lack of political support from the OAS. This indicates that there is something different about the IACtHR that supersedes logistical circumstances.

The founders of the IACtHR deliberately created a wider-reaching system of human rights protection to respond to the acute challenges of the region. As a result, the IACtHR has become a consequential actor in domestic debates about how to investigate and remedy human rights atrocities, including those arising from state actions committed preaccession. The IACtHR has continued to employ evidentiary standards that recognize the inherent obstacles that victims of state violence may face in providing evidence to support their claims. The IACtHR's rejection of the "beyond reasonable doubt" standard may be a product of precedents set in the Court's early years when state violence plagued the region. Still, the continued prominence of PI violations in the Court's case law gives judges little motivation to reevaluate this approach. Consistent with its founding social purpose, the IACtHR maintains sweeping authority to flexibly interpret its jurisdiction and mandate remedies in cases of severe fundamental rights violations. Furthermore, IACtHR judges created a new legal doctrine, the conventionality control, which has no textual basis outside of case law but intensifies the Court's influence in domestic legal systems. Consistent with theorized expectations, even amid a rising workload and state criticism, the IACtHR is not inclined to pull back its judicial authority.

The African Court on Human and Peoples' Rights

While the ACtHPR has ruled on only a relatively small number of cases involving alleged PI rights violations, judges have seized those opportunities to clarify the contours of the Court's authority. In *Ally Rajabu and Others v. Tanzania* (2019), the Court was faced with one of the most contentious challenges in international human rights law: adjudicating if the death penalty can ever be compatible with the right to life. The applicant in this case had been convicted of murder and sentenced to death by hanging. The Tanzanian penal code imposes mandatory death sentences in all cases of murder. The applicant alleged that these sentencing mandates violate the African Charter's right to life (Article 4) and respect of human dignity (Article 5). The Court's judgment reviewed existing international jurisprudence, noting that "despite a global trend towards the abolition of the death penalty . . . the prohibition of the death sentence in international law is still not absolute."[80] The Court ultimately determined that while it could not establish a basis for a total ban of the death penalty in the Charter, imposing the death penalty as an automatic, mandatory sentence constituted an arbitrary deprivation of life in violation of Article 4. Furthermore, the Court ruled that hanging is a form of torture in violation of the Charter's protection of human dignity. Sending a clear signal of its willingness to intervene domestically in this issue, the Court mandated that Tanzania remove the mandatory imposition of the death penalty from its penal code and provide the applicant with a new sentencing hearing.[81]

The ACtHPR again asserted authority to intervene in domestic legal affairs in the aforementioned case of *Sébastien Germain Ajavon v. Benin* (2020). The Court ruled that Benin had violated the right to life and prohibition of torture in connection with May 2019 postelection violence. When citizens had taken to the streets to protest election irregularities, the army opened fire on crowds, killing dozens. The government then passed an amnesty law that blocked investigation into these events and granted impunity to the perpetrators. The ACtHPR ordered Benin to repeal that amnesty law, as well as amend several other provisions within national legislation.[82] The ACtHPR's willingness to order states to amend and repeal legislation follows the example of the IACtHR, while the ECtHR has solidly rejected assuming that authority.

The ACtHPR is still developing its delineation of its temporal jurisdiction. However, existing case law indicates that the Court is adopting a flexible approach to admitting preaccession violations with continuing effects, and a case-by-case approach to applying the six-month rule. This balance is observable in *Chananja Luchagula v. Tanzania* (2020). The applicant was a former death row inmate who had recently been released through a presidential pardon. The applicant alleged that the court that had sentenced him to death had erred and claimed several PI violations connected to his sentencing and imprisonment. The applicant's sentencing had occurred in 2003, seven years before Tanzania acceded to the ACtHPR. The Court recognized the continuing effects of that sentencing as falling within its temporal jurisdiction. Nevertheless, the application was ultimately still declared inadmissible on temporal grounds because of noncompliance with the six-month rule. The Court noted that the applicant did not provide evidence to justify why he had waited over three years after exhausting domestic remedies to approach the ACtHPR.[83] This statement suggests that, had he provided evidence, the Court may have been open to granting an exception to the six-month rule. Particularly given the Court's flexible interpretation of its temporal jurisdiction in the aforementioned *Zongo v. Burkina Faso* case, which dealt with preaccession state-sponsored killings, the ACtHPR has the potential to take on a central role in reckoning with past state violence in the region.

Additionally, the ACtHPR has demonstrated flexibility in applying the six-month rule in cases where applicants face structural barriers to pursuing justice through domestic court systems.[84] The applicant in *Lucien Ikili Rashidi v. Tanzania* (2019) was a national of the Democratic Republic of Congo who, with his wife and children, had fled wartime violence to live in Dar es Salaam. The family were arrested in 2006 on charges of illegally residing in Tanzania. The applicant's wife and children had entered the country as refugees,[85] and the applicant had previously been issued a visa that remained valid at the time of his arrest. However, he had lost physical possession of that visa when he lost his passport, which he reported to Tanzanian authorities prior to his date of arrest. Tanzanian courts ended up taking nearly seven years to reach a final judgment in the applicant's immigration case, after which he was deported and reunited with his family in Burundi. Following that traumatic episode, the applicant filed a case at the ACtHPR alleging violation of his rights to residence and free movement (Article 12(1)) and his right to be tried in a reasonable amount of time (Article 7(1)). Additionally, the applicant alleged that, during his initial arrest in 2006, Tanzanian police subjected him to an anal search in front of his two sons, in violation of his right to human dignity (Article 5). In proceedings at the ACtHPR, the government argued that the applicant had filed the case out of time, as just over a year had passed between the final deportation order in 2014 (considered by the government to mark the exhaustion of domestic remedies) and the applicant's filing with the ACtHPR in 2015. ACtHPR judges rejected this argument, emphasizing that the six-month rule is not actually specified in the Charter, and that the Court maintains discretion to evaluate temporal jurisdiction on a case-by-case basis.[86] The judges unanimously found Tanzania responsible for all the Charter violations that had been alleged by the applicant, and went even further to find that the anal search performed by Tanzanian police violated Article 4 of the Charter by degrading the applicant's physical integrity of person.[87]

As with its temporal jurisdiction, the ACtHPR is still grappling with establishing evidentiary standards. In *Andrew Ambrose Cheusi v. Tanzania* (2020), the Court found no violation of Article 5 on the grounds that the applicant, who claimed to have been tortured in police custody, provided no corroborating evidence. It should be noted, however, that the applicant did not even provide specific descriptions of the alleged torture.[88] In another PI case, *Léon Mugesera v. Rwanda* (2020), the ACtHPR demonstrated openness to shifting the burden of proof to the government. The applicant, Mr. Mugesera, alleged he had been subjected to death threats and denied food and medicine while in prison. Mugesera had been convicted by Rwandan courts in 2016 of inciting genocide. He had then petitioned the ACtHPR in February 2017, before Rwanda's withdrawal from the Court went into force; consequently the Court could still admit the case. When asked by the ACtHPR to provide documentation in connection with *Mugesera*, the Rwandan government responded "reminding the Court of its withdrawal" and declined to participate in the proceedings. The Court then issued provisional measures ordering Rwanda to allow Mugesera access to his lawyers and correct the complained-of issues regarding his treatment in prison. The ACtHPR eventually decided to render a judgment on the case in *suo motu*, without the acknowledgment or participation of the Rwandan state.[89]

The *Mugesera* judgment offers important insight into the ACtHPR's allocation of the burden of proof. The Court noted that Mugesera's detailed descriptions of his mistreatment in prison and documented attempts to appeal to domestic authorities "justify shifting the burden of proof to the Respondent State, given that the Applicant is in prison and that it is difficult for him to produce additional evidence beyond the steps he claims to have taken."[90] This statement demonstrates the Court's cognizance of the inherent power differentials between prisoners and state agents. On these grounds, the ACtHPR ruled that Rwanda had violated Article 5.

The ACtHPR has already developed a distinct approach to navigating the level of deference it affords to member governments. Despite a recent spate of withdrawals, the Court has rejected requiring proof beyond reasonable doubt to rule against governments. As seen in *Mugesera*, the Court does not appear interested in going easy on withdrawn governments to attempt to win back their membership. The ACtHPR has also developed a (cautiously) flexible interpretation of its temporal jurisdiction and an unabashedly interventionist approach to mandating remedies for established PI violations. As the Court's jurisprudence develops, it will be interesting to see whether the ACtHPR decides to take on a transitional justice-oriented role akin to that of the IACtHR in addressing past state violence.

Interviews conducted at the ACtHPR indicated that Court officials are generally very attuned to developments in the other two regional courts and see these courts as important sources of jurisprudential guidance. One ACtHPR judge specified that, while the African Court is in no manner bound to follow the examples of the other regional courts, the young age of the Court necessitates openness to learning from older courts and being willing to engage in cross-court jurisprudential dialogue: "No court exists in isolation."[91] A lawyer interviewed also pointed to the Court's youth as an important factor in this process, stating that referencing other courts' precedents is helpful "particularly if the African Court does not yet have jurisprudence on the issue. . . . The older the Court gets, the less it has to rely on others."[92] These statements provide supportive evidence for the hypothesis that international judges are more likely to cite jurisprudence from other courts in the context of issue areas in which their own court has relatively less experience.

Another lawyer commented that while the ACtHPR is attentive to jurisprudence from both the ECtHR and the IACtHR, referencing IACtHR jurisprudence is often "more relevant," as that court addresses "more similar issues" to those faced by the ACtHPR.[93] This remark is crucial for understanding how international courts relate to one another. When looking for jurisprudential guidance, court officials look to examples set by other courts that they perceive to be facing similar challenges. The IACtHR and ACtHPR have both had to navigate geopolitical environments riddled with antagonism toward the very concepts of human rights and international governance. These environments, while different from one another in important ways, have both been shaped by shared challenges of a magnitude not experienced by the ECtHR. It makes sense that the ACtHPR might be more inclined to look toward its Latin American counterpart for jurisprudential inspiration.

The ECtHR and IACtHR's starkly divergent approaches to defining temporal jurisdiction represent one of the most consequential fissures across international jurisprudence on PI rights protections. This disparity can be traced to each court's unique interpretation of the boundaries of its authority over member governments, rooted in the courts' founding moments. The ECtHR and IACtHR were both founded to reckon with state-sponsored violence and to advance democratization, but they adopted very different strategies for doing so based on the exigencies of their geopolitical contexts. The ECtHR's founders designed the Court to institutionalize closure on a recent era of mass violence and illuminate the path for a visionary regional integration project. This mission necessitated a forward-thinking approach to human rights adjudication, shutting the door tight on the demons of the past. Consequently, the ECtHR has adopted a deferential approach that largely leaves it up to governments to determine whether and/or how to address past human rights atrocities. The ECtHR's persistently narrow interpretation of its temporal jurisdiction is a product of this ingrained deference. At the creation of the IACtHR, on the other hand, the demons were still in the house. The drafters of the American Convention and the IACtHR's founding judges faced pervasive, ongoing state-sponsored violence. Meeting the unique challenges of the moment required the IACtHR to adopt an interventionist conceptualization of its authority and broadly interpret its temporal jurisdiction. The IACtHR continues to assert that authority today, as PI rights violations still dominate the court's caseload. The ACtHPR's case law indicates that it is positioned to follow the example of the IACtHR more closely than that of the ECtHR when interpreting its temporal jurisdiction. Still, the ACtHPR has remained attentive to international consensus on this issue, despite the African Charter's lack of temporal constraints on case admissibility.

While the IACtHR and ACtHPR have always maintained flexible evidentiary standards, the ECtHR has held fast to requiring "proof beyond reasonable doubt" to rule against governments in most cases. Over the past decade or so, however, the ECtHR has demonstrated increased willingness to shift the burden of proof to governments in cases of PI rights violations in which applicants face systemic impediments to procuring evidence to support their claims. This shift recognizes the inherently different dynamics and aims of international human rights adjudication relative to domestic legal proceedings. The ECtHR's loosening of evidentiary standards has unfolded amid vocal government critique of the Court in the post-Brighton era, indicating that the expectation that deferential courts will be more responsive to accusations of judicial overreach does not appear to hold true in the case of PI rights violations. This is likely due to the unique gravity of these violations, as the *jus cogens* status of PI rights allows comparatively little room for judicial discretion. ECtHR judges have not directly cited IACtHR jurisprudence in several key PI cases that reevaluated the burden of proof. Still, it is possible that the IACtHR's repeated insistence on flexible evidentiary standards has influenced ECtHR judges' shifting views on allocating the burden of proof in PI cases.

JUDGMENTS ON GENDER IDENTITY AND SEXUAL ORIENTATION DISCRIMINATION

In March 2021, the IACtHR delivered a historic ruling advancing legal protections for transgender individuals in one of the most dangerous places in the world to be trans. Vicky Hernández, a Honduran trans woman, had been murdered amid widespread attacks on trans individuals following a 2009 military coup that deposed the Honduran president. After over a decade of state refusal to investigate Ms. Hernández's murder and broad impunity for antitrans violence in Honduras, the IACtHR ordered the government to reopen Hernández's case, prosecute those responsible for her killing, and pay reparations to her family. The Court also ordered Honduras to implement extensive measures aimed at dignifying the legal personhood of trans individuals and preventing future antitrans violence, including developing a national database for tracking violence against LGBT persons, implementing an antidiscrimination training program for state agents, creating a system to allow trans individuals to amend the sex notated on their official identification documents, and establishing a national education scholarship for trans women in Hernández's name. Rosa Hernández, Vicky's mother, reflected on the implications of the IACtHR's ruling while speaking to *The New York Times*: "It's so significant that there will always be this memory of her. We are always going to remember that she was the one that created a before and after."[1]

International law surrounding LGBT rights has evolved dramatically in recent years. The ECtHR and IACtHR have been at the forefront of this progress. While both courts have developed expanded rights protections for LGBT people, they have pursued starkly different approaches to doing so. ECtHR judges have espoused a deferential disposition to ruling on issues such as same-sex marriage and transgender identification rights, prioritizing attention to regional socio-legal consensus and reinforcing the ECtHR's subsidiary role relative to national authorities.[2] IACtHR judges have largely rejected the cautious incrementalism espoused by their European counterparts. Over the past decade, the IACtHR has rapidly elaborated states' human rights obligations to LGBT people and mandated intensive domestic policy reforms.

Protections against discrimination based on sexual orientation and gender identity were not included in any of the regional courts' constitutive documents. Between the 1950s and 1980s, when the European Convention, American Convention, and African Charter were drafted, discrimination against homosexual and transgender people was not widely considered within international legal bodies to be a pressing human rights issue. As domestic and transnational social movements supporting LGBT rights have grown, the regional courts have had to decide where they stand. Because LGBT rights were not contemplated at the founding of each court, judges have not been bound by precedent or written law in this area to the same extent as in other established areas of case law. Consequently, examining the development of LGBT rights jurisprudence offers a unique opportunity to observe how and when regional courts' interpretations of their authority change in the context of "new" human rights issues.

In previous chapters, I have explored whether changes in the types of rights violations faced by a court, state backlash against court decisions, and jurisprudential developments in other human rights courts might push judges to adopt more deferential or interventionist interpretations of the boundaries of their court's jurisdiction. The following passages devote particular attention to these factors while reviewing regional jurisprudence on LGBT issues. For the ECtHR, I have applied the same case selection technique as in previous chapters, focusing on discussion of cases that have set particularly influential precedent. Because the IACtHR has ruled on only a handful of cases involving sexual orientation and gender identity issues, I discuss each one of these cases in turn. The ACtHPR has not yet had the opportunity to rule on any LGBT rights cases. I take this opportunity to review the challenges that have impeded development of LGBT rights in the African system. Then, drawing from the experiences of the ECtHR and IACtHR, I sketch out a few potential pathways for overcoming those roadblocks and getting LGBT rights cases in front of the ACtHPR.

The following analysis reveals that, while the ECtHR has become increasingly interventionist in its approach to developing pro-LGBT rights jurisprudence over time, it has consistently demonstrated greater restraint in this area relative to the IACtHR. In doing so, the ECtHR has pursued a strategy of cautious incrementalism with close attention to evolving domestic social consensus, in keeping with its founding commitments to deferential authority. The IACtHR, in contrast, has rapidly expanded the scope of LGBT rights in Latin America, controversially leveraging its advisory jurisdiction to impose upon states new obligations that are not codified in the American Convention and are supported by scant international precedent.

The European Court of Human Rights

As discussed in chapter 3, several key judgments in the 1980s developed the ECtHR's case law on LGBT rights. The Court repeatedly found laws criminalizing homosexuality to violate the European Convention's Article 8 protections of private life.[3] However, the Court unequivocally denied extending the right to marry (protected by Article 12) to same-sex couples and declined to require states to allow transgender individuals to change their legal sex. With regard to both same-sex marriage and transgender identification, the majority of judges noted the lack of European consensus on these issues and emphasized that governments should retain primary authority to define the scope of LGBT rights. Judges did acknowledge rapidly evolving social norms in this area and signaled an openness to reconsidering the issue of transgender identification rights in the future. They did not indicate, however, that reinterpretation of Article 12 to extend to same-sex marriage was possible.[4]

The ECtHR's engagement with LGBT rights accelerated significantly in the 1990s. The first LGBT rights case of that decade, *Cossey v. the United Kingdom* (1990), was factually similar to the aforementioned *Rees v. the United Kingdom* case. The applicant, a transgender woman, wished to change the sex listed on her birth certificate and enter into a legal marriage with a man. Ms. Cossey invoked Article 8's protections of private life to argue for her right to change her birth certificate. She claimed that her inability to do so produced a further violation of Article 12 because UK law did not permit same-sex marriage. Additionally, Cossey alleged that the government was in violation of Article 14, the Convention provision that prohibits discrimination. The ECtHR declined to consider the Article 14 component of Cossey's complaint, further entrenching the view that transgender concerns were to be treated as aspects of private life and therefore not examined as potential violations of the rights to equality and nondiscrimination.[5] The majority upheld the *Rees* precedent and ruled that the government had not violated Articles 8 or 12.[6]

The final judgment, however, was more contentious in *Cossey* as compared to *Rees*. In *Rees*, only three out of fifteen judges had dissented to the majority's finding of no violation of Article 8, and the ruling of no violation of Article 12 was unanimous. In *Cossey*, however, eight out of eighteen judges voted that there had in fact been a violation of Article 8, and four out of eighteen judges voted that there had been a violation of Article 12. Among the dissenters, Judges MacDonald and Spielmann argued that finding no violation of Article 8 lacked attention to important social and legal changes that had advanced popular conceptualizations of transgender rights since the *Rees* judgment: "We consider that since 1986 there have been, in the law of many of the member States of the Council of Europe, not 'certain developments' but clear developments. We are therefore of the opinion that, although the principle of the States' 'wide margin of appreciation' was at a pinch acceptable in the Rees case, this is no longer true today."[7] This argument reveals stark differences of opinion among ECtHR judges regarding how to apply the margin of appreciation to defer to national authority, as well as divergent understandings of how legal protections for transgender people were progressing at the domestic level.

Judge Martens, in what is perhaps one of the most prolific dissenting opinions in the history of the ECtHR, launched a scathing critique of the *Rees* judgment in his dissent to *Cossey*: "A true reconsideration of the issues arising under Articles 8 and 12 should have led [the Court] to conclude that the Rees judgment was wrong—or at least that present day conditions warranted a different decision in the Cossey case."[8] Judge Martens then analyzed domestic legislative reforms both within and outside of the Council of Europe that had permitted transgender people to change the sex listed on their identification documents. This was followed by a lengthy castigation of ECtHR precedent, including sections titled "Why the Rees Case Should Have Been Decided Differently as Regards Article 8," a companion section regarding Article 12, and "Why the Court in the Cossey Case Should Have Overruled Its Decision in the Rees Case." It is rare for ECtHR judges to criticize their colleagues so acutely and extensively. Judge Martens concluded his dissent with the following appeal: "There is an ever-growing awareness of the essential importance of everyone's identity and of recognising the manifold differences between individuals that flow therefrom. With that goes a growing tolerance for, and even comprehension of, modes of human existence which differ from what is considered 'normal.' . . . These tendencies are certainly not new, but I have a feeling that they have come more into the open especially in recent years."[9] Marten's dissent reflected the frustration of those who felt that the ECtHR had lost touch with domestic realities and was moving too slowly in recognizing LGBT rights. His dissent also demonstrated confidence that, like society, the Court could change.

The ECtHR got a chance to revise its precedent on transgender identification in *B. v. France* (1992). Like Ms. Cossey, Ms. B. alleged that refusal to amend the sex listed on her identification documents amounted to a violation of Article 8.

The judges discussed whether the facts of B's case and/or predominant socio-legal norms sufficiently diverged from those present in *Brees* and *Cossey* to establish an Article 8 violation. The Court majority was convinced of the disproportionate severity of this incursion into B.'s private life "even having regard to the State's margin of appreciation," and, for the first time in the Court's history, established that refusal to allow transgender people to change their official sex identification violated Article 8.[10] The decision was not unanimous. Six out of twenty-one judges voted that there had been no violation. Still, the *B.* case marked a distinct shift in the ECtHR's disposition toward transgender rights.

A key challenge of the Council of Europe's expansion in the 1990s was instilling shared conceptualizations of European human standards across member states. This was a herculean task. Member states' varied cultural heritages encompassed diverse understandings of what "human rights" should look like and the responsibilities that governments held to implement those rights. This challenge was intensified in areas such as LGBT rights, where there was no prevailing consensus even among the Court's founding member states regarding the scope or necessity of such rights. In 1998, no CoE member state had yet legalized same-sex marriage, although seven states (Denmark, Norway, Sweden, Iceland, France, Belgium, and the Netherlands) had legalized some form of registered same-sex partnership or civil union. All seven of these states were Western European, founding members of the CoE. In the new crop of Eastern European member states, social attitudes regarding LGBT issues tended to be more conservative. The eastward expansion of the CoE coincided with major developments in LGBT rights debates worldwide in the late 1990s and early 2000s, setting the stage for contentious legal battles within the ECtHR.

The first major LGBT rights issue that the ECtHR confronted after the 1998 Protocol 11 reforms was discharging military members on the basis of sexuality. In September 1999, the ECtHR issued judgments on two cases, *Smith and Grady v. the United Kingdom* and *Lustig-Prean and Beckett v. the United Kingdom*, in which members of the Royal Air Force and Royal Navy had been discharged after commanding officers discovered their homosexuality. At that time, military law banned British service members from participating in homosexual acts.[11] All four applicants in *Smith and Grady* and *Lustig-Prean and Beckett* had been subjected to invasive interviews by their command prior to ultimately being discharged. These interviews involved questions on deeply private topics, including the applicants' sexual histories and the personal information of other homosexual people known to the applicants.[12] In both cases, the government submitted that discharging gay and lesbian service members was justified to protect the "nation's security," arguing that "admitting homosexuals to the armed forces at this time would have a significant and negative effect on the morale of armed forces' personnel and, in turn, on the fighting power and the operational effectiveness of the armed forces."[13]

ECtHR judges were unconvinced. While the Court acknowledged that governments are afforded a particularly wide margin of appreciation with regard to military affairs, it found the government's argument lacking in evidence. In both cases, the Court unanimously ruled that the military's investigations into the applicants' sexual histories constituted excessive interference in their privacy in violation of Article 8, and ruled 6–1 that the applicants' subsequent discharge violated Article 8.[14] The Court unanimously declined, however, to rule on whether the applicants had experienced discrimination in violation of Article 14.[15] This was consistent with ECtHR jurisprudence at the time, which tended to relegate concerns regarding the treatment of LGBT people to the category of "private life" rather than abject discrimination.

However, it was not long before the tendency to sideline discrimination concerns would deteriorate. In December 1999, the Court unanimously ruled in *Salgueiro da Silva Mouta v. Portugal* that refusing to grant custody to a divorced parent on the grounds that the parent was living with a same-sex partner violated Article 14's protection against discrimination.[16] This case established a precedent that, although the Convention drafters did not include sexual orientation as a protected category under Article 14, times had changed. The ECtHR now recognized states' distinct obligation to prevent discrimination on the basis of sexual orientation.

The Netherlands became the first country in the world to legalize same-sex marriage on April 1, 2001. The ECtHR next had the opportunity to weigh in on the development of LGBT rights in *I. v. the United Kingdom* and *Christine Goodwin v. the United Kingdom*, two cases finalized on the same day in July 2002. Both cases involved transgender women who reported suffering interference in their private and professional lives due to not being permitted to change their legal sex.[17] Both women also argued that their inability to change their legal sex violated their right to marry under Article 12, as UK law still banned same-sex marriage. Recall that, in the aforementioned *Rees* (1986) and *Cossey* (1990) judgments, the ECtHR upheld states' authority to deny transgender individuals the ability to marry partners of the same sex-at-birth. In both *I.* and *Goodwin*, the Court upheld its *B. v. France* (1992) precedent and found a violation of Article 8 for not allowing the applicants to change their legal sex.[18] When it came to transgender marriage rights, the Court was willing to revise its past reasoning. In both judgments, the Court highlighted changing social and medical understandings of transgenderism: "There have been major social changes in the institution of marriage since the adoption of the Convention as well as dramatic changes brought about by developments in medicine and science in the field of transsexuality. . . .

The Court would also note that Article 9 of the recently adopted Charter of Fundamental Rights of the European Union departs, no doubt deliberately, from the wording of Article 12 of the Convention in removing the reference to men and women."[19] Of particular note here is the judges' attention to gender-neutral language in recently adopted European Union marriage rights protections. In both *I.* and *Goodwin*, the ECtHR Grand Chamber unanimously found a violation of the right to marry under Article 12.[20]

These judgments marked monumental advancements in transgender rights in the CoE. The judges resoundingly endorsed interpreting the Convention as a "living instrument" and correspondingly expanded the scope of Article 12, even in the face of government opposition. However, despite the fact that the applicants in these cases had attested to experiencing discriminatory treatment as a result of their gender identity and alleged violations of Article 14, the ECtHR decided that these allegations "raised no separate issues" and once again declined to consider the cases from a discrimination perspective.[21]

As European states continued to be on the global forefront of the fight for marriage equality throughout the early 2000s, LGBT citizens turned to the ECtHR seeking rulings that would bolster domestic progress. Central to these disputes was the question of whether denying homosexual couples the same rights as heterosexual couples could be considered legitimate for protecting "family life" under Article 8. A key example is *Karner v. Austria* (2003), which the ECtHR ruled on one month after Belgium became the second country in the world to legalize same-sex marriage. The applicant in *Karner*, a gay man, challenged an Austrian Supreme Court ruling that denied his ability to retain the tenancy of his male life partner following the partner's death. In defense of that ruling, the government argued before the ECtHR that excluding homosexual couples from tenancy rights protections was necessary for the "protection of the traditional family unit." The government submitted that this differential treatment thus fulfilled a legitimate aim under Article 8's protection of "family life."[22]

The ECtHR had maintained a heteronormative definition of "the family" in previous cases involving LGBT applicants. In *Karner*, however, judges reconsidered the scope of Article 8 in the new millennium. Referencing recent precedent establishing sexual orientation as a protected category under Article 14, the majority underscored that unequal treatment must be proportionate to legitimate aims:

> In cases in which the margin of appreciation afforded to States is narrow, as is the position where there is a difference in treatment based on sex or sexual orientation, the principle of proportionality does not merely require that the measure chosen is in principle suited for realising the aim sought. It must also be shown that it was necessary in

order to achieve that aim to exclude certain categories of people—in this instance persons living in a homosexual relationship.... The Court cannot see that the Government have advanced any arguments that would allow such a conclusion.[23]

Here, we see clear evidence that the margin of appreciation had narrowed for unequal treatment of homosexual couples to the point where discrimination on the basis of sexual orientation was considered equally unacceptable as discrimination on the basis of sex itself. This statement signaled a shift in the ECtHR's approach to deferring to governments in the area of LGBT rights. By a vote of 6–1, the ECtHR found Austria in violation of Articles 14 and 8 in *Karner*.

The ECtHR continued to build up its authority to demand equal treatment for homosexual couples in the 2000s. The Court again found governments in violation of Article 14 for discriminating against homosexual couples in cases involving adoption (*E. B. v. France*, 2008)[24] and surviving tenant rights (*Kozak v. Poland*, 2010).[25] In the meantime, Spain became the third country in the world to legalize same-sex marriage in 2005, followed by Sweden in 2009 and Portugal and Iceland in 2010. Additionally, twelve CoE member states legalized some form of registered partnership or civil union for same-sex couples between 2000 and 2010.[26]

Amid this shifting legal landscape in the 2000s, the margin of appreciation undoubtedly narrowed with regard to certain types of anti-LGBT discrimination covered by Articles 8 and 14. However, the ECtHR repeatedly refused to intervene in domestic decisions about extending the full rights of marriage to same-sex couples. Recall that the aforementioned *I.* and *Christine Goodwin* judgments in 2002 had expanded marriage rights for couples in which one partner had transitioned into the opposite sex of the other partner. However, these judgments ultimately entrenched an interpretation of Article 12 that would deny marriage rights to same-sex couples.

For example, in November 2006, the ECtHR ruled on two cases involving transgender applicants who had transitioned into the *same* gender as their spouse. In both cases, *Parry v. the United Kingdom* and *R. and F. v. the United Kingdom*, the applicants wished to change the sex listed on their official identification documentation to reflect their post-transition identity. Doing so, however, would invalidate the legality of their existing marriages, as the UK did not permit same-sex marriage. The ECtHR unanimously declared both cases to be inadmissible on the grounds that the applicants' complaints were "manifestly ill-founded." In defense of this decision, the judges addressed evolving domestic conceptualizations of marriage:

> While it is true that there are a number of Contracting States which have extended marriage to same-sex partners, this reflects their own vision of

the role of marriage in their societies and does not, perhaps regrettably to many, flow from an interpretation of the fundamental right as laid down by the Contracting States in the Convention in 1950. The Court cannot but conclude therefore that the matter falls within the appreciation of the Contracting State as how to regulate the effects of the change of gender in the context of marriage.[27]

In this passage, the judges appear to throw out the idea of the Convention as a "living instrument" that had been emphasized in previous LGBT rights cases. Rather, the judges explicitly directed attention to the Convention drafters' intentions in 1950. These judgments demonstrate how the deferential interpretation of the ECtHR's authority espoused by its founders has continued to motivate judges' reasoning in the twenty-first century, even amid domestic changes in conceptualizing human rights.[28]

The ECtHR had another opportunity to address same-sex marriage rights in *Schalk and Kopf v. Austria* in 2010. The applicants, a gay couple, alleged that Austria's nonrecognition of same-sex marriage violated their rights to private and family life (Article 8), the right to marry (Article 12), and furthermore constituted discrimination (Article 14). Referencing the precedent set in *Christine Goodwin* and reinforced in *Parry* and *R. and F.*, the Court unanimously declared that Austria had not violated Article 12 by refusing to recognize same-sex marriages. This decision was rooted in prioritizing deference to governments: "The Court reiterates that it must not rush to substitute its own judgment in place of that of the national authorities, who are best placed to assess and respond to the needs of society."[29]

LGBT rights cases at the ECtHR in the 1980s through the 2000s tended to focus on issues of privacy and family life. However, the ECtHR began to face cases involving more public facets of anti-LGBT discrimination in the 2010s, including alleged violations of freedom of expression and assembly rights. For example, in *Identoba and Others v. Georgia* (2015), the ECtHR was tasked with determining whether Georgian authorities had made sufficient efforts to prevent and investigate homophobic violence against LGBT protesters. The applicants were a group of LGBT activists who had been injured when counterprotesters attacked them during a peaceful demonstration in 2012. The activists had obtained prior municipal approval to hold their demonstration and were assured that police would be present to provide security. The ECtHR majority found that state authorities failed to fulfill their "positive obligation to provide the peaceful demonstrators with heightened protection from attacks by private individuals."[30] Furthermore, by failing to approach investigation into the protesters' injuries with specific attention to the potential for homophobic motivations, Georgian authorities had failed to fulfill their procedural obligations under Article 3 (the prohibition of inhuman and degrading treatment).[31] This case set an important precedent clarifying that states have positive obligations to both prevent homophobic violence and specifically investigate the role of sexual orientation discrimination in attacks aimed at LGBT individuals.

The majority of LGBT rights cases at the ECtHR in the 2010s were provoked by the Russian government's increasingly antagonistic attitude toward homosexuality. For example, Nicolay Alekseyev, a Russian gay rights activist, petitioned the ECtHR after Moscow authorities forcibly repressed demonstrations his organization held in support of the LGBT community. ECtHR judges unanimously ruled that Russia had violated Articles 11 and 14 in this case.[32]

The Parliamentary Assembly of the CoE suspended Russia's voting rights in 2014 following the invasion of Crimea, after which Russia threatened to withdraw from the CoE entirely.[33] Russia stopped paying its yearly dues to the CoE in 2017 in protest and repeated its threats of withdrawal (including, at one point, asserting that it would not consider ECtHR judgments to be legally binding).[34] Russia only agreed to resume payments and return to the Parliamentary Assembly in 2019 after President Vladimir Putin essentially coerced Assembly members into revising the body's Rules of Procedure to limit the conditions under which the CoE can impose sanctions on member states. The Assembly granted these concessions despite no efforts by Russia to improve conditions in Crimea, a move that cast doubt on the CoE's ability to rein in rogue member states.[35]

In June 2013, Putin had signed into law a controversial federal mandate commonly known as the "gay propaganda law." The law criminalized publishing information about "nontraditional sexual relations." The ECtHR confronted Russia's anti-LGBT legislation in the case of *Bayev and Others v. Russia*, which the Court ruled on in June 2017. The applicants were three gay rights activists, including the aforementioned Mr. Alekseyev. The men claimed to be victims of several regional antigay propaganda laws that had been implemented between 2006 and 2011, prior to the federal law in 2013. While this case did not directly invoke the 2013 law, ECtHR judges took this opportunity to evaluate the general compatibility of laws that criminalize public displays of homosexuality with the Convention. The ECtHR found Russia in violation of Articles 10 (freedom of expression) and 14 (prohibition of discrimination) in a 6–1 vote.[36] The timing of the *Bayev* judgment was critical. The case was the first major LGBT rights challenge at the ECtHR after Russia stopped paying its CoE dues and renewed its threats to withdraw from the Council of Europe.

At least with regard to Russia, the expectation that ECtHR judges are likely to be responsive to governments who accuse the Court of judicial overreach does not hold. The Court continued to condemn Russian anti-LGBT discrimination

even as the state was withholding substantial funds from the CoE and threatening to leave the institution entirely.[37] However, Russia had long been a thorn in
the CoE's side, even prior to the government's clashes with the ECtHR in the
late 2010s. The ECtHR's refusal to soften its approach with a member state that
repeatedly deviates from regional normative consensus might actually support
the argument that the ECtHR's founding social purpose leads the Court to be
uniquely responsive to domestic authorities. The prioritization of consensus
is a pillar of the founders' deferential interpretation of the ECtHR's authority.
Over the past thirty years, ECtHR judges have carefully calibrated their decisions
expanding LGBT rights protections with attention to socio-legal developments
across the CoE. While such rights protections were progressing in the majority
of member states, they were rapidly backsliding in Russia. Consequently, when
given the opportunity, ECtHR judges cracked down on Russian deviance.

By the summer of 2021, 63 percent of CoE member states recognized some
form of same-sex partnership, ranging from registered partnerships and civil
unions to full marriage rights.[38] In a landmark July 2021 decision, *Fedotova and
Others v. Russia*, the ECtHR unanimously ruled that Russia's lack of any form
of legal recognition for same-sex couples constituted a violation of Article 8's
protections of private and family life. The judges declared that the situation of
same-sex couples in Russia created "a conflict between the social reality of the
applicants who live in committed relationships based on mutual affection, and
the law, which fails to protect the most regular of 'needs' arising in the context of
a same-sex couple."[39] Even just ten years earlier, it would have been unthinkable
for the Court to rule that states had positive obligations to legally recognize same-
sex unions. Still, the *Fedotova* ruling is not necessarily surprising, as it aligns with
the Court's historical attention to social consensus when applying the margin of
appreciation.

Nevertheless, the ECtHR has remained steadfast in deferring to governments
to adjudicate the full rights of marriage. Although the applicants in *Fedotova*
alleged discriminatory treatment, the ECtHR found that, having established
an Article 8 violation, it was "not necessary to examine whether . . . there had
also been a violation of Article 14."[40] Despite greater recognition of discrimination concerns within the ECtHR's case law on LGBT rights in recent years, the
Fedotova ruling demonstrates that the Court still conceptualizes homosexual
identities and experiences as predominantly confined to private life. In repeatedly declaring that finding violations of the right to private life is sufficient
for upholding the Convention in cases involving discriminatory treatment
of gay and lesbian individuals, the ECtHR reinforces a public/private binary
that denies homosexual couples equal legal recognition of their committed
relationships.

In *Fedotova*, ECtHR judges made it clear that it is *regional* social consensus, not domestic consensus, that carries the most weight when allocating deference to governments. The judges acknowledged the government's assertion that the majority of Russians disapprove of same-sex unions but declared that assertion irrelevant to the case: "It is true that popular sentiment may play a role in the Court's assessment when it comes to the justification on the grounds of social morals. However . . . it would be incompatible with the underlying values of the Convention, as an instrument of the European public order, if the exercise of Convention rights by a minority group were made conditional on its being accepted by the majority."[41]

Critics of the margin of appreciation doctrine have argued that relying on social consensus to adjudicate appropriate state practice defies the ECtHR's mission to uphold the rights of minorities who may be neglected under majority rule in democratic regimes (let alone under authoritarians like Putin).[42] In *Fedotova*, the judges offered a rebuke to that critique by definitively stating that domestic social consensus does not justify widening the margin of appreciation. In doing so, the judges reaffirmed the founding mission of the ECtHR as an agent for European integration. The Convention's purpose was to guide CoE member states toward shared democratic principles, thereby engineering a cohesive European identity that would ensure the success of the integration project. Russia, in not keeping up with the times, had become an obstacle to the ever-evolving integration process. Hence, at least with respect to LGBT rights, the ECtHR abandoned deference and condemned the domestic status quo. This approach demonstrates an important caveat to the theoretical expectation that the ECtHR is likely to constrict its interpretation of its authority in response to member state backlash. When the objecting state deviates from regional norms, the ECtHR will intervene to try to push that state toward behavior that aligns with the regional consensus. This strategy may have also resulted from a sense that Russia's days as a CoE member were numbered and thus that ECtHR judges had little to lose by repeatedly condemning Putin's regime.

Over the past three decades, the ECtHR has expanded the scope of LGBT rights under the Convention by gradually building up supportive precedent.[43] Of notable exception is the ECtHR's swift dismantling of established precedent that had blocked transgender individuals from marrying partners of the same sex-at-birth. This sudden reversal of course is rare in the ECtHR, reflective of a schism between judges who view the Convention as a "living instrument" and others who prioritize attention to the Convention drafters' intentions in 1950. The latter approach still dominates within same-sex marriage jurisprudence, as the Court has consistently deferred to national authorities in this area. Still, judges have demonstrated acute sensitivity to changing domestic legislation and social attitudes. The margin of appreciation in this area has narrowed significantly in recent years, as the Court has developed stringent obligations for governments to prevent discriminatory treatment of LGBT individuals.

There is no evidence that the ECtHR shirked contentious LGBT rights cases as a result of increasing caseloads or institutional reforms. Some of the Court's most pivotal judgments against governments (for example, condemning the UK for discharging gays and lesbians from the military) occurred in the late 1990s as CoE membership was quickly expanding and Protocol 11 reformed the case-processing system. There is also no indication that state backlash to Court judgments has had any substantive impact on the Court's decision-making in this area.

However, the ECtHR is only willing to go so far. It is critical to note that the ECtHR did not order states to provide remedies beyond financial reparations in *any* of the cases discussed above. Even in *Fedotova*, where the ECtHR declared that Russia's denial of legal recognition for same-sex couples violated Article 8, the Court did not order Russia to implement any sort of legislative changes. In fact, the ECtHR even declined the applicants' requests for financial reparations in that case, deciding instead that the ruling itself constituted a sufficient remedy.[44] While the ECtHR has encouraged changes in domestic LGBT rights policy, the Court has firmly declined mandating specific remedies to achieve those changes.[45]

The Inter-American Court of Human Rights

The ECtHR has several decades of experience adjudicating disputes involving LGBT rights claims. For the IACtHR, this area of case law is still relatively new terrain. Nevertheless, in the decade since the IACtHR ruled on its first gay rights case, the Court has developed innovative precedent strengthening LGBT rights in Latin America. The Court has done so by widely interpreting the scope of its authority, particularly through the use of its advisory jurisdiction. Legal protections for LGBT people vary widely by region within Latin America. While Mexico and much of South America have seen significant advancements in LGBT rights over the past decade, legal protections for LGBT people in most of Central America and the Caribbean are severely lacking. As of 2025, homosexuality is still illegal in five states across Latin America and the Caribbean.[46] None of those states are subject to the jurisdiction of the IACtHR. In 2010, Argentina became the first state in Latin America (and only the tenth country in the world) to legalize same-sex marriage on the federal level. Argentina was quickly followed by Mexico later that year. Since then, Brazil, Chile, Colombia, Costa Rica, Cuba, Ecuador, and Uruguay have also legalized same-sex marriage.

The IACtHR did not confront its first case involving LGBT rights until 2012, in *Atala Riffo and Daughters v. Chile*. The applicant, a divorced lesbian mother, had lost custody of her three daughters after moving in with her female partner. The primary argument the girls' father advanced in the domestic custody lawsuit was that the "sexual choice made by the mother would disrupt the healthy, fair, and normal coexistence to which [the daughters] have a right." Additionally, the father claimed that, by living with a lesbian couple, the girls would be "under constant risk of contracting sexually transmitted diseases such as herpes and AIDS."[47] The family's custody battle made it all the way to the Chilean Supreme Court. The Supreme Court ultimately ruled that permanent custody was to be granted to the girls' father. In that decision, the Supreme Court asserted that the girls were in a "situation of risk" because "their unique family environment differs significantly from that of their school companions . . . exposing them to ostracism and discrimination, which would also affect their personal development."[48] Facing the loss of her daughters, Ms. Atala turned to the IACtHR.

In contrast to the ECtHR's hesitation to evaluate discrimination concerns in LGBT rights cases, the IACtHR foregrounded the rights to equality and nondiscrimination in its first-ever case dealing with homosexuality. The IACtHR judges first considered Article 1(1) of the Convention, which prohibits "discrimination for reasons of race, color, sex, language, religion, political or other opinion, national or social origin, economic status, birth, or any other social condition." Like the European Convention, the American Convention does not list sexual orientation as a protected category. Referencing the aforementioned *Salgueiro da Silva v. Portugal* case (as well as developments in the UNCESCR and UN General Assembly), the IACtHR declared sexual orientation to constitute a protected category under Article 1(1).[49]

With regard to the rights to privacy and family life (protected under Articles 11 and 17 of the American Convention, respectively), the IACtHR again invoked ECtHR precedent to clarify that these guarantees encompass an individual's "right to establish and develop relationships with other people and their social environment, including the right to establish and maintain relationships with people of the same sex."[50] Furthermore, building on the ECtHR's discussion in *Karner v. Austria* of what constitutes a "traditional family," the IACtHR declared that "the language used by the Supreme Court of Chile regarding the girls' alleged need to grow up in a 'normally structured family' . . . reflects a limited, stereotyped perception of the concept of the family, which has no basis in the Convention, since there is no specific model of family."[51]

The IACtHR unanimously ruled that Chile had violated Articles 1(1) (the prohibition of discrimination), 8 (the right to a fair trial), 11 (the right to privacy), 19 (the rights of the child), and 24 (equality before the law). Reliance on ECtHR precedent was crucial for arriving at this outcome. In addition to financial compensation for Atala and her daughters, the IACtHR ordered Chile to provide them with free medical and psychological care, publish an acknowledgment of its responsibility for the rights violations, and implement a nationwide training program for public officials aimed at "overcoming gender stereotypes of LGBTI persons and homophobia."[52] These measures sought not only to push the state to rectify Atala's individual situation but also to implement structural reforms that would prevent future sexual orientation discrimination.

While only a few cases involving LGBT rights disputes reached the IACtHR in the 2010s, the Court continued to build precedent supporting antidiscrimination protections in surviving partner benefits/pension law[53] and military law. Particularly with regard to military regulations banning homosexual service members, the IACtHR has leaned heavily on ECtHR precedent. *Flor Freire v. Ecuador* (2016) concerned an Ecuadorian army officer who had been discharged after his colleagues accused him of participating in homosexual acts.[54] Mr. Flor Freire denied that he identified as homosexual. Still, as he was discharged from the army on the basis of perceived homosexual orientation, the IACtHR was tasked with evaluating the compatibility of Ecuadorian military regulations with the Convention.

The IACtHR unanimously ruled that Ecuador had violated the prohibition of discrimination (Articles 1(1) and 24) as well as the right to honor and dignity (Article 11) with respect to Flor Freire. The Court cited ECtHR precedent in the aforementioned *Lustig-Prean* and *Smith and Grady* cases, as well as recent legal developments in Argentina, Chile, Colombia, Brazil, and Peru that had amended policies discriminating against homosexual service members. However, the IACtHR's ruling contrasts with the ECtHR's approach in *Lustig-Prean* and *Smith and Grady* in that, while the ECtHR declined to consider the service members' discrimination allegations, the IACtHR centered discrimination as a concern in *Flor Freire*.[55] By the time of the IACtHR judgment, Ecuador had already undertaken reforms to remove the rule under which Flor Freire had been discharged. Even so, the IACtHR mandated that Ecuador provide Flor Freire with financial compensation, restore him to his military position, strike the discharge from his military record, and implement training programs for members of the armed forces aimed at eliminating sexual orientation discrimination within the ranks.[56]

In January 2018, the IACtHR issued a landmark advisory opinion that dramatically accelerated the development of LGBT rights in Latin America. The government of Costa Rica had submitted the request for the advisory opinion, which was titled "State Obligations Concerning Change of Name, Gender Identity, and Rights Derived from a Relationship Between Same-Sex Couples" (hereafter referred to as "OC-24/17"). Costa Rica asked the IACtHR to answer five central questions in this advisory opinion:

1. Are states obligated to recognize and facilitate the name change of an individual in accordance with his or her gender identity?
2. If so, are states required to provide administrative procedures to facilitate name changes (as opposed to judicial procedures)?
3. Are states required to provide administrative name change procedures that are free, prompt, and accessible?
4. Are states obligated to recognize patrimonial rights derived from a relationship between persons of the same sex?
5. Must states provide a legal institution that regulates relationships between persons of the same sex in order to recognize all the patrimonial rights that derive from that relationship?[57]

These are wide-ranging questions that invited the Court to develop declarative stances on critical LGBT rights concerns. The IACtHR answered these questions in a sweeping discussion that referenced domestic socio-legal developments, ECtHR precedent, statements submitted by nearly one hundred academic experts, civil society leaders, and nongovernmental organizations, as well as reports by international organizations ranging from the United Nations Committee Against Torture to the World Health Organization.

The IACtHR unanimously concluded that individuals' ability to change their name and relevant identity documents to conform to their "self-perceived gender identity" constituted a right protected by Articles 1(1), 3, 7(1), 11(2), 18, and 24 of the American Convention. Consequently, all state parties to the American Convention must provide individuals wishing to change the annotation of their gender, sex, name, or photograph on their identification documents with a free, accessible, prompt, and confidential procedure for doing so. While this procedure is not required to be administrative, the judges noted that administrative procedures are preferable to judicial procedures. States must not require individuals to provide evidence of surgery and/or hormonal therapy in order to amend identification documents. Furthermore, the Court unanimously concluded that all protections of private and family life under Articles 11 and 17 were to be afforded to same-sex couples. In a 6–1 vote, the Court ruled that "States must ensure full access to all the mechanisms that exist in their domestic law, *including the right to marriage*, to ensure the protection of the rights of families formed by same-sex couples, without discrimination in relation to those that are formed by heterosexual couples" (my italics).[58]

In defense of these groundbreaking conclusions, the IACtHR judges emphasized that expanding the scope of the Convention's human rights protections honored both the nature of the Convention as a "living instrument" and the Convention drafters' founding intentions:

> Those who drafted and adopted the American Convention did not presume to know the absolute scope of the fundamental rights and freedoms recognized therein. Accordingly, the Convention confers on the States and the Court the task of identifying and protecting the scope in accordance with the passage of time. Thus, the Court considers that it is not diverging from the initial intention of the States that signed the Convention; to the contrary, by recognizing this [same-sex] family relationship, the Court is adhering to the original intention.[59]

Not every judge agreed that OC-24/17's conclusions regarding same-sex marriage aligned with the IACtHR's founding social purpose. Judge Vio Grossi was the sole opponent to the vote in favor of requiring state parties to legalize same-sex marriage. He attached a partially dissenting opinion to OC-24/17 that argued that the IACtHR had stretched its authority too far by interfering in domestic marriage policy.

Vio Grossi articulated two main concerns regarding the IACtHR's order to legalize same-sex marriage: first, that the Court was attempting to regulate an area which, by wide international legal consensus, fell within the "internal, domestic or exclusive jurisdiction of the State," and second, that the Court was attempting to do so through an advisory opinion, when the Court had very little binding jurisprudence related to same-sex relationships.[60] In a particularly acute critique, Vio Grossi asserted that OC-24/17 defied Article 31 of the Vienna Convention on the Law of Treaties by according "no importance to the fact that the States Parties agreed to sign the Convention in good faith" and failing to consider the "context" of the terms of the Convention.[61] Consequently, the interpretation of the Convention advanced in the OC-24/17 "runs the risk of affecting the principle of legal certainty."[62] Judge Vio Grossi supported OC-24/17's order to extend civil rights to same-sex couples through other forms of legal partnerships, but he objected that "it cannot be considered, in light of contemporary international law, that it would be discriminatory if the domestic laws of the States of the Americas did not allow marriage between persons of the same sex."[63] Advisory opinions are not technically legally binding. But these opinions have a "preventative nature" in that they signal appropriate application of the Convention.[64] If a state does not comply with the terms of an advisory opinion, that state is vulnerable to receiving an adverse, binding judgment if an applicant brings a contentious case to the Court based on that noncompliance. In Vio Grossi's view, exposing states to those risks and obligations through an advisory opinion supported by scant jurisprudential precedent was a step too far. At least one prominent international legal scholar has accused the IACtHR of "misuse" of its advisory jurisdiction to expand LGBT rights protections at the risk of undermining the Court's legitimacy and provoking government backlash.[65]

OC-24/17 reflected a boldly interventionist interpretation of the IACtHR's authority. The Court risked government ire by issuing an advisory opinion that imposed intensive new obligations on states with little international legal precedent. Some backlash did materialize. The governments of Argentina, Brazil, Chile, Colombia, and Paraguay issued a statement accusing the IACtHR of judicial overreach and calling for the Court to recognize a "margin of appreciation." However, this statement appears to have had negligible impact, as domestic political crises quickly overshadowed those states' standoff with the IACtHR.[66] The domestic policy consequences of OC-24/17 are still evolving, but the record so far is mixed. Three member states that did not previously recognize same-sex marriages (Chile, Costa Rica, and Ecuador) have federally legalized such marriages since OC-24/17 was issued. Additionally, four states (Mexico, Costa Rica, Brazil, and Chile) have implemented nationwide legislation allowing transgender individuals to change their legal name and gender identity (without providing proof of surgery) in direct response to OC-24/17.[67] For now, however, the states that have historically most intensely resisted recognizing LGBT rights have not demonstrated significant legal advancements post-OC-24/17.

The IACtHR bolstered protections for LGBT parental rights in *Ramírez Escobar et al. v. Guatemala*, decided three months after OC-24/17. The applicants in this case were Maria Ramírez Escobar and Gustavo Tobar Fajardo, parents whose two sons had been abducted by the government and later adopted out to separate families in the context of massive irregularities in Guatemalan international adoptions. Between 1990 and 2007, Guatemalan state agents, doctors, social workers, and international adoption agencies participated in now widely documented fraudulent adoptions for financial gain. These schemes typically targeted poor, single mothers such as Ms. Escobar. Through various tactics, including false claims of neglect or abandonment, physical threats, tricking parents into transferring sick children to complicit hospitals, and kidnapping, Guatemalan authorities systematically acquired children to sell through international adoption agencies. Most of these children were likely adopted by families in the United States.[68]

Escobar and Fajardo had a son together when they were teenagers. They later ended their romantic relationship but remained in contact. Ms. Escobar then had another son. Both children lived with her. Mr. Fajardo visited periodically and provided financial support. In 1997, state agents forcibly took both boys. The authorities reported that they had received a complaint that Escobar neglected the children. Despite a lengthy legal battle in which Escobar and Fajardo repeatedly attempted to regain custody, the boys were declared "abandoned" and adopted out to families in Illinois and Pennsylvania.[69] As part of the effort to get the boys back, Escobar's mother (the children's grandmother) had attempted to gain custody. The courts rejected this request, asserting that the grandmother's lesbian lifestyle would compromise the "values" that would be passed on to her grandsons.[70]

Citing the *Atala* judgment and OC-24/17's definition of the "family," the IACtHR unanimously found Guatemala in violation of the rights to privacy (Article 11), family life (Article 17), and the prohibition on discrimination (Article 1(1)).[71] The Court ordered Guatemala to provide a wide range of remedies, including free medical and psychological care for the parents, children, and grandmother, family reunification efforts, prosecution of those responsible for the boys' abduction and subsequent legal malpractice, public acknowledgment of international responsibility for the systematic abduction of children, and reforms of the national adoption system. This case reinforced the IACtHR's legal conceptualization of "the family" in custody rights disputes to include extended family, regardless of sexual orientation.

The IACtHR has historically held states to stringent standards for preventing and investigating violence against marginalized populations. States have positive "due diligence" obligations to recognize patterns of violence, state-sponsored or otherwise, devote resources to interrupting those violence patterns, and investigate violent acts with attention to potential bias motivations.[72] In *Azul Rojas Marín v. Peru* (2020), the IACtHR applied these principles for the first time in a case of explicitly homophobic violence. The victim, who at the time identified as a gay man, was arbitrarily detained by police and subjected to physical and mental violence, including homophobic threats, beatings, and rape.[73] Police subsequently conducted an investigation into these events, but the investigation was marred by negligence, police harassment, and a further alleged assault of the victim by a forensic investigator.[74] In a ruling that cited the aforementioned *Identoba and Others v. Georgia* case,[75] the IACtHR unanimously ruled that Peru had violated the Convention's prohibition of discrimination (Article 1), the prohibition of torture (Article 5), and the rights to personal liberty (Article 7), fair trial (Article 8), and judicial protection (Article 25). In addition to financial reparations and free medical and psychological care for the victim, the IACtHR ordered Peru to develop new protocols on "investigation and administration of justice in criminal proceedings involving LGBTI victims of violence" and create a national database system to track violence against LGBTI people.[76] The *Azul Rojas Marín* judgment laid the foundation for the groundbreaking case of Vicky Hernández highlighted in the opening of this chapter.

In February 2022, the IACtHR delivered another unprecedented ruling expanding antidiscrimination protections for sexual orientation minorities in Latin America. The complainant in the case was Sandra Cecilia Pavez Pavez, a Catholic religion teacher who had been removed from her teaching position at a public high school in Chile after her "certificate of suitability" was revoked by the local Catholic diocese following the revelation that she was a lesbian. The IACtHR ruled that, in legislatively empowering the Catholic Church to dictate the removal of public employees on the basis of sexual orientation, Chile had illegally discriminated against Ms. Pavez in contravention of the American Convention. Specifically, the Court found that by removing Pavez from her position as well as exposing her to an invasive investigation of her intimate relationships by Catholic authorities, Chile had violated Articles 1(1) and 24 regarding the rights to equality and nondiscrimination and Article 11(2) regarding the right to privacy. The IACtHR mandated that Chile pay Pavez financial reparations, implement antidiscrimination training for officials evaluating teachers, and reform domestic appeal procedures for religious education teachers facing the removal of their certificates of suitability.[77] Commenting on the outcome of the case, Pavez declared, "I am very happy because from now on, with this sentence, in no country in America will teachers, and in particular religion teachers, be able to be discriminated against because of their sexual orientation or gender identity. . . . This is a historic moment not for me, but for all discriminated people."[78]

As with the ECtHR, there is no evidence that the IACtHR's interpretation of its authority in LGBT rights disputes has been tempered by practical exigencies related to rising caseloads or member state backlash. The 2012 *Atala* judgment came during a time when the Court was facing an unprecedented level of case submissions as well as major political fallout from Venezuela's withdrawal. Advisory Opinion OC-24/17, which represents the most expansive interpretation of LGBT human rights protections by any international court to date, was issued in a year when the IACtHR ruled on a record number of cases. In 2021, the Honduran legislature approved a constitutional amendment aimed at impeding any future efforts to overturn the state's constitutional ban on same-sex marriage.[79] But just a few months afterward, the IACtHR still condemned Honduras in the Vicky Hernández case and mandated intensive policy reforms. This persistence even in the face of government resistance is emblematic of the IACtHR's interventionist interpretation of its authority. This interpretation was forged in the Court's founding years and has only intensified. As a result, the IACtHR has developed the most comprehensive framework for LGBT rights protections in modern international law.

The African Court on Human and Peoples' Rights

LGBT rights in Africa remain severely restricted. Of the African Union's fifty-five member states, thirty still criminalize homosexual acts. In four of those states (Mauritania, Nigeria, Somalia, and Uganda), homosexuality is punishable by death in certain circumstances. In May 2023, Ugandan President Yoweri Museveni's administration passed legislation criminalizing homosexuality and imposing some of the world's most draconian penalties for same-sex relations. This development is a troubling indicator of the trajectory for LGBT rights in the African Union. Of the eight states that currently allow citizens to directly petition the ACtHPR, half (the Gambia, Ghana, Malawi, and Tunisia) still criminalize homosexuality. South Africa is the only state in the African Union that has legalized same-sex marriages performed domestically. Namibia's Supreme Court ruled in May 2023 to recognize same-sex marriages performed in foreign countries between Namibian citizens and foreign nationals, making Namibia the only African country other than South Africa to recognize any form of legal same-sex union.

The ACtHPR has not had the opportunity to rule on any cases involving claims of anti-LGBT discrimination. Thus, unlike the above discussions of the ECtHR and IACtHR's case laws, the following section will not discuss jurisprudential developments. Rather, it will review the unique challenges that face LGBT Africans seeking international legal recourse. These challenges primarily stem from three sources: the language of the African Charter, the role of the African Commission in gatekeeping cases from the ACtHPR, and Africans' limited access to the individual petition mechanism. Then, drawing from the ECtHR and IACtHR's experiences, I will discuss how the ACtHPR might yet become an influential force in developing LGBT rights in the region.

One potential barrier to advancing LGBT rights within the ACtHPR is the wording of the African Charter. First, there is no explicit right to privacy in the African Charter as there is in the European and American Conventions. Appeals to the right to privacy have been crucial for developing jurisprudence in support of LGBT rights protections in the ECtHR and IACtHR. This has particularly been the case in the ECtHR. It took several decades for the ECtHR to start to recognize states' unique human rights obligations to transgender and homosexual people. When this eventually happened, the ECtHR almost exclusively relegated those rights to the realm of "private life." It was not until the 2010s that the ECtHR began to take up anti-LGBT discrimination as an issue of public life, primarily in the context of the freedoms of expression and assembly. Based on the ECtHR's example, filing complaints under the right to private life might be a promising avenue for transgender and homosexual Africans while ACtHPR judges have not yet clarified their stances on LGBT rights. Although the African Charter does not protect privacy, appeals to the right to private life may still be possible within the ACtHPR because of the Court's uniquely expansive jurisdiction. Recall that ACtHPR judges can rule not only on violations of the African Charter but also on violations of *any other human rights instrument* that the state in question has ratified. A citizen of any state that has ratified both the African Charter and the International Covenant on Civil and Political Rights (ICCPR) could submit a petition to the African Commission or the ACtHPR directly (depending on the state) alleging a violation of the ICCPR's right to privacy. While somewhat convoluted, this strategy represents a potential path for kick-starting the ACtHPR's engagement with LGBT rights. The ACtHPR has exercised its jurisdiction to rule on violations of the ICCPR on numerous occasions in the past.[80]

Another potential hurdle to LGBT rights recognition is the African Charter's emphasis on the family as "the custodian of morals and traditional values recognized by the community."[81] The Charter's protections of "traditional" family values may complicate efforts to expand the ACtHPR's definition of the family beyond the heteronormative standard. In at least one instance, domestic officials have pointed to the African Charter to justify restricting LGBT rights. After eleven men were detained on sodomy charges in Cameroon in 2005, the Cameroonian minister of justice referenced the Charter's promotion of "African cultural values" and the "moral well-being of society" to claim that "by virtue of the African culture, homosexuality is not a value accepted in the Cameroonian society."[82] Scholars have pushed back on the assumption that "African values" are monolithic and necessarily opposed to homosexuality. Murray and Viljoen emphasize that laws criminalizing homosexuality "were unknown in pre-colonial Africa, and coincided with the imposition of Victorian moral law as part of the British colonial project."[83]

Particularly given the fact that so few states allow citizens to petition the ACtHPR directly, the African Commission is a formidable stumbling block for citizens who are trying to get their cases in front of the Court. Historically, the African Commission has been demonstrably opposed to incorporating LGBT rights into the African human rights framework. For example, in 2010, the African Commission refused to grant observer status to the NGO Coalition of African Lesbians, citing that "the activities of the said Organization do not promote and protect any of the rights enshrined in the African Charter."[84] The commissioners' lack of independence also deters individuals from bringing LGBT rights complaints before the African Commission. Many commissioners throughout the institution's history have simultaneously held government positions, including within governments that have been openly antagonistic toward LGBT rights.

At one point, the International Gay and Lesbian Human Rights Commission warned individuals against submitting complaints to the African Commission based on the risk of receiving an adverse decision: "We do not recommend sending formal complaints about violations based on sexual orientation or gender identity to the African Commission. . . . A complaint coming to it without prior preparation or lobbying might actually end with the Commission endorsing the idea that homosexuality is opposed to 'African values.' Such a precedent would be extremely difficult to reverse."[85] Wariness that approaching the Commission would backfire has undoubtedly produced a chilling effect on the development of LGBT rights within the African system. However, there have been signs that commissioners are warming up to expanding the scope of the Charter with regard to transgender and homosexual rights. In 2014, the Commission adopted an unprecedented resolution condemning violence and discrimination against LGBT persons.[86] In 2017, the Commission specifically called on states to prevent and address torture and sexual violence against "lesbian, gay, bisexual, transgender, and intersex persons."[87] These statements are encouraging, but progress has been slow-going.

While the obstacles to developing regional LGBT rights jurisprudence are daunting, there are a number of potential pathways for success. Particularly now that the African Commission has openly condemned anti-LGBT violence and discrimination, individuals and NGOs could pave a way to the ACtHPR by bringing cases that focus on more public-facing elements of discrimination. Cases alleging violations of private life, such as discrimination in legal relationship recognition, may be unlikely to succeed owing to the dual hurdles of weak protection within the Charter and persistent resistance from commissioners and/ or their government connections. But cases that focus on public discrimination against LGBT individuals rather than intimate aspects of private relationships may be more likely to gain traction within the Commission and ultimately make it to the ACtHPR. Cases that involve anti-LGBT discrimination in the broader context of rights protections that are already well established within the African system, such as the freedom of assembly or the prohibition of torture, may have better chances for success.

Another potential option could be for the ACtHPR to take a page from the IACtHR's book and issue an advisory opinion on member states' human rights obligations to LGBT people. As documented in previous chapters, the ACtHPR has been inclined to emulate the IACtHR's example to expand its judicial authority (for instance, with regard to flexible temporal jurisdiction and intensive remedial mandates). There is evidence, however, that the ACtHPR's bold attempts to expand its authority have backfired, culminating in several states withdrawing the right of their citizens to petition the Court. Issuing an advisory opinion on

LGBT rights without first building up supportive jurisprudence risks provoking further accusations of judicial overreach. Partially because of the young age of the ACtHPR, the Court has not yet built up the level of legitimacy in the eyes of governments and civil society that the IACtHR had amassed before releasing its 2018 advisory opinion. Still, in light of the African Commission's history of deterring complaints from LGBT individuals, it might be wise for the ACtHPR to leverage its advisory jurisdiction to jump-start regional support for the rights of homosexual and transgender Africans.

The ECtHR and IACtHR have both developed increasingly expansive interpretations of the scope of LGBT rights protections over time. However, true to its founding commitment to deference, the ECtHR has adopted a more cautious approach to expanding such protections, rooted in sensitivity to regional social consensus. The ECtHR has also declined to mandate that states implement specific policy remedies to address anti-LGBT discrimination. The IACtHR, in contrast, has characteristically thrown caution to the wind, leveraging its advisory jurisdiction to expand member states' obligations to LGBT people and ordering intensive remedial mandates, including legislative reforms. As a result, the IACtHR became the first international court to require member states to legalize same-sex marriage. It remains to be seen whether the ACtHPR will, as it has in the past, follow in the IACtHR's footsteps and adopt an interventionist approach to developing LGBT rights.

CONCLUSION

The founding stories of the IACtHR and the ACtHPR are marked by distinct government apathy. Political representatives repeatedly declined opportunities to provide feedback on the American Convention and African Charter. Appointees to the negotiation delegations that created those courts as well as appointees to the courts' first judicial benches had demonstrated professional and personal commitments that, in the cases of many unstable and authoritarian founding member states, appeared to be in direct contravention of government interests. Although the IACtHR and ACtHPR were founded in regions rife with systemic human rights violations perpetrated by militarism, civil conflict, and repression, these geopolitical conditions actually seem to have engendered those courts' wider-reaching judicial mandates. Lack of government participation from autocratic and unstable regimes during the founding of the IACtHR and ACtHPR—whether because of preoccupation with domestic crises, lack of diplomatic capacity, or disbelief that such courts could ever meaningfully constrain national authorities—created situations where legal bureaucrats could capture control over negotiation delegations and design courts with greater authority to intervene in domestic affairs. As a result, the written mandates of the IACtHR and ACtHPR encompass a wider range of human rights protections and impose comparatively fewer limitations on judges' latitude to self-interpret their authority relative to the written mandate of the ECtHR. In contrast, government representatives from the mostly Western European democracies that founded the ECtHR retained tight control over the negotiations to found that court. The ECtHR's founding member states perceived themselves as already exemplary protectors of human rights and were skeptical of the need for a regional court in the first place. The central goal shared by all major players in the founding of the ECtHR was for the Court to serve as an instrument of cross-national socialization that would bolster Europeans' sense of shared identity in support of the broader integration project. In order to secure political support for that project, the ECtHR's mission had to be rooted in deference to governments and attention to fostering regional consensus.

Interrogating the founding of each of the regional courts provides a more nuanced picture to complement existing explanations for why transitional democracies tend to be particularly likely to ratify human rights treaties, as well as why authoritarian regimes ratify such treaties even when it seems unlikely that they intend to comply with them. While the act of ratification itself may well be driven by the benefits that such regimes can accrue by signaling respect for human rights (for example, bolstering the regime's international reputation or fending off domestic critics), national executives may not actually be particularly attentive to the content and scope of the agreements that they are signing. Actors that are interested in promoting international governance can capitalize on this lack of government attention to craft treaties that imbue international courts with wide-reaching authority. There is perhaps no clearer example of this phenomenon than the fact that over thirty states have ratified the African Charter on Human and Peoples' Rights and its First Protocol, even though these agreements define no temporal limitations on the ACtHPR's jurisdiction! It is hard to imagine a situation in which any reasonable person would sign a legal agreement that did not explicitly define the time frame during which that agreement would be enforceable. Yet such an agreement is the foundation of the African human rights system.

The ECtHR's early case law indicates a strong commitment to respecting national authority, as judges established wide-ranging conditions under which states could legitimately restrict freedom of expression, resisted labeling aggressive interrogation practices as torture, and declined to intervene in burgeoning debates surrounding the rights of sexual orientation minorities. The ECtHR's founding social purpose required the Court to tread carefully in condemning government actions and mandating remedies for violations of international law. Early IACtHR judges, in comparison, had relatively less to lose by throwing caution to the wind. Faced with emergency conditions as military coups swept through the region, IACtHR judges were motivated by a unique moral imperative to protect vulnerable individuals from abusive governments. In service of this mission, IACtHR judges expanded the scope of their authority by engaging in flexible interpretations of the Court's substantive, temporal, and advisory jurisdiction. Early IACtHR precedent established stringent obligations for states to prevent, investigate, and remedy grave human rights violations, including past violations whose ongoing implications negatively prejudiced the well-being of victims and their families. The IACtHR's first judges quickly asserted broad authority to mandate that states provide specific and intensive remedies to respond to human rights violations. These remedial mandates aimed not only to secure reparations for individual victims but also to remediate the underlying social and political conditions that facilitated human rights violations. The ACtHPR's first judges in many ways followed the IACtHR's lead, for example by developing an implied right to domestic legal recourse that could be leveraged to stretch the Court's temporal jurisdiction in continuing violation cases, rejecting the criminalization of defamation, exerting authority to mandate domestic legislative reforms, and attempting to intervene in domestic criminal proceedings.

Regional courts' interpretations of the boundaries of their authority have evolved over time. Still, the influence of each court's founding social purpose has remained a constant fixture in its contemporary jurisprudence. Analysis of the historical development of each court's case law demonstrates that entrenched traditions of judicial deference and interventionism drive variation across how judges admit, rule on, and mandate remedies across diverse types of cases. International courts' founding interpretations of their authority exert durable influence on how those courts respond to political backlash, engage in cross-court jurisprudential dialogue, and react to dynamic caseloads.

A consistent refrain that emerged during the Second International Human Rights Forum, a virtual meeting that brought together judges from all three regional courts in March 2021, was a desire to achieve greater convergence across the courts' jurisprudences. In the words of Judge Patricio Pazmiño Freire, then vice president of the IACtHR,

> We have grasped that the developments in, and implications of, globalization mean that a single legal language needs to be used. The classic borders of international and national law are blurred. . . . In a globalized world, justice, too, must be global. We as judges have to continue rolling out and expanding spaces for dialogue, and ensuring that the law that we apply is grounded in reality and is constructed according to criteria adopted not only by us in isolation, but in conjunction with other local and international courts.

Analysis of the courts' case laws in the areas of freedom of expression, personal integrity rights, and anti-LGBT discrimination reveals that, while opportunities for cross-court coordination abound, consequential schisms in their respective approaches to defining the boundaries of their authority may pose significant challenges for future harmonization of jurisprudence. These courts' unique founding interpretations of their social purpose have fostered engrained legal philosophies that guide judges' decision-making through the present day. It may not be feasible or even normatively desirable to reconcile cross-court jurisprudential divergences for the sake of achieving a more "globalized" legal framework. Attempts at cross-regional harmonization simply for the sake of harmonization may backfire if not attentive to diverse conceptualizations of justice that persist within the regional courts' respective jurisdictions. It is critical to strike a balance between the inherent universality of human rights guarantees and local ideas as to how best to implement those guarantees.

In the creation of any international institution, the priorities and convictions of the institution's founders and the geopolitical context in which they operate will fundamentally condition not only the scope of the institution's written mandate, but also how actors working within that institution construct narratives of the source of their own legitimacy. These narratives will drive how those actors define their institution's social purpose, with long-lasting influence on how and when the institution projects authority into the domestic arena. This influence is likely to be particularly durable in international courts, as reliance on precedent and professional legal socialization favor the reproduction of established norms. The persistent influence of founding context is both inevitable and necessary for sustaining judges' confidence in the legitimacy of their court's mission and ability to speak to the needs of local populations. Scholars should be cautious not to characterize cross-institutional fragmentation in the implementation of international law as an inherently normatively positive or negative phenomenon. Rather, fragmentation is a natural feature of international law that may degrade, bolster, or be agnostic to the law's efficacy, depending on how efficacy is defined in variable contexts.

What Does "Justice" Look Like?

Perhaps the most fundamental divergence across the ECtHR, on the one hand, and the IACtHR and ACtHPR, on the other hand, is the courts' wildly disparate approaches to ordering remedies for human rights violations. This disparity has profound implications, as remedial mandates define what constitutes "compliance" with international law. Remedial mandates provide opportunities for judges to project what they believe justice substantively looks like. These projections speak to how judges perceive the broader role of their court in facilitating social reconciliation and directing public discourse surrounding human rights. In no area are the regional courts' remedial mandates more revelatory of judges' divergent conceptualizations of legal justice than in personal integrity rights cases.

Torture and death at the hands of the state are the most grievous and irreparable violations of human dignity. These acts not only inflict permanent trauma on individual victims and their loved ones but also unleash rippling breakdowns in interpersonal trust that can destroy the social fabric of communities and impede genuine reconciliation for generations.

The ECtHR, IACtHR, and ACtHPR have developed unique approaches to mandating remedies guided by each court's social purpose. The ECtHR's focus on individual financial reparations for victims of human rights violations reflects the Court's conceptualization of legal justice as based on the principle of *restitutio in integrum* ("restoring to original condition"). The European Convention is viewed as a contract between governments and individual citizens, and breaches of legal contracts are remedied by restitution in kind. In the words of one ECtHR judge, "The aim [of the Court's remedial mandates] is not symbolism, nor a general moral condemnation. They are *legal* remedies."[1] This conceptual melding of "legal" with "financial" remedies and juxtaposition of "legal" with "general moral condemnation" paints a distinctive picture of what "justice" means in the European system. That judge went on to directly contrast the ECtHR's remedial approach with that of the IACtHR, elaborating that the "Inter-American Court is based on a very different logic—a more revolutionary system." IACtHR judges "go very far" and "engage in a lot of policy-making" through their remedial mandates.[2]

This fissure between what constitutes a "legal remedy" in the ECtHR and IACtHR can be traced back to their respective founding commitments to interpreting the boundaries of their authority. "Moral condemnation" and "policy-making" fall outside the scope of the ECtHR's self-interpreted identity as an international judicial institution, and are thus conceived as extralegal. Meanwhile, remedial mandates that impose policymaking obligations on governments (for example, orders to amend domestic penal codes or establish databases to track conflict-era enforced disappearances) or express moral condemnation (for example, orders for the state to pay for a dignified reburial of a person's remains, issue a public apology for past atrocities, or construct a memorial to honor victims of state violence) are indeed cornerstones of what IACtHR judges consider to be "legal justice." The ECtHR sees itself as an institution for resolving discrete human rights disputes between the state and specific injured parties, in keeping with its mandate to be a "safety valve" or "insurance policy" whose authority supplements domestic institutions but does not supersede them. It is the ECtHR's job to condemn states when they have failed to uphold their human rights obligations but not to dictate the measures that states must take to address the sociopolitical conditions that facilitated those violations. The IACtHR, in contrast, treats specific cases as windows to reach into the domestic realm and issue remedial mandates aimed at broader social reconciliation and policy change. IACtHR judges' definition of "justice" thus transcends the traditional legal sense, in that restitution is one necessary but insufficient component to addressing human rights crimes. Real justice means creating conditions that elevate the stories of victims over the narrative created by the state and directing reforms that prevent the repetition of similar crimes in the future.

In the ACtHPR's limited but quickly growing case law, African judges have projected similar commitments to a vision of justice that goes beyond individual restitution. In recent cases, ACtHPR judges have asserted authority to intervene in domestic policymaking and public discourse by ordering states to repeal mandatory death penalty sentencing, reform election law, revise penal codes, publicly acknowledge responsibility for rights violations, and even allocate land titles to Indigenous peoples.[3] It is not surprising that the ACtHPR has followed in the IACtHR's footsteps in this area. From the beginning of negotiations to draft the African Charter, the African regional human rights system was conceived as a distinctly collectivist project, rejecting existing notions of human rights law as a contract between individuals and the state and instead viewing such rights as collective responsibilities that communities must work together to uphold. The ACtHPR's interventionist approach to issuing remedial mandates reflects the Court's founding commitment to a definition of justice that encompasses measures of social restoration and nonrepetition, in addition to individual restitution.

Even when the ECtHR expanded its authority to issue nonfinancial remedial mandates through the introduction of the pilot judgment procedure, this decision was rooted in the ECtHR's founding commitment to deference to national authorities. Facing a deluge of repetitive cases instigated by systemic domestic human rights deficiencies, the ECtHR had to find a way to reduce its case backlog. The pilot judgment procedure did not represent a reimagining of the ECtHR's authority to intervene in domestic affairs. Rather, the change was a direct response to practical and logistical exigencies aimed at sustaining the Court's case-processing capabilities. Consistent with the ECtHR's founding commitment to cooperation with domestic authorities, pilot judgments are not an interventionist power-grab. These judgments represent bargains that the ECtHR strikes with states, in which the ECtHR pauses pending cases to give governments time to enact reforms. Furthermore, typical remedial mandates contained in pilot judgments are exceedingly vague compared to those routinely issued by the IACtHR and ACtHPR. These judgments offer considerable leeway for states to decide how to implement domestic reforms, and state representatives can negotiate with the Committee of Ministers to define what constitutes "compliance" with pilot judgments.

The types of cases in which the ECtHR utilizes pilot judgments provide insight into the underlying objectives of the procedure. Recall that the first pilot judgment, *Broniowski v. Poland*, responded to ongoing deprivation of property rights stemming from a border dispute that occurred decades prior to Poland acceding to the ECtHR. While the ECtHR has repeatedly declined to admit cases involving preaccession personal integrity rights violations, and never ordered remedies beyond financial reparations in such cases, the Court mandated domestic legislative change in a preaccession property rights dispute case. This decision was a puzzling move for a court that has consistently avoided holding states accountable for past human rights violations, even when such violations have continuing effects in the present day.

However, when evaluated in light of the ECtHR's historical rejection of responsibility to address preaccession violence and conceptualization of legal "justice" as individual restitution, the *Broniowski v. Poland* pilot judgment comports with the ECtHR's founding commitment to deference. Ordering a state to provide compensation for expropriated property is much less politically sensitive, and much less likely to be interpreted as "moral condemnation," than ordering a state to go dig up the bodies of victims of political violence and return them to their families. Offering citizens money is only ever going to be politically popular for national executives. While governments might begrudge being told what to do with their money by an international court, complying with that judgment is not likely to pose a substantive threat to domestic leaders' authority. An international court ordering a government to construct a memorial or publicly acknowledge responsibility for past human rights abuses, on the other hand, represents a profoundly polemical incursion into domestic society, with potentially destabilizing political ramifications. When looking for ways to reduce a deferential court's caseload, it makes sense to target systemic issues that can be addressed by throwing money at the problem, rather than issuing judgments that could cause festering old wounds to split open. Hence, while the ECtHR has repeatedly issued pilot judgments in cases involving property restitution and improving prison conditions, judges will not apply this procedure to systemic issues that require healing broader social traumas, for example investigating unresolved conflict-era enforced disappearances.

ECtHR and IACtHR jurisprudence on LGBT rights demonstrates how an international court's founding interpretation of its authority conditions court behavior even when adjudicating contemporary issues that were not contemplated by the court's founders. Both courts have broadened the scope of human rights protections for LGBT people in recent decades, imposing new obligations on member states to allow transgender individuals to alter their official identification documents, legally recognize same-sex partnerships, and investigate and prosecute homophobic violence. The pace and extent of jurisprudential developments on these issues, however, have varied significantly across the ECtHR and IACtHR. ECtHR judges have engaged cautious incrementalism in expanding their interpretations of governments' obligations to LGBT people since the mid-1980s. Their approach has been consistently characterized by attention to domestic legal consensus and evolving social norms surrounding homosexuality and transgenderism. This process has aligned with the ECtHR's historical adherence to the margin of appreciation doctrine when determining when to defer implementation of the European Convention to domestic authorities.

IACtHR judges, in contrast, have taken it upon themselves to proactively promote LGBT rights rather than waiting on domestic consensus. The Court's 2018 advisory opinion that obligated states to implement intensive domestic legal reforms based on meager jurisprudential precedent represented a boldly interventionist assertion of judicial authority. It is not surprising, however, that IACtHR judges risked government backlash and pushed ahead with the advisory opinion. Since the early 1980s, even before the Court issued its first binding judgment, IACtHR judges have been leveraging advisory opinions to push the boundaries of the Court's jurisdiction and strengthen its authority in the region. The 2018 opinion introduced a variety of new requirements for states to uphold the human rights of LGBT people, the most contentious of which mandated that states provide full marriage rights to same-sex couples. In doing so, the IACtHR became the first court in the world to establish that depriving same-sex couples of the ability to marry constitutes a violation of international human rights law. The ECtHR has, as of the 2021 *Fedotova v. Russia* judgment, ruled that states must provide some form of legal recognition to same-sex couples. However, the ECtHR has repeatedly and unequivocally rejected the argument that states must provide such couples with the right to marry, maintaining that governments must be afforded a wide margin of appreciation to implement Article 12 of the European Convention. The ECtHR and IACtHR's divergent approaches to expanding LGBT rights protections illustrate how, even when international courts are faced with issues not contemplated by their founders, variation across founding interpretations of their authority can produce very different legal outcomes. Changing social norms influence how international judges interpret the scope of their authority, but their response to "new" norms will still be conditioned by their court's founding social purpose.

The Future of the African Court

When I traveled to the headquarters of the ACtHPR in Arusha, Tanzania, in June 2024 to interview judges and lawyers there, one constant theme permeated our conversations: anxiety about the Court's future. The cascade of withdrawals the Court has experienced in recent years and the lack of new declarations permitting individual access to the Court have clearly rattled the institution. In the stark words of one judge, "The future does not look very bright."[4] However, this judge emphasized that while there are critical issues threatening the survival of the ACtHPR that are specific to its member states, it is important not to perceive these problems as inherent to Africa. All international courts are currently threatened by the worldwide "retrogression of democracy." There are potential reforms on the table that might promote more cooperative government engagement with the ACtHPR (for example, another judge expressed support for reforming the judge selection rules so that only jurists from states that have deposited a declaration permitting individual access would be allowed to sit on the Court's bench, ideally spurring more governments to submit declarations).[5] But more fundamentally, stalling the global trend of democratic backsliding and demonstrating the value of international institutions to governments and citizens are imperative for sustaining the modern human rights project. The regional human rights courts are indispensable anchors of this endeavor. Ruminating on the tumultuous days that lie ahead, one ACtHPR lawyer reminded me that we must reject shortsighted interpretations of the current maelstrom. Attention to the long arc of history gives us reasons to be hopeful about the ACtHPR's future, and the future of regional human rights litigation more broadly: "This is a low point. But the other courts had that too, and they managed it. They moved on and up."[6] The ECtHR and IACtHR have both weathered perilous storms, particularly in their younger days. They not only survived those storms, but emerged armed with more resilient strategies for achieving their unique visions of justice. The African Court is just getting started. Give it time.

Final Thoughts

During the meeting of the three regional courts in March 2021, ECtHR Judge Anja Seibert-Fohr underscored the urgency of achieving deeper cross-court cooperation and jurisprudential coherence: "Over the past years in which, unfortunately, multilateralism seems to have lost momentum, our mutual engagement becomes even more important. This is true for our regular meetings as much as for our judicial dialogue.... By taking into account other bodies' interpretations of similar rights, the notion of universality can be enhanced. Coordination can help us to foster the notion of universal human rights protection by addressing common legal issues."[7] In this age of rising nationalism and isolationism, presenting a coordinated front may help international human rights institutions weather the storm. We may soon be embarking on a new era in which the regional human rights courts, cognizant of their role as the most direct links between international law and domestic institutions, commit to cultivating shared legal interpretations in service of truly "universal" human rights protections. Stable partnerships between international and domestic authorities will be imperative as the world confronts proliferating threats to human security. The climate change emergency, mass migration and refugee crises, fallout from the COVID-19 pandemic, and the looming threats of great power military aggression all cast in stark relief the urgency of transnational cooperation. Careful calibration of international institutional power with domestic sovereignty will be crucial for maintaining forums in which that cooperation can be realized. Understanding and appreciation of the ways in which founding context shapes international institutions' varied conceptualizations of justice can empower actors within those institutions to navigate the exigencies of the current moment. Though the regional human rights courts are each staring down formidable threats from antidemocratic forces, their renewed determination to learn from one another represents a compelling reason to have hope for the future of international justice.

Acknowledgments

This book is the culmination of personal and professional support invested in me by so many brilliant people. I will thank some of them here, but there are truly too many to name in this space, so I will start by apologizing to those not named.

I am immensely appreciative of my graduate school advisers, Nisha Fazal and Cosette Creamer, without whose sage advice and guidance I would have never embarked on this endeavor (or survived graduate school, or become a professor). I deeply value the years that Nisha and Cosette spent asking me difficult questions and pushing me to be a better researcher and writer. I would also like to thank Lisa Hilbink and Jessica Stanton for serving on my dissertation committee and, along with Nisha and Cosette, initiating the conversation that motivated me to transform that project into this book. There are many people at the University of Minnesota whose mentorship has been invaluable for me. I kind of stumbled into graduate school during a challenging time in my life. The UMN gave me a community of friends and mentors who helped me get back on my feet and achieve things I never thought possible. I am so grateful.

To my political science colleagues at Colorado College: Doug Edlin, Elizabeth Coggins, Jiun Bang, Joe Derdzinski, Sofia Fenner, Tim Fuller, John Gould, Eve Grace, Juan Lindau, Corina McKendry, Dana Wolfe, and Marla Patanelli—each of you has, in your own way, been instrumental in supporting me as I have finished this book while figuring out how to be a professor. I am so lucky to work with such a compassionate and talented group of teachers and scholars. The kindness, friendship, and wisdom you have blessed me with these past few years has meant the world to me. Thank you.

Jackie Teoh at Cornell University Press deserves immense credit for expertly guiding me through the process of turning what was, admittedly, a monster of a manuscript into this book. Her talents are profound. I would also like to thank the anonymous reviewers whose feedback was vital and constructive.

On a more personal note, my husband, Joe, is the love of my life, and I could not have done this without him. When we were teenagers sneaking out late at night to sit by the Meramec River and ponder the future, none of this was in the plan. In the many years since, he has supported my every ambition, picked me up when I am down, and been my guiding star when I have desperately needed one. Joe is my favorite person to climb mountains with, literally and metaphorically.

He is also a damn good cook, and the sole reason I did not starve while writing this book.

Perhaps the greatest gift and privilege I have ever received in my life is to have been born into a family of educators. As far as first teachers go, I hit the lottery with my parents. Their commitment to my education has empowered me immeasurably. In their personal and professional lives, they have modeled learning as liberation. Their example has shaped my sense of justice and driven me to do the work that I do.

Finally, this book is, above all else, inspired by the courage of ordinary people who have reached out to international courts to attempt to hold governments accountable for human rights abuses. In researching this book, the most moving and humbling part of the process was reading their stories. It takes incomprehensible strength to speak truth to power and persevere in the face of denigration of one's human dignity. My greatest hope is that this book teaches someone something about how to better advocate for those ordinary people.

Notes

INTRODUCTION

1. INEGI 2021.
2. INEGI 2023.
3. Tzompaxtle Tecpile and Others v. México, Judgment of November 7, 2022 (Preliminary Exception, Merits, Reparations and Costs), IACtHR.
4. Stevan Petrovič v. Serbia, App. nos. 6097/16 and 28999/19, April 20, 2021, para. 99.
5. Hamilton and Buyse 2018; Sandholtz and Feldman 2019.
6. Kampala Declaration, First International Human Rights Forum, Kampala, Uganda, October 28–29, 2019.
7. San José Declaration (II), Third International Human Rights Forum, San José, Costa Rica, May 25–26, 2023.
8. Huneeus and Madsen 2018.
9. Álvarez 2014; Moynihan 2016; Sanchez 2023.
10. Beneficiaries of Late Norbert Zongo, Abdoulaye Nikiema (Ablassé), Ernest Zongo, and Blaise Ilboudo and the Burkinabé Human and Peoples' Rights Movement v. Burkina Faso (App. no. 013/2011), Judgment of June 4, 2015.
11. Hawkins and Jacoby 2010; Hillebrecht 2014.
12. Odermatt 2018.
13. Simmons 2009, 126.
14. Guzman 2008a.
15. Pollack 2007; Guzman 2008b.
16. Abbott and Snidal 2000; Mansfield and Pevehouse 2006; Stone Sweet and Brunell 2013.
17. Milner 2006.
18. Nielson and Tierney 2003; Bertelli 2006.
19. Martin 2006.
20. Helfer and Slaughter 2005, 899.
21. Koremenos 2008, 154.
22. Simmons and Danner 2010.
23. Moravcsik 2000.
24. Hafner-Burton, Mansfield, and Pevehouse 2015.
25. Pollack 2007.
26. Keck and Sikkink 1998; Zippel 2004; Novak 2020.
27. Deitelhoff 2009.
28. Deitelhoff 2009, 50–55.
29. Steffek 2003, 261.
30. Barnett and Finnemore 2005, 174.
31. Steffek 2003, 261.
32. Barnett and Finnemore 1999; Reinalda and Verbeek 2004; Vaubel 2006; Kennard and Stanescu 2025.
33. T. Johnson 2014, 13.

34. See the discussion in Madsen (2014) of the distinct approaches adopted by diplomats and law professors for "balancing law and politics" at the Permanent Court of International Justice.

35. Candidates are not required to be nationals of states that have accepted the jurisdiction of the IACtHR.

36. The twenty-four OAS member states that are currently parties to the American Convention are Argentina, Barbados, Bolivia, Brazil, Chile, Colombia, Costa Rica, Dominica, the Dominican Republic, Ecuador, El Salvador, Grenada, Guatemala, Haiti, Honduras, Jamaica, Mexico, Nicaragua, Panama, Paraguay, Peru, Suriname, Uruguay, and Venezuela.

37. The Economic Community of West African States (ECOWAS) Community Court of Justice, while founded to adjudicate economic disputes, has gradually expanded its jurisdiction over human rights–related complaints since the early 2000s. Because of the fundamentally different types of treaties that it enforces compared to the ECtHR, IACtHR, and ACtHPR, the ECOWAS Court is not considered in this analysis. However, future work could evaluate findings from this study in light of the ECOWAS Court's unique and evolving mandate. For more on how the ECOWAS Court acquired authority to litigate human rights disputes see Alter et al. (2013).

38. The Council of Europe took a step toward gender equality within the ECtHR in 2004, when the Parliamentary Assembly adopted Resolution 1366. That resolution stated that the Assembly would not consider a state's submitted lists of judicial candidates if "the list does not include at least one candidate of each sex."

39. The thirty-two states that have ratified the protocol are Algeria, Benin, Burkina Faso, Burundi, Cameroon, Chad, the Comoros, Congo, Côte d'Ivoire, the Democratic Republic of the Congo, Gabon, the Gambia, Ghana, Guinea-Bissau, Kenya, Lesotho, Libya, Malawi, Mali, Mauritania, Mauritius, Mozambique, Niger, Nigeria, Rwanda, the Sahrawi Arab Democratic Republic, Senegal, South Africa, Tanzania, Togo, Tunisia, and Uganda.

1. THEORIZING INTERNATIONAL JUDICIAL AUTHORITY

1. Fontevecchia and D'Amico v. Argentina, Judgment of November 29, 2011 (Merits, Reparations and Costs), IACtHR.

2. Contesse 2017.

3. Neuman 2008; Soley et al. 2018.

4. Arnaiz 2018.

5. Antkowiak 2007; Cavallaro and Brewer 2008; Contreras 2012; Anagnostou and Mungiu-Pippidi 2014.

6. Bodansky 2008.

7. Meltzer 2005.

8. Neuman 2008.

9. Helfer and Alter 2013, 484–85.

10. Grossman 2013; Alter et al. 2016.

11. Ruggie 1982, 382.

12. Goldberg 1984; Arold 2007.

13. Hillebrecht 2021, 19.

14. Sandholtz and Feldman 2019, 113–19.

15. Voeten 2010.

16. Laffranque 2008, 1291–92.

17. HUDOC database, https://hudoc.echr.coe.int/.

18. The Commission admitted only eighteen cases during the first decade of the Court's existence, between 1959 and 1969. The vast majority of petitions submitted to the Commission during this time were declared inadmissible, often for incompatibility with basic admissibility requirements (for example, the exhaustion of domestic remedies).

19. By 1969, the Council of Europe had eighteen member states, eleven of which had recognized the right of individuals to petition the ECtHR. (These were the Netherlands, Belgium, Luxembourg, Denmark, Norway, Sweden, the UK, Ireland, Iceland, West Germany, and Austria.)

20. HUDOC. These numbers include all decisions made by Chambers and the Plenary Court. Committee decisions are not included because data on inadmissibility decisions are not available.

21. A list of these states and their dates of admission into the CoE: Hungary (1990), Poland (1991), Bulgaria (1992), Estonia, Lithuania, Slovenia, Czech Republic, Slovakia, Romania (1993), Andorra (1994), Latvia, Moldova, Albania, Ukraine, North Macedonia (1995), Russia, Croatia (1996), Georgia (1999), Armenia, Azerbaijan (2001), Bosnia and Herzegovina (2002), and Serbia and Montenegro (2003).

22. Minutes of the 89th Session of the Committee of Ministers (CoM), 1991, CM (91) PV 4, pp. 21–27.

23. CM (91) PV 4 (1991), pp. 9, 24, 39.

24. CM (91) PV 4 (1991), p. 9.

25. *Explanatory Report*, ETS 155—Protocol 11, pp. 10–11. By 1990, acceptance of individual petition was already a de facto requirement for CoE admission.

26. ECtHR lawyer, interview by the author, Strasbourg, France, June 2019.

27. See *Protocol No. 14 to the European Convention on Human Rights; First Report of Session 2004–05*, House of Lords House of Commons Joint Committee on Human Rights, p. 7.

28. *Explanatory Report to Protocol No. 14 to the Convention for the Protection of Human Rights and Fundamental Freedoms, Amending the Control System of the Convention*, CETS 194, Strasbourg, 13.V.2004, para. 20.

29. *Explanatory Report*.

30. *Explanatory Report*, para. 7.

31. *Explanatory Report*.

32. *Explanatory Report*, para. 26.

33. Russia's prolonged refusal to ratify the Protocol was primarily responsible for this six-year delay.

34. Parliamentary Assembly of the Council of Europe, Recommendation 1649 (2004).

35. *Explanatory Report*, para. 50.

36. *Protocol No. 14 to the Convention for the Protection of Human Rights and Fundamental Freedoms, Amending the Control System of the Convention*, ETS 194, Strasbourg, 13.V.2004, Art. 7(1).

37. *Protocol No. 14*, Art. 8(1).

38. *Protocol No. 14*, Art. 12.

39. *Explanatory Report*, para. 39.

40. Shelton 2016.

41. *Explanatory Report*, para. 34. This is despite the fact that the IACtHR had been (relatively successfully) exercising advisory jurisdiction for over thirty years at this point.

42. *Protocol No. 14*, ETS 194, Art. 16(4).

43. Case of Khadija Ismayilova v. Azerbaijan, App. nos. 65286/13 and 57270/14, January 10, 2019.

44. Bates 2012. The *Hirst v. United Kingdom* (No. 2) judgment of October 2005, in which the Court ruled that the UK's blanket ban on convicted prisoners voting violated the Convention, sparked particularly vociferous domestic backlash. See Bates 2015.

45. Madsen 2018, 204.

46. Arnardóttir 2018, 224.

47. Brighton Declaration, High Level Conference on the Future of the European Court of Human Rights, April 2012, para. 12 (a, b). Protocol 15, which entered into force in 2021, amended the Preamble of the European Convention to include a reference to the margin of appreciation.

48. Madsen 2018.

49. Stiansen and Voeten 2020.

50. Brighton Declaration, para. 21.

51. Brighton Declaration, para. 25 (a–c).

52. Brighton Declaration, para. 23.

53. "Evaluation of the Workings of the Inter-American System for the Protection and Promotion of Human Rights with a View to Its Improvement and Strengthening," OAE/Ser.P/AG/Res. 1701 (XXX-O/00), June 5, 2000.

54. Inter-American Commission Rules of Procedure (2001), Arts. 43–44.

55. Gómez 2001; Dulitzky 2011, 151.

56. Soley and Steininger 2018, 247–48.

57. Huneeus 2010, 127–29.

58. Huneeus 2012.

59. Soley and Steininger 2018, 252.

60. Huneeus 2012.

61. Soley and Steininger 2018, 248–49.

62. *Resolución de la Corte Interamericana de Derechos Humanos de 12 de marzo de 2019: Caso de Las Niñas Yean Bosico y Caso de Personas Dominicanas y Haitianas Expulsadas vs. República Dominicana. Supervisión de Cumplimiento de Sentencias y Competencia*, para. 42–43.

63. Navarro 2014.

64. Ally Rajabu and Others v. United Republic of Tanzania (App. no. 007/2015), Judgment of November 28, 2019, ACtHPR.

65. ACtHPR lawyer, interview by the author, Arusha, Tanzania, June 2024.

66. Kirabira 2019.

67. Magubira 2020.

68. Anami 2021.

69. "African Court Commends Tanzania for Construction of Permanent Premises," ACtHPR press release, June 8, 2023, https://www.african-court.org/wpafc/african-court-commends-tanzania-for-construction-of-permanent-premises/.

70. ACtHPR judges, interviewed by the author, Arusha, Tanzania, June 2024.

71. Soro and Others v. Côte d'Ivoire (App. no. 012/2020), Provisional Measures Order of April 22, 2020, ACtHPR.

72. Africanews 2020.

73. Africanews 2020.

2. FOUNDING MOMENTS OF THE REGIONAL HUMAN RIGHTS COURTS

1. The founding members of the CoE were Belgium, Denmark, France, Ireland, Italy, Luxembourg, the Netherlands, Norway, Sweden, and the United Kingdom. Greece and Turkey joined later in 1949, followed by Iceland and Germany in 1950. While Turkey is the obvious outlier here, its early inclusion in the CoE made more sense at the time than

it might today. Turkey held its first free elections in 1950, which were won by the opposition Democratic Party. At the time, Turkey's status as a promising transitional democracy geographically surrounded by communist and other nondemocratic regimes made it an attractive candidate for inclusion in the CoE. See Reynolds 2012, 4.

2. Simpson 2004.

3. The European Movement Convention, Article 1. Original draft reproduced in Simpson 2004, 660.

4. Simpson 2004, 654–55.

5. The Consultative Assembly was the institutional predecessor to the modern Parliamentary Assembly of the CoE. However, the Consultative Assembly did not have any of the decision-making powers that the Parliamentary Assembly now possesses. The Consultative Assembly was merely a deliberative body made up of parliamentarians from each member state. Its primary function was to hold debates and present policy proposals to the Committee of Ministers, which held all substantive decision-making authority.

6. Bates 2010, 58–63.

7. Bates 2010, 80–82.

8. Wildhaber 2007, 523.

9. Bates 2010, 104–5.

10. Simpson 2004, 294–99. To relieve this point of tension, the draft convention was eventually amended to preclude the right of individual petition from residents of colonial possessions.

11. Quoted in Bates 2010, 12.

12. Bates 2010, 104–5.

13. Bates 2010, 14.

14. Quoted in Bates 2010, 105.

15. Bates 2010, 14. See also *Travaux Préparatoires to the European Convention on Human Rights* (hereafter, *Travaux préparatoires*), CDH (72) 27, p. 2, https://www.echr.coe.int/documents/library_travPrep_table_eng.pdf.

16. Spano 2018, 490.

17. O'Donnell 1982, 475.

18. Gerards 2011.

19. Property rights protections ended up being added to the Convention shortly afterward in Article 1 of Protocol 1, adopted in 1952.

20. *Travaux préparatoires*, DH (57) (5), p. 18, paras. 14–16.

21. *Travaux préparatoires*, CDH (72) (27), p. 6.

22. *Travaux préparatoires*, CDH (70) 30, p. 29.

23. The Commission did declare several cases inadmissible *ratione temporis* during the first decade of its tenure on the grounds that the alleged violations occurred prior to state accession. See X. v. Sweden (App. no. 172/56), Nielsen v. Denmark (App. no. 343/57), X. v. Germany (App. no. 2038/63), X. v. Austria (App. no. 913/60).

24. Treaty of Berlin (1878), Art. 29; Havana Convention on Treaties (1928), Art. 8; Harvard Draft Convention on the Law of Treaties (1928), Art. 11. See also Vienna Convention on the Law of Treaties (1969), Art. 28.

25. *Travaux préparatoires*, CDH (72) 27, p. 2.

26. *Travaux préparatoires*, CDH (72) 27.

27. Council of Europe 1960, 137–51.

28. Herz 2011, 8.

29. Carnegie Endowment for International Peace, Division of International Law 1940, 3–4.

30. Herz 2011, 10–11.

31. Sikkink 2017.

32. Glendon 2003.

33. Morsink 1999, 130; Sikkink 2015.

34. Fifth Meeting of Consultation of Ministers of Foreign Affairs, Final Act, 1960, Resolution VIII, Art. 1.

35. Cabranes 1968.

36. Herz 2011, 14–15.

37. Cabranes 1968, 901–3.

38. Cuba's OAS membership was suspended in 1962.

39. Cabranes 1968, 904.

40. *Travaux Préparatoires to the Inter-American Convention on Human Rights*, OEA/Ser.K/XVI/1.2, pp. 3

41. Rouquié and Vale 1973.

42. *Travaux Préparatoires to the Inter-American Convention on Human Rights*, OEA/Ser.K/XVI/1.2, pp. 215, 299.

43. McSherry 2007, 21.

44. Forero 2006.

45. Ginger 1967.

46. For the purposes of this analysis I only describe the backgrounds of the presidents of each state delegation, not any other subordinate delegates. Some states sent larger delegations than others (Paraguay, Peru, the Dominican Republic, and Trinidad and Tobago sent only one delegate each), but the delegation president was generally responsible for directing negotiation discussions. For a complete manifest of the members of all delegations see the *Travaux préparatoires*, OEA/Ser.K/XVI/1.2, "Lista de Participantes" (Doc. 22 Rev 2), pp. 525–34.

47. I was unfortunately not able to locate credible background information on the delegation presidents from Peru and Trinidad and Tobago. Bolivia is not listed as having representatives present at the San José conference.

48. Perón was arrested in 2007 on charges of human rights abuses stemming from her connections to right-wing death squads during her 1974–1976 presidency (Carroll 2007).

49. In Magnet's case this repression occurred after San José, under the Pinochet dictatorship.

50. Richard Kearney of the US delegation could conceivably be included in this category. Given that the US never ratified the Convention or acceded to the Court, it is not clear how much influence Kearney's professional background had on Convention negotiations.

51. *Travaux préparatoires* de la Conferencia Especializada Interamericana sobre Derechos Humanos, San José, Costa Rica (hereafter, *Travaux préparatoires* San José), OEA/Ser.K/XVI/1.2, pp. 432–34; Buergenthal et al. 1982, 67–71.

52. Buergenthal 1980, 166.

53. The protection of property, codified in the original American Convention, was not codified in the original European Convention but incorporated through Protocol 1 shortly afterward, in 1952. The freedom of movement, similarly included in the American Convention but not the original European Convention, was incorporated in the European Convention through Protocol 4 in 1963. These amendments to the European Convention narrowed the substantive rights differential between the two systems to 23–15 at the time of the IACtHR's founding.

54. The "right to equal protection before the law" is also codified in the American Convention but not the European Convention. I did not include the right to equal protection in this list of rights unique to the American Convention because I think it can be argued that the right is sufficiently implied in the European Convention, while not explicitly designated as a distinct "right."

55. *Travaux préparatoires* San José, OEA/Ser.K/XVI/1.2, p. 22.

56. *Travaux préparatoires* San José, p. 41, para. 13.

57. *Travaux préparatoires* San José, p. 263.

58. The ECtHR eventually was granted the authority to issue advisory opinions, but not until the implementation of Protocol 16 in 2018.

59. Between the adoption of the American Convention in 1969 and the IACtHR's establishment in 1979, four more states joined the OAS: Grenada, Suriname, Dominica, and Saint Lucia.

60. Segado 2002.

61. Pinto 2019.

62. "Convinced that this was a hoax and that the caller was a student in my seminar, I thanked the caller and asked him for his phone number, ostensibly to enable me to call him back after I had had a chance to discuss the matter with my wife." Buergenthal 2005, 4.

63. Buergenthal 2005, 4.

64. Associated Press 2003.

65. Ventura Robles 2021, 174.

66. IACtHR 2021.

67. Buergenthal 2005, 5.

68. Buergenthal 2005, 6.

69. Buergenthal 2005, 5–6.

70. Buergenthal 2005, 5.

71. Contreras 2012, 64.

72. "Regional integration" is only mentioned once in the *travaux*, by a Brazilian delegate. OEA/Ser.K/XVI/1.2, p. 375.

73. Bermúdez 2018.

74. *African Conference on the Rule of Law, Lagos (Nigeria), 3–7 January 1961—Report on the Work of the Conference,* "Law of Lagos," 1961. Geneva International Commission of Jurists (ICJ), p. 11.

75. In fact, Nigeria, the state in which the conference took place, officially achieved independence only three months before the conference!

76. Ouguergouz 2003, 82–83.

77. African Conference on the Rule of Law (ACRL), "Introductory Report to the Third Committee—the Responsibility of the Judiciary and of the Bar for the Protection of the Rights of the Individual in Society," 1961, Herbert W. Chitepo, Geneva ICJ, p. 71.

78. ACRL, "Introductory Report to the First Committee—Human Rights and Government Security—the Legislature, Executive, and Judiciary," 1961, Abdoulaye Wade, Geneva ICJ, pp. 56–68.

79. ACRL, "General Report," 1961, T. O. Elias, Geneva ICJ, p. 54.

80. ACRL, "Foreword," 1961, Jean-Flavien LaLive, Geneva ICJ, pp. 5–6.

81. Seminar on Human Rights in Developing Countries (hereafter, UN Dakar Seminar), Dakar (Senegal), February 8–22, 1966, United Nations, UNDOC ST/TAO/HR/25, paras. 239–41. See pp. 1–6 for a full list of conference participants.

82. UN Dakar Seminar, para. 241.

83. Seminar on the Establishment of Regional Commissions on Human Rights with Special Reference to Africa (hereafter, UN Cairo Seminar), Cairo (Egypt), September 2–15, 1969, UNDOC ST/TAO/HE/38. See pp. 20–25 for a full list of conference participants.

84. UN Cairo Seminar, para. 65(a–f).

85. Heyns 2004, 685.

86. *Report of the Secretary-General on the Draft African Charter on Human and Peoples' Rights,* reprinted in Heyns 2002, 92.

87. *Address Delivered by Léopold Sédar Senghor, President of the Republic of Senegal,* meeting of African experts preparing the draft African Charter in Dakar, Senegal, November 28–December 8, 1979. Reprinted in Heyns 2002, 78–79.

88. *Address Delivered by Léopold Sédar Senghor,* 1979.

89. *Address Delivered by Léopold Sédar Senghor,* 1979.

90. Heyns 2002.

91. Akinyemi 1985, 223.

92. Heyns 2004, 686.

93. Assembly of the Heads of State and Government of the OAU, 1994, AHG/Res.230 (XXX): 2.

94. Ouguergouz 2003, 85.

95. Ouguergouz 2003, 85–87.

96. *Third Government Legal Experts Meeting (Enlarged to Include Diplomats),* reprinted in Heyns 2002, 287.

97. I have not been able to locate records of the submitted comments from Senegal, Algeria, Burundi, Niger, and Togo.

98. *Comments and Observations Received from Member States on the Draft Protocol on the Establishment of an African Court on Human and Peoples' Rights,* reprinted in Heyns 2002, 275.

99. *Third Government Legal Experts Meeting,* reprinted in Heyns 2002, 287.

100. Ouguergouz 2003, 88–89.

101. In 2002, between the adoption and the entry into force of the Protocol, the OAU was reconstituted as the African Union (AU), the name under which the organization operates today.

102. Protocol to the African Charter on Human and Peoples' Rights (hereafter, First Protocol), Art. 3.

103. The Organization of African Unity (OAU) was reconstituted as the African Union (AU) in 2001.

104. First Protocol, Art. 4.

105. With one notable exception: The right to privacy is not included in the African Charter, despite the fact that privacy has been widely recognized as a fundamental human right since the mid-twentieth century.

106. Information on judges' professional profiles can be found on the ACtHPR's website, https://www.african-court.org/en/index.php/judges/former-judges.

3. THE COURTS' EARLY YEARS

1. These include violations of the right to life as well as the right to humane treatment / prohibition of torture.

2. Figure 3.1 only includes cases that were declared admissible, and includes cases where the respective violation was alleged, not necessarily established. One might ask why, given the frequency of fair-trial violations, I have not selected this right as a primary area of analysis. I have not done so because the IACtHR found a violation of the right to free trial in 77 percent of cases from 1998 through 2001 (100 percent of the instances that violation was alleged), while the ECtHR found a violation of the right to free trial in 40 percent of cases from 1961 through 1989 (60 percent of the instances in which that violation was alleged). These disparate proportions suggest significantly different standards for establishing a violation of the right to free trial across the IACtHR and ECtHR, complicating the ability to draw meaningful comparisons. Also, the right to privacy is not included in the African Charter, but the right to family life is (Art. 18). The ACtHPR does have jurisdiction over the right to privacy as codified in other human rights treaties ratified

by member states (for example, the International Covenant on Civil and Political Rights). Freedom from ex post facto laws is included within the right to fair trial in the African Charter, so alleged violations of those rights are combined under the fair trial column for the ACtHPR in this chart.

3. The exception to this statement is a pair of cases originating in the Northern Irish conflict, *Lawless v. Ireland* (1961) and *Ireland v. United Kingdom* (1978), which are discussed later.

4. Case of Ireland v. the United Kingdom (App. no. 5310/71), Judgment of January 18, 1978, ECtHR (Chamber), paras. 157–59.

5. *Ireland v. UK*, para. 96.

6. *Ireland v. UK*, para. 167.

7. Spjut 1979; Cullen 2003.

8. Case of Ireland v. the United Kingdom (App. no. 5310/71), Report of the European Commission, adopted January 25, 1976, p. 402.

9. Case of Ireland v. the United Kingdom (App. no. 5310/71), Judgment (Revision) of March 20, 2018, ECtHR (Third Section).

10. Case of Lawless v. Ireland (No. 3) (App. no. 332/57), Judgment of July 1, 1961, ECtHR (Chamber).

11. Gross and Ní Aoláin 2001.

12. Case of Tyrer v. the United Kingdom (App. no. 5856/72), Judgment of April 25, 1978, ECtHR (Chamber), para. 35.

13. Case of X and Y v. the Netherlands (App. no. 8978/80), Judgment of March 26, 1985, ECtHR (Chamber), paras. 7–13.

14. X and Y v. the Netherlands, paras. 31–36.

15. Case of Soering v. the United Kingdom (App. no. 14038/88), Judgment of July 7, 1989, ECtHR (Plenary), paras. 101–4.

16. *Soering v. UK*, Concurring Opinion of Judge De Meyer.

17. *Soering v. UK*, paras. 106–11. Ultimately, after receiving assurances that Soering would not be sentenced to death, the UK fulfilled the US's extradition request. Soering was found guilty on two charges of capital murder. He was released on parole in 2019.

18. Pauwelyn 1996, 415.

19. Case of De Becker v. Belgium (App. no. 214/5), Judgment of March 27, 1962, ECtHR (Chamber), para. 8.

20. Case of Engel and Others v. the Netherlands (App. nos. 5100/71, 5101/71, 5102/71, 5354/72, 5370/72), Judgment of June 8, 1976, ECtHR (Chamber), paras. 43–51.

21. Engel and Others v. the Netherlands, paras. 97–98.

22. Engel and Others v. the Netherlands, paras. 97–98.

23. Case of Handyside v. the United Kingdom (App. no. 5493/72), Judgment of December 7, 1976, ECtHR (Chamber), para. 46.

24. *Handyside v. UK*, paras. 31, 34.

25. *Handyside v. UK*, para. 48.

26. *Handyside v. UK*, para. 50.

27. Case of Müller and Others v. Switzerland (App. no. 10737/84), Judgment of May 24, 1988, ECtHR (Chamber), paras. 36–44.

28. Case of *Sunday Times* v. the United Kingdom (App. no. 6538/74), Judgment of April 26, 1979, ECtHR (Chamber), para. 66.

29. *Sunday Times v. UK*, para. 65.

30. *Sunday Times v. UK*, para. 67.

31. The European Commission's role in gatekeeping cases is primarily responsible for the fact that no cases concerning gay rights reached the ECtHR until the 1980s. The

Commission dismissed at least six petitions involving complaints of sexual orientation discrimination prior to the *Dudgeon* case.

32. Case of Dudgeon v. the United Kingdom (App. no. 7525/76), Judgment of October 22, 1981, ECtHR (Plenary), paras. 42–45.

33. *Dudgeon v. UK*, para. 60.

34. *Dudgeon v. UK*, paras. 23–24.

35. A June 2021 article in the *Irish Post* commemorating the twenty-eighth anniversary of the decriminalization of homosexuality in Ireland named the ECtHR's *Norris* judgment as a "significant victory" in the long fight for gay and lesbian liberation: https://www.irishpost.com/news/homosexuality-was-decriminalised-in-ireland-28-years-ago-today-187564.

36. These states are Andorra, Austria, Belgium, Denmark, Estonia, Finland, France, Germany, Greece, Iceland, Ireland, Lichtenstein, Luxembourg, Malta, the Netherlands, Norway, Portugal, Slovenia, Spain, Sweden, Switzerland, and the United Kingdom.

37. These states are Croatia, the Czech Republic, Cyprus, Hungary, Italy, Latvia, Monaco, Montenegro, and San Marino.

38. P. Johnson 2011, 361.

39. Case of Rees v. the United Kingdom (App. no. 9532/81), Judgment of October 17, 1986, ECtHR (Plenary), para. 37.

40. *Rees v. UK*, paras. 41–46.

41. *Rees v. UK*, para. 31.

42. *Rees v. UK*, paras. 49–51.

43. Opinión Consultiva OC-3/83 del 8 de Septiembre de 1983, *Restricciones a la Pena de Muerte (Arts. 4.2 y 4.4 Convención Americana sobre Derechos Humanos)*, IACtHR, para. 10.

44. OC-3/83, para. 28.

45. OC-3/83, para. 76.

46. Buergenthal 2005, 8.

47. Case of Velásquez-Rodríguez v. Honduras, Judgment of July 29, 1988 (Merits), IACtHR, paras. 174, 184.

48. Velásquez-Rodríguez v. Honduras, para. 55.

49. Velásquez-Rodríguez v. Honduras, paras. 187–88.

50. García Chavarría 2019.

51. Case of Blake v. Guatemala, Judgment of January 24, 1998 (Merits), IACtHR, paras. 65–67.

52. Blake v. Guatemala, para. 86.

53. Case of Blake v. Guatemala, Judgment of July 2, 1996 (Preliminary Objections), IACtHR, para. 24.

54. Case of Blake v. Guatemala (Merits), paras. 109–16.

55. Case of Barrios Altos v. Peru, Judgment of March 14, 2001 (Merits), IACtHR, para. 51.

56. Caso de Nicholas Chapman Blake (Demanda no. 11.219), Decisión de 3 de Agosto de 1995, Comisión Interamericana de Derechos Humanos.

57. Case of Blake v. Guatemala (Merits), paras. 109–16.

58. Case of "The Last Temptation of Christ" v. Chile, Judgment of February 5, 2001 (Merits, Reparations and Costs), IACtHR, para. 45.

59. "The Last Temptation of Christ" v. Chile, paras. 65, 89.

60. "The Last Temptation of Christ" v. Chile, paras. 68–69.

61. Case of Ivcher-Bronstein v. Peru, Judgment of February 6, 2001 (Merits, Reparations and Costs), para. 62(a).

62. Ivcher-Bronstein v. Peru, para. 62(b).

63. Ivcher-Bronstein v. Peru, para. 76.

64. Ivcher-Bronstein v. Peru, para. 155.

65. Ivcher-Bronstein v. Peru, para. 191.

66. Tanganyika Law Society, Legal and Human Rights Center, and Rev. Christopher Mtikila v. Tanzania (App. nos. 009/2011 and 011/2011), Judgment of June 14, 2013, ACtHPR, para. 84.

67. *TLS, LHRC, and Rev. Christopher Mtikila v. Tanzania*, para. 82.

68. *TLS, LHRC, and Rev. Christopher Mtikila v. Tanzania*, para. 126(3).

69. African Commission on Human and Peoples' Rights v. Libya (App. no. 002/2013), Judgment of June 2, 2016, ACtHPR, para. 97(v).

70. Beneficiaries of Late Norbert Zongo, Abdoulaye Nikiema (Ablassé), Ernest Zongo, and Blaise Ilboudo and the Burkinabé Human and Peoples' Rights Movement v. Burkina Faso (App. no. 013/2011), Judgment of June 4, 2015, ACtHPR, paras. 2–4.

71. *Zongo v. Burkina Faso*, para. 32.

72. *Zongo v. Burkina Faso*, paras. 174–76.

73. *Zongo v. Burkina Faso*, para. 203(5).

74. Joint Declaration of Judges Gérard Niyungeko, Fatsah Ouguergouz, El Hadji Guisse, and Kimelabalou Aba (App. no. 013/2011), para. 6.

75. *Zongo v. Burkina Faso*, para. 156.

76. *Zongo v. Burkina Faso*, para. 117.

77. *Zongo v. Burkina Faso*, para. 203(3).

78. Lohé Issa Konaté v. Burkina Faso (App. no. 004/2013), Judgment of June 2, 2016, ACtHPR, paras. 3–6.

79. *Konaté v. Burkina Faso*, paras. 146–47.

80. *Konaté v. Burkina Faso*, para. 154.

81. *Konaté v. Burkina Faso*, paras. 158–59.

82. *Konaté v. Burkina Faso*, para. 176.

83. Lohé Issa Konaté v. Burkina Faso (App. no. 004/2013), Judgment of June 2, 2016, ACtHPR, Separate Opinion of Justices Elsie N. Thompson, Sophia A. B. Akuffo, Bernard M. Ngoepe, and Duncan Tambala, para. 4.

84. *Konaté v. Burkina Faso*, Separate Opinion, para. 5.

4. JUDGMENTS ON THE RIGHT TO FREEDOM OF EXPRESSION

1. Case of Magyar Jeti Zrt v. Hungary (App. no. 11257/16), Judgment of December 4, 2018, ECtHR (Fourth Section), para. 18.

2. Goldberg 1984; Arold 2007.

3. Voeten 2010; Sandholtz and Feldman 2019.

4. Case of Oberschlick v. Austria (App. no. 11662/85), Judgment of May 23, 1991, ECtHR (Plenary), paras. 11–19.

5. Oberschlick v. Austria, paras. 59–63.

6. Oberschlick v. Austria, para. 73.

7. Oberschlick v. Austria, Partly Dissenting Opinion of Judge Thor Vilhjalmsson; Partly Dissenting Opinion of Judge Matscher, Approved by Judge Bindschedler-Robert, para. 2.

8. Oberschlick v. Austria, Partly Dissenting Opinion of Judge Thor Vilhjalmsson.

9. Case of *Bladet Tromsø* and Stensaas v. Norway (App. no. 21980/93), Judgment of May 20, 1999, ECtHR (Grand Chamber), para. 58.

10. *Bladet Tromsø* and Stensaas v. Norway, paras. 9–14, 27, 35.

11. *Bladet Tromsø* and Stensaas v. Norway. paras. 30–31.

12. *Bladet Tromsø* and Stensaas v. Norway. para. 68.

13. *Bladet Tromsø* and Stensaas v. Norway, para. 73.

14. *Bladet Tromsø* and Stensaas v. Norway, Joint Dissenting Opinion of Judges Palm, Fuhrmann, and Baka.

15. Case of Dalban v. Romania (App. no. 28114/95), Judgment of September 28, 1999, ECtHR (Grand Chamber), para. 44.

16. Dalban v. Romania, para. 49.

17. See Case of Lingens v. Austria (App. no. 9815/82), Judgment of July 8, 1986, para. 42.

18. Case of Perna v. Italy (App. no. 48898/99), Judgment of July 25, 2001, ECtHR (Second Section), paras. 6–11.

19. Perna v. Italy, paras. 40–41.

20. Case of Perna v. Italy (App. no. 48898/99), Judgment of May 6, 2003, ECtHR (Grand Chamber), para. 47.

21. Case of Cumpănă and Mazăre v. Romania (App. no. 33348/96), Judgment of June 10, 2003, ECtHR (Second Section), para. 25.

22. Cumpănă and Mazăre v. Romania, para. 55.

23. Cumpănă and Mazăre v. Romania, Joint Dissenting Opinion of Judges Costa and Thomassen.

24. Case of Cumpănă and Mazăre v. Romania (App. no. 33348/96), Judgment of December 17, 2004, ECtHR (Grand Chamber), paras. 94, 120.

25. High Level Conference on the Future of the ECtHR, 2012, Brighton Declaration, para. 5.

26. Case of Sanoma Uitgevers B.V. v. the Netherlands (App. no. 38224/03), Judgment of March 31, 2009, ECtHR (Third Section), paras. 5–18.

27. Sanoma Uitgevers B.V. v. the Netherlands, para. 44.

28. Sanoma Uitgevers B.V. v. the Netherlands, para. 60.

29. Case of Sanoma Uitgevers B.V. v. the Netherlands (App. no. 38224/03), Judgment of September 14, 20010, ECtHR (Grand Chamber), para. 92.

30. Sanoma Uitgevers B.V. v. the Netherlands (Grand Chamber), Concurring Opinion of Judge Myjer.

31. Case of Kasabova v. Bulgaria (App. no. 22385/03), Judgment of April 19, 2011, ECtHR (Fourth Section), para. 71.

32. Kasabova v. Bulgaria, para. 68.

33. Case of Alex Springer AG v. Germany (App. no. 399954/08), Judgment of February 7, 2012, ECtHR (Grand Chamber), paras. 89–95.

34. Alex Springer AG v. Germany, para. 88.

35. Case of Medžlis Islamske Zajednice Brčko and Others v. Bosnia and Herzegovina (App. no. 17224/11), Judgment of October 13, 2015, ECtHR (Fourth Section), paras. 5–17.

36. *Brčko and Others v. Bosnia and Herzegovina*, para. 35.

37. *Brčko and Others v. Bosnia and Herzegovina*, Joint Dissenting Opinion of Judges Nicolaou, Tsotsoria, and Vehabović.

38. Case of Herrera-Ulloa v. Costa Rica, Judgment of July 2, 2004 (Preliminary Objections, Merits, Reparations and Costs), IACtHR, para. 66(a).

39. Herrera-Ulloa v. Costa Rica, paras. 14–26.

40. Herrera-Ulloa v. Costa Rica, para. 103(f).

41. Herrera-Ulloa v. Costa Rica, paras. 66(c–d), 137(4a).

42. Herrera-Ulloa v. Costa Rica, para. 133.

43. Case of Ricardo Canese v. Paraguay, Judgment of August 31, 2004 (Merits, Reparations and Costs), IACtHR, para. 2.

44. *Canese v. Paraguay*, para. 71.

45. *Canese v. Paraguay*, para. 87.

46. *Canese v. Paraguay*, paras. 89–90.

47. *Canese v. Paraguay*, para. 106.

48. Case of Palamara-Iribarne v. Chile, Judgment of November 22, 2005 (Merits, Reparations and Costs), IACtHR, para. 88.

49. Palamara-Iribarne v. Chile, para. 63(18).

50. Palamara-Iribarne v. Chile, para. 75.

51. Case of Mémoli v. Argentina, Judgment of August 22, 2013 (Preliminary objections, Merits, Reparations and Costs), IACtHR, para. 139.

52. Mémoli v. Argentina, paras. 114–16.

53. Mémoli v. Argentina, para. 140.

54. Mémoli v. Argentina, Joint Partially Dissenting Opinion of Judges Manuel E. Ventura Robles, Eduardo Vio Grossi, and Eduardo Ferrer Mac-Gregor Poisot, Section I.

55. Mémoli v. Argentina, para. 146.

56. The 2011 *Fonteveccia and D'Amico v. Argentina* case involving President Carlos Menem (discussed in chapter 2) is another example of the IACtHR's greater scrutiny of restrictions on expression targeted at public officials relative to private citizens.

57. Case of Álvarez Ramos v. Venezuela, Judgment of August 30, 2019 (Preliminary objections, Merits, Reparations and Costs), IACtHR, para. 16.

58. Álvarez Ramos v. Venezuela, para. 1.

59. Álvarez Ramos v. Venezuela, para. 109.

60. Álvarez Ramos v. Venezuela, para. 129.

61. Álvarez Ramos v. Venezuela, para. 124.

62. Human Rights Watch 2012; Amnesty International 2013.

63. Amnesty International 2013, 6.

64. Human Rights Watch 2016.

65. Ingabire Victoire Umuhoza v. Rwanda (App. no. 003/2014), Ruling on Jurisdiction, Decision of June 3, 2016, ACtHPR, para. 4.

66. Windridge 2018, 249.

67. Ingabire Victoire Umuhoza v. Rwanda, paras. 36–37.

68. Ingabire Victoire Umuhoza v. Rwanda, para. 52.

69. Ingabire Victoire Umuhoza v. Rwanda, paras. 63–65.

70. Ingabire Victoire Umuhoza v. Rwanda, paras. 68–69.

71. Ingabire Victoire Umuhoza v. Rwanda, Dissenting Opinion of Judges Gérard Niyungeko and Augustino S. L. Ramadhani, para. 13.

72. Ingabire Victoire Umuhoza v. Rwanda (App. no. 003/2014), Judgment of November 24, 2017, ACtHPR, para. 172.

73. Ingabire Victoire Umuhoza v. Rwanda (App. no. 003/2014), Judgment on Reparations of December 7, 2018, ACtHPR, para. 74.

74. Ingabire Victoire Umuhoza v. Rwanda (2017), para. 167.

75. The ACtHPR again asserted its authority to hear prewithdrawal cases involving freedom of expression submitted by Rwandan nationals in the 2021 case of *Laurent Munyandilikirwa v. Rwanda* (App. no. 023/2015), although this case was ultimately dismissed owing to lack of exhaustion of domestic remedies.

76. Sébastien Germain Marie Aikoué Ajavon v. Republic of Benin (App. no. 013/2017), Provisional Measures Order of December 7, 2018, ACtHPR, paras. 1–9.

77. Sébastien Germain Marie Aikoué Ajavon v. Republic of Benin (App. no. 013/2017), Judgment of March 29, 2019, ACtHPR, para. 292.

78. France 24 2019.

79. The only other case submitted to the ACtHPR that has alleged violations of the freedom of expression in the context of government repression of protests was *Emil Touray and Others v. Republic of Ghana* (App. no. 026/2020). In 2022, the ACtHPR declined to admit this case in accordance with international legal custom because it was already being tried by the ECOWAS Court.

80. Sébastien Germain Marie Aikoué Ajavon v. Republic of Benin (App. no. 062/2019), Provisional Measures Order of April 17, 2020, ACtHPR, operative para. 5.

81. IJRC 2020.

82. Sébastien Germain Marie Aikoué Ajavon v. Republic of Benin (App. no. 062/2019), Judgment of December 4, 2020, ACtHPR, para. 369.

83. *Ajavon v. Republic of Benin* (2020), paras. 121–28.

84. Sébastien Germain Marie Aikoué Ajavon v. Republic of Benin (App. no. 013/2017), Separate Opinion of Judge Gerard Niyungeko, March 29, 2019, ACtHPR, para. 29.

85. Côte d'Ivoire's withdrawal is discussed in chapter 2.

86. XYZ v. Benin (App. no. 010/2020), Judgment of November 27, 2020, ACtHPR, para. 15.

87. XYZ v. Benin, paras. 107–21.

88. XYZ v. Benin, para. 159 (xiv–xv).

89. Houngue Éric Noudehouenou v. Republic of Benin (App. no. 028/2020), Judgment of December 1, 2022, ACtHPR, paras. 114, 203.

90. In October 2021, Benin's minister for justice and legislation, Séverin Maxime Quenum, met with the ACtHPR president, Justice Imani Daud Aboud, to communicate Benin's commitment to "strengthening human rights and good governance, and that it will work very closely with the [ACtHPR] to attain this objective." Minister Quenum urged the Court to "undertake reforms to make it more effective by reviewing the structure of the Court and its Registry as well as conditions of service of judges." Benin has not yet announced any plans to reverse its withdrawal. See http://www.african-court.org/wpafc/republic-of-benin-to-work-closely-with-the-african-court-on-human-and-peoples-right-to-strengthen-human-rights/.

91. ACtHPR lawyer, interview by the author, Arusha, Tanzania, June 2024.

5. JUDGMENTS ON PERSONAL INTEGRITY RIGHTS

1. *Querella 4591/2010*, N.N. por genocidio y/o crímenes de lesa humanidad cometidos en España por la dictadura franquista, Juzgado Nacional en lo Criminal y Correccional Federal Nro. 1, Buenos Aires, Argentina.

2. Baquero 2020.

3. Sikkink 2011.

4. Binder 2011; Ceia 2015.

5. Van Pachtenbeke and Haeck 2010; Heri 2014; Moynihan 2016.

6. Claude 2010; Citroni 2016, 37.

7. ECtHR judge, interview by the author, Strasbourg, France, June 2019.

8. McCann and Others v. the UK (App. no. 1898491), ECtHR, Judgment of September 27, 1995, paras. 157–62.

9. Kaya v. Turkey (App. nos. 158/1996/777/978), ECtHR, Judgment of February 19, 1998, paras. 76–77, 92.

10. Tanrikulu v. Turkey (App. no. 23763/94), ECtHR, Judgment of July 8, 1999, paras. 49–51, 99, 110–11, 120–21.

11. Kurt v. Turkey (App. no. 24276/94), ECtHR, Judgment of May 25, 1998, paras. 106–9, 116–17, 133.

12. Caraher v. the United Kingdom (App. no. 24520/94), ECtHR, Judgment of January 11, 2000.

13. See Tomasi v. France (App. no. 12850/87), Ribitsch v. Austria (App. no. 18896/91).

14. Yagiz v. Turkey (App. no. 19092/91), ECtHR, Judgment of August 7, 1996, para. 28.

15. *Minutes of the 89th Session of the Committee of Ministers*, CM (91) PV 4 (1991), 21–27.

16. CM (91) PV 4 (1991), 39, 24.

17. CM (91) PV 4 (1991), 9.

18. Göç v. Turkey (App. no. 36590/97), ECtHR, Judgment of April 6, 2000.

19. Labita v. Italy (App. no. 26772/95), ECtHR, Judgment of April 6, 2000.

20. See also Loizidou v. Turkey (App. no. 15318/89).

21. Blečič v. Croatia (App. no. 59532/00), ECHR 2006 [13–33].

22. Blečič v. Croatia, para. 92.

23. Šilih v. Slovenia (App. no. 71463/01), Judgment of April 9, 2009, paras. 147, 159.

24. Šilih v. Slovenia, para. 152.

25. Šilih v. Slovenia, paras. 114–18.

26. Šilih v. Slovenia, para. 159.

27. Šilih v. Slovenia, para. 163.

28. ECtHR lawyers, interview by the author, Strasbourg, France, June 2019.

29. ECtHR lawyer, interview by the author, Strasbourg, France, June 2019.

30. The African Charter and its Protocol do not actually codify any time limits for submitting applications, but ACtHPR judges have developed a practice of recognizing a six-month rule. As of the implementation of Protocol 15 to the European Convention in February 2022, applicants must now submit petitions to the Court within four months of exhausting domestic remedies.

31. Varnava and Others v. Turkey (App. nos. 16064/90, 16065/90, 16066/90, 16068/90, 16069/90, 16070/90, 16071/90, 16072/90 and 16073/90), ECtHR, Judgment of September 18, 2009, paras. 154–59.

32. Varnava and Others v. Turkey, paras. 157, 158.

33. Álvarez 2014, 143–46.

34. Hilbink 2015, 194.

35. Antonio Gutiérrez Dorado and Carmen Dorado Ortiz v. Spain (App. no. 30141/09), ECHR, Judgment of March 27, 2012, paras. 34–36.

36. Jimeno 2017.

37. Citroni 2016, 37.

38. Association "21 December 1989" and Others v. Romania (App. no. 33810/07), ECtHR, Judgment of May 4, 2011, para. 118; Mocanu and Others v. Romania (App. nos. 10865/09, 45885/07, 32431/08), ECtHR, Judgment of September 17, 2014, paras. 204, 352.

39. Janowiec and Others v. Russia (App. nos. 55508/07 and 29520/09), ECtHR, Judgment of October 21, 2013.

40. Janowiec and Others v. Russia, para. 150.

41. Janowiec and Others v. Russia, para. 160.

42. Chong and Others v. the United Kingdom (App. no. 29753/16), ECtHR, Decision of September 11, 2018.

43. Grinenko v. Ukraine (App. no. 33627/06), ECtHR, Judgment of November 15, 2012, para. 55.

44. Grinenko v. Ukraine, paras. 58, 62–63.

45. Askhabova v. Russia (App. no. 54765/09), ECtHR, Judgment of April 4, 2013, para. 131.

46. Askhabova v. Russia, para. 133.

47. Askhabova v. Russia, paras. 135–38.

48. Askhabova v. Russia, paras. 143, 160–67.

49. ECtHR Press Unit 2021.

50. ECtHR judge, interview by the author, Strasbourg, France, June 2019.

51. Case of Broniowski v. Poland (App. no. 31443/96), Judgment of June 22, 2004, ECtHR Grand Chamber.

52. These cases are Ilaşcu and Others v. Moldova and Russia (App. no. 48787/99), Neshkov and Others v. Bulgaria (App. nos. 36925/10, 21487/12, 72893/12, 73196/12, 77718/12,

and 9717/13), Varga and Others v. Hungary (App. nos. 14097/12, 45135, 73712/12, 34001/13, 44055/13, and 64586/13), Sukachov v. Ukraine (App. no. 14057/17), Ananyev and Others v. Russia (App. nos. 42525/07 and 60800/08), Rezmiveş and Others v. Romania (App. nos. 61467/12, 39516/13, 48231/13, 68191/13), and Torreggiani and Others v. Italy (App. nos. 43517/09, 35315/10, 37818/10, 46882/09, 55400/09, 57875/09, 61535/09).

53. Case of Tunikova and Others v. Russia (App. nos. 55794/16, 53118/17, 27484/18, and 28011/19), Judgment of December 14, 2021, ECtHR Third Section.

54. Case of Tunikova and Others v. Russia, paras. 151–58.

55. See, for example, González et al. ("Cotton Field") v. Mexico, Judgment of November 16, 2009; Rosendo Cantú et al. v. Mexico, Judgment of August 31, 2010; Vicky Hernández et al. v. Honduras, Judgment of March 26, 2021.

56. Juan Humberto Sánchez v. Honduras, IACtHR, Judgment of June 7, 2003, para. 106.

57. *Sánchez v. Honduras*, paras. 100–111.

58. 19 Merchants v. Colombia, IACtHR, Judgment of July 5, 2005, para. 65.

59. Norín Catrimán et al. v. Chile, IACtHR, Judgment of May 29, 2014, para. 98.

60. *Catrimán et al. v. Chile*, paras. 390–400.

61. 19 Merchants v. Colombia, operative paras. 8–9.

62. Tibi v. Ecuador, IACtHR, Judgment of September 7, 2004, operative para. 13.

63. Aroca Palma and Others v. Ecuador (Series C, No. 2022), IACtHR, Judgment of November 8, 2022.

64. See Contesse 2017; Soley and Steininger 2018; Contesse 2019.

65. These cases are Landaeta Mejías Brothers et al. v. Venezuela, Judgment of August 27, 2014; Ortiz Hernández et al. v. Venezuela, Judgment of August 22, 2017; López Soto et al. v. Venezuela, Judgment of September 26, 2018; Díaz Loreto et al. v. Venezuela, Judgment of November 19, 2019; Olivares Muñoz et al. v. Venezuela, Judgment of November 10, 2020; Mota Abarullo et al. v. Venezuela, Judgment of November 18, 2020; Guerrero, Molina et al. v. Venezuela, Judgment of June 3, 2021; and González et al. v. Venezuela, Judgment of September 20, 2021.

66. Serrano-Cruz Sisters v. El Salvador, IACtHR, Judgment of March 1, 2005, paras. 113–15, 172, 218.

67. Serrano-Cruz Sisters v. El Salvador, operative paras. 6–14.

68. ECtHR lawyer, interview by the author, Strasbourg, France, June 2019.

69. IACtHR lawyer, Skype interview by the author, May 2020.

70. Gelman v. Uruguay, IACtHR, Judgment of February 24, 2011, paras. 244–66.

71. Gelman v. Uruguay, operative para. 11.

72. Almonacid-Arellano et al. v. Chile, IACtHR, Judgment of September 26, 2006, paras. 49–59, 160; operative paras. 5–6.

73. Almonacid-Arellano et al. v. Chile, para. 124.

74. González Domínguez 2017.

75. IACtHR lawyer, Skype interview by the author, May 2020.

76. Binder 2011, 1204.

77. Dulitzky 2015.

78. Gonzalez-Ocantos 2018.

79. Because of the ECtHR's practice of not publishing the majority of its inadmissibility decisions, it is unfortunately impossible to gather comparative statistics on the number of continuing rights violation petitions the ECtHR has admitted/rejected.

80. Ally Rajabu and Others v. United Republic of Tanzania (App. no. 007/2015), Judgment of November 28, 2019, para. 96.

81. *Rajabu and Others v. Tanzania*, paras. 114–19, operative paras. xv–xvi.

82. Sébastien Germain Marie Aikoué Ajavon v. Benin (App. no. 062/2019), Judgment of December 3, 2020, paras. 158, 172–73.

83. Chananja Luchagula v. United Republic of Tanzania (App. no. 039/2016), Ruling on Jurisdiction and Admissibility of September 25, 2020.

84. While the African Charter does not specify a time limit for submitting petitions following the exhaustion of domestic remedies, the ACtHPR has adopted the six-month rule based on existing international standards.

85. The ACtHPR's judgment is unclear as to why the wife and children were considered to be illegally residing in Tanzania at their time of arrest, although their choice to reside with the applicant in Dar es Salaam rather than designated refugee camps may have invalidated their refugee status.

86. Lucien Ikili Rashidi v. United Republic of Tanzania (App. no. 009/2015), Judgment of March 28, 2019, paras. 50–56.

87. *Rashidi v. Tanzania*, operative para. 160.

88. Andrew Ambrose Cheusi v. United Republic of Tanzania (App. no. 004/2015), Judgment of June 26, 2020, paras. 131–36.

89. Léon Mugesera v. Republic of Rwanda (App. no. 012/2017), Judgment of November 27, 2020, paras. 6–9.

90. *Mugesera v. Rwanda*, para. 88.

91. ACtHPR judge, interview by the author, Arusha, Tanzania, June 2024.

92. ACtHPR lawyer, interview by the author, Arusha, Tanzania, June 2024.

93. ACtHPR lawyer, interview by the author, Arusha, Tanzania, June 2024.

6. JUDGMENTS ON GENDER IDENTITY AND SEXUAL ORIENTATION DISCRIMINATION

1. Lopez 2021.

2. Cooper 2011; Shahid 2017.

3. See Dudgeon v. the United Kingdom (1981) and Norris v. Ireland (1988). The Court again upheld this position in Modinos v. Cyprus (App. no. 15070/89), Judgment of April 22, 1993.

4. See Rees v. the United Kingdom (1986), discussed in chapter 3.

5. Cossey v. the United Kingdom (App. no. 10843/84), Judgment of September 27, 1990.

6. Cossey v. the United Kingdom, paras. 38–42.

7. Cossey v. the United Kingdom, Joint Partly Dissenting Opinion of Judges MacDonald and Spielmann, para. 2.

8. Cossey v. the United Kingdom, Dissenting Opinion of Judge Martens, para. 1.1.

9. Cossey v. the United Kingdom, Dissenting Opinion of Judge Martens, para. 5.5.

10. B. v. France (App. no. 13343/87), Judgment of March 25, 1992, ECtHR, paras. 59–63.

11. Case of Lustig-Prean and Beckett v. the United Kingdom (App. no. 31417/96; 32377/96), Judgment of September 27, 1999, ECtHR (Third Section), para. 37.

12. Case of Smith and Grady v. the United Kingdom (App. no. 33985/96; 33986/96), Judgment of September 27, 1999, ECtHR (Third Section), paras. 11–28; Lustig-Prean and Beckett v. the United Kingdom, paras. 11–21.

13. Smith and Grady v. the United Kingdom, paras. 77–78; Lustig-Prean and Beckett v. the United Kingdom, paras. 69–71.

14. Smith and Grady v. the United Kingdom, paras. 88–112; Lustig-Prean and Beckett v. the United Kingdom, paras. 82–105.

15. The ECtHR later upheld this interpretation in *Perkins v. the United Kingdom* (App. no. 43208/98; 44875/98), where the applicants' discharges from the armed forces were found to violate Article 8 but the Court again declined to rule on a potential Article 14 violation.

16. Case of Salgueiro da Silva Mouta v. Portugal (App. no. 33290/96), Judgment of December 21, 1999, ECtHR (Fourth Section).

17. Case of I. v. the United Kingdom (App. no. 25680/94), Judgment of July 11, 2002, ECtHR (Grand Chamber), paras. 12–19; case of Christine Goodwin v. the United Kingdom (App. no. 28957/95), Judgment of July 11, 2002, ECtHR (Grand Chamber), paras. 12–19.

18. This precedent mandating that states allow transgender individuals to amend the sex listed on official identification documents has since been repeatedly upheld, notably in *Grant v. the United Kingdom* (App. no. 32570/03), Judgment of May 23, 2006, and *L. v. Lithuania* (App. no. 27527/03), Judgment of September 1,1 2007.

19. I. v. the United Kingdom, para. 80; Christine Goodwin v. the United Kingdom, para. 100.

20. Both these cases had been relinquished to the Grand Chamber by the Chamber formation to which they were originally assigned. There was no lower Chamber judgment in either case.

21. I. v. the United Kingdom (n 25), at 85–88; Christine Goodwin v. the United Kingdom (n 25), at 105–8.

22. Case of Karner v. Austria (App. no. 40016/98), Judgment of July 24, 2003, ECtHR (First Section), paras. 38–41.

23. Karner v. Austria, para. 41.

24. Case of E. B. v. France (App. no. 43546/02), Judgment of January 22, 2008, ECtHR (Grand Chamber).

25. Case of Kozak v. Poland (App. no. 13102/02), Judgment of March 2, 2010, ECtHR (Fourth Section).

26. These states were Andorra, Austria, the Czech Republic, Denmark, Finland, Germany, Hungary, Ireland, Luxembourg, Slovenia, Switzerland, and the United Kingdom.

27. Case of Parry v. the United Kingdom (App. no. 42971/05), Judgment of November 28, 2006, ECtHR (Fourth Section), Section B; case of R. and F. v. the United Kingdom (App. no. 35748/05), Judgment of November 28, 2006, ECtHR (Fourth Section), Section B.

28. The ECtHR again upheld this precedent in 2014 in *Hämäläinen v. Finland* (App. no. 37359/09), in which Finland refused to allow the transgender applicant to change her legal sex identification unless her marriage to her spouse, who was a cisgender woman, was first converted into a civil partnership. The ECtHR found no violation of Articles 8, 14, or 12 in this case.

29. Case of Schalk and Kopf v. Austria (App. no. 30141/04), Judgment of June 24, 2010, ECtHR (First Section), para. 62.

30. Case of Identoba and Others v. Georgia (App. no. 73235/12), Judgment of May 12, 2015, ECtHR (Fourth Section), paras. 6–9, 73.

31. Identoba and Others v. Georgia, para. 77.

32. Alekseyev v. Russia, App. no. 4916/07, 25924/09, and 14599/09, Judgment of October 21, 2010, ECtHR, para. 83.

33. Harding 2014.

34. Batchelor 2017; Radio Free Europe 2017.

35. Glas 2019.

36. Case of Bayev and Others v. Russia (App. no. 67667/09; 44092/12; 56717/12), Judgment of June 20, 2017, ECtHR (Third Section), paras. 82–92.

37. In 2019 the ECtHR also found Russia in violation of the freedom of assembly (Article 11) and prohibition of discrimination (Article 14) for refusing to allow various LGBT activism organizations to register for nonprofit status: Case of Zhdanov and Others v. Russia (App. no. 12200/08; 35949/11; 58282/12), Judgment of July 16, 2019, ECtHR (Third Section).

38. The states that recognized full marriage rights as of summer 2021 were Austria, Belgium, Denmark, Finland, France, Germany, Iceland, Ireland, Luxembourg, Malta, the Netherlands, Norway, Portugal, Spain, Sweden, and the United Kingdom. The states that recognized other forms of same-sex partnership (but not the full rights of marriage) were Andorra, Croatia, Cyprus, the Czech Republic, Estonia, Greece, Hungary, Italy, Liechtenstein, Monaco, Montenegro, San Marino, Slovenia, and Switzerland.

39. Case of Fedotova and Others v. Russia (App. no. 40792/10; 30538/14; 43439/14), Judgment of July 13, 2021, ECtHR (Third Section), para. 51.

40. Fedotova and Others v. Russia, para. 57.

41. Fedotova and Others v. Russia, para. 52.

42. Benvenisti 1999; Brauch 2005.

43. Helfer and Voeten 2014.

44. Fedotova and Others v. Russia, Judgment of July 13, 2021, paras. 62–64, operative para. 5.

45. See also case of R. K. v. Hungary (App. no. 54006/20), Judgment of June 22, 2023, ECtHR (First Section).

46. Homosexuality is illegal in the Caribbean states of Grenada, Jamaica, Saint Lucia, and Saint Vincent and the Grenadines, in addition to the South American state of Guyana. There are signs of a regional shift: Antigua and Barbuda, Barbados, and Saint Kitts and Nevis legalized homosexuality in 2022, followed by Dominica in 2024.

47. Case of Atala Riffo and Daughters v. Chile (Merits, Reparations and Costs), Judgment of February 24, 2012, IACtHR, para. 31.

48. Atala Riffo and Daughters v. Chile, para. 57.

49. Atala Riffo and Daughters v. Chile, paras. 87–95.

50. Atala Riffo and Daughters v. Chile, para. 135.

51. Atala Riffo and Daughters v. Chile, para. 145.

52. Atala Riffo and Daughters v. Chile, paras. 272, 314.

53. Case of Duque v. Colombia (Preliminary Objections, Merits, Reparations and Costs), Judgment of February 26, 2016, IACtHR.

54. Case of Flor Freire v. Ecuador (Preliminary Objections, Merits, Reparations and Costs), Judgment of August 31, 2016, IACtHR, paras. 102–3.

55. Flor Freire v. Ecuador, paras. 130–36.

56. Flor Freire v. Ecuador, operative paras. 9–13.

57. Advisory Opinion OC-24/17 of November 24, 2017, requested by the Republic of Costa Rica, *Gender Identity, and Equality and Non-Discrimination of Same-Sex Couples: State Obligations Concerning Change of Name, Gender Identity, and Rights Derived from a Relationship Between Same-Sex Couples (Interpretation and Scope of Articles 1(1), 3, 7, 11(2), 13, 17, 18, and 24, in relation to Article 1, of the American Convention on Human Rights)*, para. 3.

58. OC-24/17, Section IX, paras. 2–8.

59. OC-24/17, para. 193.

60. OC-24/17, Separate Opinion of Judge Eduardo Vio Grossi, paras. 66–71.

61. OC-24/17, Separate Opinion, paras. 84–85.

62. OC-24/17, Separate Opinion, para. 97.

63. OC-24/17, Separate Opinion, para. 108.

64. OC-24/17, Separate Opinion, para. 71.

65. Contesse 2021.

66. See Statement from the Governments of Argentina, Brazil, Chile, Colombia, and Paraguay, submitted to the Inter-American Commission on Human Rights (April 11, 2019), at https://www.mre.gov.py/index.php/noticias-de-embajadas-y-consulados/gobiernos-de-argentina-brasil-chile-colombia-y-paraguay-se-manifiestan-sobre-el-sistema-interamericano-de-derechos-humanos. See also Contesse 2021, 365–69.

67. Argentina, Bolivia, and Uruguay implemented legislation codifying name and gender change rights prior to OC-24/17: See Alvarado 2018; Reid 2018; Ghoshal 2018; Human Rights Campaign 2020.

68. Case of Ramírez Escobar and Others v. Guatemala (Merits, Reparations and Costs), Judgment of March 9, 2018, IACtHR, paras. 61–71. See also *Report of a Fact-Finding Mission to Guatemala in Relation to Intercountry Adoption*, Hague Conference on Private International Law (May 2007).

69. Ramírez Escobar and Others v. Guatemala, Judgment of March 9, 2018, paras. 83–113.

70. Ramírez Escobar and Others v. Guatemala, paras. 95–98, 300–303.

71. Ramírez Escobar and Others v. Guatemala, operative para. 5. The Court ruled that Guatemala violated a number of additional rights in this case, including the rights to fair trial, judicial protection, personal liberty, personal integrity, and the right to an identity and name.

72. See, e.g., González and Others ("Cotton Fields") v. México, Judgment of November 16, 2009, involving a pattern of gender-based violence ("feminicidio").

73. Case of Azul Rojas Marín et al. v. Peru (Preliminary Objections, Merits, Reparations and Costs), Judgment of March 12, 2020, IACtHR, paras. 52–53.

74. *Marín et al. v. Peru*, paras. 60–69.

75. *Marín et al. v. Peru*, para. 96.

76. *Marín et al. v. Peru*, operative paras. 4–17.

77. Case of Pavez Pavez v. Chile (Merits, Reparations and Costs), Judgment of February 4, 2022, IACtHR.

78. Guzmán (2022).

79. Reuters 2021.

80. See, e.g., Lohé Issa Konaté v. Republic of Burkina Faso (App. no. 004/2013), Judgment of June 2, 2016, ACtHPR; Houngue Eric Noudehouenou v. Republic of Benin (App. no. 003/2020), Judgment of December 4, 2020, ACtHPR.

81. African Charter on Human and People's Rights, Article 18(2).

82. Murray and Viljoen 2007, 93.

83. Murray and Viljoen 2007, 94.

84. P. Johnson 2013, 258.

85. Cited in Murray and Viljoen 2007, 106.

86. ACHPR/Res.275(LV)2014, Resolution on Protection Against Violence and Other Human Rights Violations Against Persons on the Basis of Their Real or Imputed Sexual Orientation or Gender Identity, 55th Ordinary Session, Luanda, Angola, April 28 to May 12, 2014.

87. General Comment No. 4 on the African Charter on Human and Peoples' Rights: The Right to Redress for Victims of Torture and Other Cruel, Inhuman, or Degrading Punishment or Treatment (Article 5), 21st Extra-Ordinary Session of the African Commission on Human and Peoples' Rights, Banjul, the Gambia, February 23 to March 4, 2017, para. 59.

CONCLUSION

1. ECtHR judge, interview by the author, Strasbourg, France, June 2019.

2. ECtHR judge, interview by the author, Strasbourg, France, June 2019.

3. The African Commission on Human and Peoples' Rights v. Republic of Kenya (App. no. 006/2012), Judgment of June 22, 2022, ACtHPR.

4. ACtHPR judge, interview by the author, Arusha, Tanzania, June 2024.

5. ACtHPR judge, interview by the author, Arusha, Tanzania, June 2024.

6. ACtHPR lawyer, interview by the author, Arusha, Tanzania, June 2024.

7. Statement by ECtHR Judge Anja Seibert-Fohr at the Second International Human Rights Forum in Strasbourg, France, March 2021.

Works Cited

Abbott, Kenneth W., and Duncan Snidal. 2000. "Hard and Soft Law in International Governance." *International Organization* 54 (3): 421–56.

Africanews. 2020. "Ivory Coast Withdraws from African Human Rights and Peoples Court." https://www.africanews.com/2020/04/30/ ivory-coast-withdraws-from-african-human-rights-and-peoples-court//.

Akinyemi, A. Bolaji. 1985. "The African Charter on Human and Peoples' Rights: An Overview." *Indian Journal of Political Science* 46 (2): 207–38.

Alter, Karen J., Laurence R. Helfer, and Mikael Rask Madsen. 2016. "How Context Shapes the Authority of International Courts." *Law and Contemporary Problems* 79 (1): 1–36.

Alter, Karen J., Laurence R. Helfer, and Jacqueline McAllister. 2013. "A New International Human Rights Court for West Africa: The ECOWAS Community Court of Justice." *American Journal of International Law* 107:737–79.

Alvarado, Laura. 2018. "Transgender Population in Costa Rica Will Be Able to Choose the Name Shown in Their ID." *Costa Rica Star News*. https://news.co.cr/ transgender–population–in–costa–rica–will–be–able–to–choose–the–name– shown–in–their–id/73032/.

Álvarez, Javier Chinchón. 2014. "La competencia ratione temporis del Tribunal Europeo de Derechos Humanos sobre la obligación de investigar (art. 2. derecho a la vida): De *De Becker c. Bélgica* a *Canales Bermejo c. España.*" *Revista Española de Derecho Internacional* 66 (1): 125–58.

Amnesty International. 2013. *Rwanda: Justice in Jeopardy; The First Instance Trial of Victoire Ingabire*. https://www.amnesty.org/en/documents/afr47/001/2013/en/.

Anagnostou, Dia, and Alina Mungiu-Pippidi. 2014. "Domestic Implementation of Human Rights Judgments in Europe: Legal Infrastructure and Government Effectiveness Matter." *European Journal of International Law* 25 (1): 205–27.

Anami, Luke. 2021. "Tanzania Reverses Decision to Withdraw from the African Court." *East African*. https://www.theeastafrican.co.ke/tea/news/east-africa/ tanzania-reverses-decision-to-withdraw-from-the-african-court-3415592.

Antkowiak, Thomas M. 2007. "Remedial Approaches to Human Rights Violations: The Inter-American Court of Human Rights and Beyond." *Columbia Journal of Transnational Law* 46:351–419.

Arnaiz, Alejandro Saiz. 2018. "Estrasburgo en Buenos Aires: Citas irrelevantes y omisiones sobresalientes de la doctrina del Tribunal Europeo de Derechos Humanos para justificar el incumplimiento por la Corte Suprema de Justicia de la Nación Argentina de una sentencia de la Corte Interamericana." In *Human Rights in a Global World: Essays in Honor of Luis López Guerra*, edited by G. Raimondi, I. Motoc, P. P. Vilanova, and C. M. Gómez. Wolf Legal.

Arnardóttir, Oddný Mjöll. 2018. "The Brighton Aftermath and the Changing Role of the European Court of Human Rights." *Journal of International Dispute Settlement* 9 (2): 223–39.

Arold, Nina-Louisa. 2007. "The European Court of Human Rights as an Example of Convergence." *Nordic Journal of International Law* 76 (2–3): 305–22.

Associated Press. 2003. "Carlos Roberto Reina, 77, President of Honduras in the 1990's." *New York Times*. https://www.nytimes.com/2003/08/21/world/carlos-roberto-reina-77-president-of-honduras-in-the-1990-s.html.

Baquero, Juan Miguel. 2020. "Diez años de Querella Argentina: El único juicio en el mundo contra el franquismo." *ElDiario.es*. https://www.eldiario.es/sociedad/querella-argentina-unico-juicio-franquismo_1_2258964.html.

Barnett, Michael N., and Martha Finnemore. 1999. "The Politics, Power, and Pathologies of International Organizations." *International Organization* 53 (4): 699–732.

Barnett, Michael N., and Martha Finnemore. 2005. "The Power of Liberal International Organizations." In *Power in Global Governance*, edited by Michael Barnett and Raymond Duvall. Cambridge University Press.

Batchelor, Tom. 2017. "Russia Cancels Council of Europe Payments After Saying It Is 'Persecuted.'" *Independent*. https://www.independent.co.uk/news/world/europe/russia-cancels-council-europe-payment-members-persecuted-a7816951.html.

Bates, Ed. 2010. *The Evolution of the European Convention on Human Rights: From Its Inception to the Creation of a Permanent Court of Human Rights*. Oxford University Press.

Bates, Ed. 2012. "The Brighton Declaration and the 'Meddling Court.'" *UK Human Rights Blog*. https://ukhumanrightsblog.com/2012/04/22/the-brighton-declaration-and-the-meddling-court/.

Bates, Ed. 2015. "The Continued Failure to Implement Hirst v UK." *EJIL: Talk!* https://www.ejiltalk.org/the-continued-failure-to-implement-hirst-v-uk/.

Benvenisti, Eyal. 1999. "Margin of Appreciation, Consensus, and Universal Standards." *New York University Journal of International Law and Politics* 31 (4): 843–54.

Bermúdez, Ángel. 2018. "Por qué en América Latina no ha habido una integración regional como en la Unión Europea." https://www.bbc.com/mundo/noticias-america-latina-43916189.

Bertelli, Anthony M. 2006. "Delegating to the Quango: Ex Ante and Ex Post Ministerial Constraints." *Governance* 19 (2): 229–49.

Binder, Christina. 2011. "The Prohibition of Amnesties by the Inter-American Court of Human Rights." *German Law Journal* 12:1203–30.

Bodansky, Daniel. 2008. "Legitimacy." In *The Oxford Handbook of International Environmental Law*, edited by Daniel Bodansky, Jutta Brunnée, and Ellen Hey. Oxford University Press.

Brauch, Jeffrey A. 2005. "The Margin of Appreciation and the Jurisprudence of the European Court of Human Rights: Threat to the Rule of Law." *Columbia Journal of European Law* 11 (1): 113–50.

Buergenthal, Thomas. 1980. "The American and European Conventions on Human Rights: Similarities and Differences." *American University Law Review* 30:155–66.

Buergenthal, Thomas. 2005. "Remembering the Early Years of the Inter-American Court of Human Rights." *Center for Human Rights and Global Justice, New York University School of Law* 1:1–17.

Buergenthal, Thomas, Robert E. Norris, and Dinah Shelton. 1982. *Protecting Human Rights in the Americas: Selected Problems*. N. P. Engel.

Cabranes, José A. 1968. "The Protection of Human Rights by the Organization of American States." *American Journal of International Law* 62 (4): 889–908.

Carnegie Endowment for International Peace; Division of International Law. 1940. *The International Conferences of American States, 1889–1928: A Collection of the Conventions, Recommendations, Resolutions, Reports, and Motions Adopted by the First Six International Conferences of the American State, and Documents Relating to the Organization of the Conferences. Supplement.* Oxford University Press.

Carroll, Roy. 2007. "Isabel Perón Arrested over Accusations of Human Rights Abuses." *Guardian.* http://www.theguardian.com/world/2007/jan/13/argentina. rorycarroll.

Cavallaro, James L., and Stephanie Erin Brewer. 2008. "Reevaluating Regional Human Rights Litigation in the Twenty-First Century: The Case of the Inter-American Court." *American Journal of International Law* 102 (4): 768–827.

Ceia, Eleonora Mesquita. 2015. "The Contributions of the Inter-American Court of Human Rights to the Development of Transitional Justice." *Law and Practice of International Courts and Tribunals* 14 (3): 457–75.

Citroni, Gabriella. 2016. "Missing Persons and Victims of Enforced Disappearance in Europe." Issue Paper for the Council of Europe Commissioner of Human Rights.

Claude, Ophelia. 2010. "A Comparative Approach to Enforced Disappearances in the Inter-American Court of Human Rights and the European Court of Human Rights Jurisprudence." *Intercultural Human Rights Law Review* 5:407–62.

Contesse, Jorge. 2017. "The Final Word? Constitutional Dialogue and the Inter-American Court of Human Rights." *International Journal of Constitutional Law* 15 (2): 414–35.

Contesse, Jorge. 2019. "Resisting the Inter-American Human Rights System." *Yale Journal of International Law* 44 (2): 179–238.

Contesse, Jorge. 2021. "The Rule of Advice in International Human Rights Law." *American Journal of International Law* 115 (3): 367–408.

Contreras, Pablo. 2012. "National Discretion and International Deference in the Restriction of Human Rights: A Comparison Between the Jurisprudence of the European and the Inter-American Court of Human Rights." *Northwestern University Journal of International Human Rights* 11 (1): 29–82.

Michael Coppedge et al. 2023. "V-Dem Dataset v13" Varieties of Democracy (V-Dem) Project. https://doi.org/10.23696/vdemds23.

Cooper, Sarah Lucy. 2011. "Marriage, Family, Discrimination and Contradiction: An Evaluation of the Legacy and Future of the European Court of Human Rights' Jurisprudence on LGBT Rights." *German Law Journal* 12 (10): 1746–63. https://doi.org/10.1017/S2071832200017545.

Council of Europe. 1960. *Yearbook of the European Convention on Human Rights / Annuaire de la Convention Européenne des Droits de l'Homme: The European Commission and European Court of Human Rights / Commission et Cour Européennes des Droits de l'Homme.* 1st ed. Dordrecht Springer Netherlands.

Deitelhoff, Nicole. 2009. "The Discursive Process of Legalization: Charting Islands of Persuasion in the ICC Case." *International Organization* 63 (1): 33–65.

Dulitzky, Ariel E. 2011. "The Inter-American Human Rights System Fifty Years Later: Time for Changes." *Quebec Journal of International Law.* September Special Issue, 127–64.

Dulitzky, Ariel E. 2015. "An Inter-American Constitutional Court? The Invention of the Conventionality Control by the Inter-American Court of Human Rights." *Texas International Law Journal* 50 (1): 45–94.

ECtHR Press Unit. 2021. "Pilot Judgements Fact Sheet." https://www.echr.coe.int/documents/fs_pilot_judgments_eng.pdf.

Forero, Juan. 2006. "Details of Mexico's Dirty Wars from 1960s to 1980s Released." *Washington Post*, November 21.

France 24. 2019. "'Unopposed Election': Benin Voters Shun Polls
    with Only One Choice." France 24. https://www.france24.com/
    en/20190429-benin-voters-boycott-election-opposition-talon.
García Chavarría, Ana Belem. 2019. "Debates sobre la prueba en el litigio ante la Corte
    Interamericana." *Anuario Mexicano de Derecho Internacional* 19:293–325.
Gerards, Janneke. 2011. "Pluralism, Deference and the Margin of Appreciation
    Doctrine: European Law Journal." *European Law Journal* 17 (1): 80–120.
Ghoshal, Neela. 2018. "Mexico Transgender Ruling a Beacon for Change."
    Human Rights Watch. https://www.hrw.org/news/2018/10/29/
    mexico-transgender-ruling-beacon-change.
Ginger, Henry. 1967. "Salvador Elects President Today." *New York Times*, March 5.
Glas, Lize R. 2019. "Russia Left, Threatened and Won: Its Return to the Assembly
    Without Sanctions." *Strasbourg Observers*, July 2. https://strasbourgobservers.
    com/2019/07/02/russia-left-threatened-and-has-won-its-return-to-the-
    assembly-without-sanctions/.
Glendon, Mary Ann. 2003. "The Forgotten Crucible: The Latin American Influence
    on the Universal Human Rights Idea." *Harvard Human Rights Journal*
    16:27–40.
Goldberg, Susan L. 1984. "Judicial Socialization: An Empirical Study." *Journal of
    Contemporary Law* 11 (2): 423–52.
Gómez, Verónica. 2001. "Inter-American Commission on Human Rights and the
    Inter-American Court of Human Rights: New Rules and Recent Cases." *Human
    Rights Law Review* 1 (1): 111–26.
González Domínguez, Pablo. 2017. "La doctrina del control de convencionalidad a la
    luz del principio de subsidiariedad." *Estudios constitucionales* 15 (1): 55–98.
Gonzalez-Ocantos, Ezequiel. 2018. "Communicative Entrepreneurs: The Case of
    the Inter-American Court of Human Rights' Dialogue with National Judges."
    International Studies Quarterly 62 (4): 737–50.
Gross, Oren, and Fionnuala Ní Aoláin. 2001. "From Discretion to Scrutiny: Revisiting
    the Application of the Margin of Appreciation Doctrine in the Context of
    Article 15 of the European Convention on Human Rights." *Human Rights
    Quarterly* 23 (3): 625–49.
Grossman, Nienke. 2013. "The Normative Legitimacy of International Courts." *Temple
    Law Review* 86 (1): 61–106.
Guzman, Andrew T. 2008a. *How International Law Works: A Rational Choice Theory.*
    Oxford University Press.
Guzman, Andrew T. 2008b. "International Tribunals: A Rational Choice Analysis."
    University of Pennsylvania Law Review 157:171–235.
Guzmán, Esteban. 2022. "Inter-American Court Rules in Favor
    of Lesbian Religion Teacher in Chile." *Washington Blade*,
    April 23. https://www.washingtonblade.com/2022/04/23/
    inter-american-court-rules-in-favor-of-lesbian-religion-teacher-in-chile.
Hafner-Burton, Emilie M., Edward D. Mansfield, and Jon C. W. Pevehouse. 2015.
    "Human Rights Institutions, Sovereignty Costs and Democratization." *British
    Journal of Political Science* 45 (1): 1–27.
Hamilton, Michael, and Antoine Buyse. 2018. "Human Rights Courts as Norm-
    Brokers." *Human Rights Law Review* 18 (2): 205–32.
Harding, Luke. 2014. "Russia Delegation Suspended from Council of Europe
    over Crimea." *Guardian.* http://www.theguardian.com/world/2014/apr/10/
    russia–suspended–council–europe–crimea–ukraine.

Hawkins, Darren G., David A. Lake, Daniel L. Nielson, and Michael J. Tierney, eds. 2006. *Delegation and Agency in International Organizations.* Cambridge University Press.

Hawkins, Darren G., and Wade Jacoby. 2010. "Partial Compliance: A Comparison of the European and Inter-American Courts of Human Rights." *Journal of International Law and International Relations* 6:35–85.

Helfer, Laurence R., and Karen J. Alter. 2013. "Legitimacy and Lawmaking: A Tale of Three International Courts." *Theoretical Inquiries in Law* 14 (2): 479–503.

Helfer, Laurence R., and Anne-Marie Slaughter. 2005. "Why States Create International Tribunals: A Response to Professors Posner and Yoo." *California Law Review* 93:899.

Helfer, Laurence R., and Erik Voeten. 2014. "International Courts as Agents of Legal Change: Evidence from LGBT Rights in Europe." *International Organization* 68 (1): 77–110.

Heri, Corina. 2014. "Enforced Disappearance and the European Court of Human Rights' *ratione temporis* Jurisdiction: A Discussion of Temporal Elements in *Janowiec and Others v. Russia.*" *Journal of International Criminal Justice* 12 (4): 751–68.

Herz, Mônica. 2011. *The Organization of American States (OAS): Global Governance Away from the Media.* London: Routledge.

Heyns, Christof. 2002. *Human Rights Law in Africa 1999.* Martinus Nijhoff.

Heyns, Christof. 2004. "The African Regional Human Rights System: The African Charter." *Penn State Law Review* 108 (3): 679–702.

Hilbink, Lisa. 2015. "When You Wish upon a Star: Baltasar Garzón and the Frustration of Legal Accountability for Franco-Era Crimes." In *Legacies of Violence in Contemporary Spain: Exhuming the Past, Understanding the Present*, edited by Ofelia Ferrán and Lisa Hilbink. Routledge.

Hillebrecht, Courtney. 2014. *Domestic Politics and International Human Rights Tribunals: The Problem of Compliance.* Cambridge University Press.

Hillebrecht, Courtney. 2021. *Saving the International Justice Regime: Beyond Backlash Against International Courts.* Cambridge: Cambridge University Press. https://doi.org/10.1017/9781009052610.

Human Rights Campaign. 2020. "Gender Identity Law Takes Effect in Chile." Human Rights Campaign, January 10. Update of November 28, 2018, blog. https://www.hrc.org/news/gender-identity-law-takes-effect-in-chile.

Human Rights Watch. 2012. "Rwanda: Eight-Year Sentence for Opposition Leader." Human Rights Watch. https://www.hrw.org/news/2012/10/30/rwanda-eight-year-sentence-opposition-leader.

Human Rights Watch. 2016. "Dispatches: Rwanda Turns the Clock Back on Access to Justice." Human Rights Watch. https://www.hrw.org/news/2016/03/11/dispatches-rwanda-turns-clock-back-access-justice.

Huneeus, Alexandra. 2010. "Rejecting the Inter-American Court: Judicialization, National Courts, and Regional Human Rights." In *Cultures of Legality*, edited by Javier Couso, Alexandra Huneeus, and Rachel Sieder. Cambridge: Cambridge University Press.

Huneeus, Alexandra. 2012. "Venezuela's Exit from the Inter-American Court." *I-CONnect, Journal of Constitutional Law Blog.* http://www.iconnectblog.com/2012/10/venezuelas-exit-from-the-inter-american-court/.

Huneeus, Alexandra, and Mikael Rask Madsen. 2018. "Between Universalism and Regional Law and Politics: A Comparative History of the American, European, and African Human Rights Systems." *International Journal of Constitutional Law* 16 (1): 136–60.

IACtHR (Inter-American Court of Human Rights). 2021. Biografías de los jueces. https://www.corteidh.or.cr/tablas/jueces/HEM.pdf; https://www.corteidh.or.cr/tablas/jueces/MCS.pdf; https://www.corteidh.or.cr/tablas/jueces/COQ.pdf.

IJRC (International Justice Resource Center). 2020. "Benin and Côte d'Ivoire to Withdraw Individual Access to African Court." International Justice Resource Center, May 6. https://ijrcenter.org/2020/05/06/benin–and–cote–divoire–to–withdraw–individual–access–to–african–court/.

INEGI (National Institute of Statistics and Geography). 2021. *Encuesta Nacional de Población Privada de la Libertad,* December. https://www.inegi.org.mx/contenidos/programas/enpol/2021/doc/enpol2021_presentacion_nacional.pdf.

INEGI. 2023. Censo Nacional de Sistema Penitenciario Federal y Estatales. https://www.inegi.org.mx/contenidos/programas/cnspef/2023/doc/cnsipef_2023_resultados.pdfhttps://www.inegi.org.mx/contenidos/programas/enpol/2021/doc/enpol2021_presentacion_nacional.pdf.

Jimeno, Roldán. 2017. *Amnesties, Pardons and Transitional Justice: Spain's Pact of Forgetting.* Routledge.

Johnson, Paul. 2013. "Homosexuality and the African Charter on Human and Peoples' Rights: What Can Be Learned from the History of the European Convention on Human Rights?" *Journal of Law and Society* 40 (2): 249–79.

Johnson, Tana. 2014. *Organizational Progeny: Why Governments Are Losing Control over the Proliferating Structures of Global Governance.* Oxford University Press.

Keck, Margaret E., and Kathryn Sikkink. 1998. *Activists Beyond Borders: Advocacy Networks in International Politics.* Cornell University Press.

Kennard, Amanda, and Diana Stanescu. 2025. "Do International Bureaucrats Matter? Evidence from the International Monetary Fund." *Journal of Politics.* https://doi.org/10.1086/735705.

Kirabira, Tonny. 2019. "Tanzania's Withdrawal of Access to the African Court: Further Retrogression in Human Rights Protection in East Africa." https://ohrh.law.ox.ac.uk/tanzanias–withdrawal–of–access–to–the–african–court–further–retrogression–in–human–rights–protection–in–east–africa/.

Koremenos, Barbara. 2008. "When, What, and Why Do States Choose to Delegate?" *Law and Contemporary Problems* 71:151–92.

Laffranque, Julia. 2008. "Judicial Borrowing: International and Comparative Law as Nonbinding Tools of Domestic Legal Adjudication with Particular Reference to Estonia." *International Lawyer* 42 (4): 1287–1302.

Lopez, Oscar. 2021. "International Court Rules in Favor of Trans Rights in Honduras." *New York Times,* June 28. https://www.nytimes.com/2021/06/28/world/americas/honduras-trans-rights-ruling.html.

Madsen, Mikael R. 2014. "The International Judiciary as Transnational Power Elite." *International Political Sociology* 8 (3): 332–34.

Madsen, Mikael R. 2018. "Rebalancing European Human Rights: Has the Brighton Declaration Engendered a New Deal on Human Rights in Europe?" *Journal of International Dispute Settlement* 9 (2): 199–222.

Magubira, Patty. 2020. "Tanzania Sets in Motion Its Exit from Rights Court." *East African,* July 6. https://www.theeastafrican.co.ke/tea/news/east-africa/tanzania-sets-in-motion-its-exit-from-rights-court-1432330.

Mansfield, Edward D., and Jon C. Pevehouse. 2006. "Democratization and International Organizations." *International Organization* 60 (1): 137–67.

Marshall, M. G., and T. R. Gurr. 2020. *Polity v Project, Political Regime Characteristics and Transitions, 1800–2018.* Center for Systemic Peace. https://datafinder.qog.gu.se/dataset/p.

Martin, Lisa. 2006. "Distribution, Information, and Delegation to International Organizations: The Case of IMF Conditionality." In Hawkins et al., *Delegation and Agency in International Organizations.*

McSherry, J. Patrice. 2007. "Death Squads as Parallel Forces: Uruguay, Operation Condor, and the United States." *Journal of Third World Studies* 24 (1): 13–52.

Meltzer, Joshua. 2005. "State Sovereignty and the Legitimacy of the WTO." *University of Pennsylvania Journal of International Economic Law* 26:693–733.

Milner, Helen. 2006. "Why Multilateralism? Foreign Aid and Domestic Principal-Agent Problems." In Hawkins et al., *Delegation and Agency in International Organizations.*

Moravcsik, Andrew. 2000. "The Origins of Human Rights Regimes: Democratic Delegation in Postwar Europe." *International Organization* 54 (2): 217–52.

Morsink, Johannes. 1999. *The Universal Declaration of Human Rights: Origins, Drafting, and Intent.* University of Pennsylvania Press.

Moynihan, Harriet. 2016. "Regulating the Past: The European Court of Human Rights' Approach to the Investigation of Historical Deaths Under Article 2 ECHR." *British Yearbook of International Law* 86 (1): 68–100.

Murray, Rachel, and Frans Viljoen. 2007. "Towards Non-Discrimination on the Basis of Sexual Orientation: The Normative Basis and Procedural Possibilities Before the African Commission on Human and Peoples' Rights and the African Union." *Human Rights Quarterly* 29 (1): 86–111.

Navarro, Andrés. 2014. "Canciller apoya que se revise sistema de DDHH." *Listín Diario.* https://listindiario.com/la-republica/2014/11/24/346397/canciller-apoya-que-se-revise-sistema-de-ddhh.

Neuman, Gerald L. 2008. "Import, Export, and Regional Consent in the Inter-American Court of Human Rights." *European Journal of International Law* 19 (1): 101–23.

Nielson, Daniel L., and Michael J. Tierney. 2003. "Delegation to International Organizations: Agency Theory and World Bank Environmental Reform." *International Organization* 57 (2): 241–76.

Novak, Andrew. 2020. "Applying the Lens of Transnational Advocacy Networks to Human Rights Litigation." In *Transnational Human Rights Litigation: Challenging the Death Penalty and Criminalization of Homosexuality in the Commonwealth.* Ius Gentium: Comparative Perspectives on Law and Justice. Cham, Switzerland: Springer International.

Odermatt, Jed. 2018. "Patterns of Avoidance: Political Questions Before International Courts." *International Journal of Law in Context* 14 (2): 221–36.

O'Donnell, Thomas A. 1982. "The Margin of Appreciation Doctrine: Standards in the Jurisprudence of the European Court of Human Rights." *Human Rights Quarterly* 4 (4): 474–96.

Ouguergouz, Fatsah. 2003. "The Establishment of an African Court of Human and Peoples' Rights: A Judicial Premiere for the African Union." *African Yearbook of International Law Online* 11 (1): 79–141.

Pauwelyn, Joost. 1996. "The Concept of a 'Continuing Violation' of an International Obligation: Selected Problems." *British Yearbook of International Law* 66 (1): 415–50.

Pinto, Mónica. 2019. "Murió el jurista Pedro Nikken, una pérdida irreparable para la búsqueda de diálogo en Venezuela." *infobae.* https://www.infobae.com/america/

opinion/2019/12/10/murio-el-jurista-pedro-nikken-una-perdida-irreparable-para-la-busqueda-de-dialogo-en-venezuela/.

Pollack, Mark A. 2007. "Principal-Agent Analysis and International Delegation: Red Herrings, Theoretical Clarifications and Empirical Disputes." *SSRN Electronic Journal*. http://www.ssrn.com/abstract=1011324.

Radio Free Europe. 2017. "Russia to Reject Strasbourg Court If Not Allowed to Help Select Judges." Radio Free Europe. https://www.rferl.org/a/russia-to-reject-strasbourg-court-if-not-allowed-to-select-judges/28794729.html.

Reid, Graeme. 2018. "Brazil Boosts Transgender Legal Recognition." *Human Rights Watch*. https://www.hrw.org/news/2018/03/14/brazil-boosts-transgender-legal-recognition.

Reinalda, Bob, and Bertjan Verbeek. 2004. *Decision Making Within International Organisations*. Routledge.

Reuters. 2021. "Congreso de Honduras aprueba enmienda para impedir legalización del aborto y el matrimonio igualitario." *El Economista*. https://www.eleconomista.com.mx/internacionales/Congreso-de-Honduras-aprueba-enmienda-para-impedir-legalizacion-del-aborto-y-el-matrimonio-igualitario-20210128-0046.html.

Reynolds, Douglas. 2012. *Turkey, Greece, and the "Borders" of Europe: Images of Nations in the West German Press 1950–1975*. Frank & Timme.

Rouquié, Alain, and Michel Vale. 1973. "Honduras–El Salvador, the War of One Hundred Hours: A Case of Regional 'Disintegration.'" *International Journal of Politics* 3 (3): 17–51.

Ruggie, John Gerard. 1982. "International Regimes, Transactions, and Change: Embedded Liberalism in the Postwar Economic Order." *International Organization* 36 (2): 379–415.

Sanchez, Maria A. 2023. "Admitting (to) the Past: Transitional Justice in the European and Inter-American Courts of Human Rights." *International Journal of Human Rights* 27 (8): 1244–66.

Sandholtz, Wayne, and Adam Feldman. 2019. "The Trans-Regional Construction of Human Rights." In *Contesting Human Rights: Norms, Institutions and Practice*, edited by Alison Brysk and Michael Stohl. Edward Elgar.

Segado, Francisco Fernández. 2002. "Rodolfo E. Piza Escalante in Memoriam." *Ministerio de la Presidencia, relaciones con las cortes y memoria democrática*. http://www.cepc.gob.es/sites/default/files/2021-12/1415aib006005.pdf.

Shahid, Masuma. 2017. "The Right to Same-Sex Marriage: Assessing the European Court of Human Rights' Consensus-Based Analysis in Recent Judgments Concerning Equal Marriage Rights." *Erasmus Law Review* 10:184–98.

Shelton, Dinah. 2015. "The Rules and the Reality of Petition Procedures in the Inter-American Human Rights System." *Notre Dame Journal of International and Comparative Law* 5 (1): 1–28.

Shelton, Dinah. 2016. "Significantly Disadvantaged? Shrinking Access to the European Court of Human Rights." *Human Rights Law Review* 16 (2): 303–22.

Sikkink, Kathryn. 2011. *The Justice Cascade: How Human Rights Prosecutions Are Changing World Politics*. Norton Series in World Politics. W. W. Norton.

Sikkink, Kathryn. 2015. "Latin America's Protagonist Role in Human Rights." *Sur—International Journal on Human Rights* 22:207–19.

Sikkink, Kathryn. 2017. *Evidence for Hope: Making Human Rights Work in the 21st Century*. Princeton University Press.

Simmons, Beth A. 2009. *Mobilizing for Human Rights: International Law in Domestic Politics*. Cambridge University Press.

Simmons, Beth A., and Allison Danner. 2010. "Credible Commitments and the International Criminal Court." *International Organization* 64 (2): 225–56.

Simpson, A. W. Brian. 2004. *Human Rights and the End of Empire: Britain and the Genesis of the European Convention.* Oxford University Press.

Soley, Ximena, and Silvia Steininger. 2018. "Parting Ways or Lashing Back? Withdrawals, Backlash and the Inter-American Court of Human Rights." *International Journal of Law in Context* 14 (2): 237–57.

Spano, Robert. 2018. "The Future of the European Court of Human Rights— Subsidiarity, Process-Based Review and the Rule of Law." *Human Rights Law Review* 18 (3): 473–94.

Spjut, R. J. 1979. "Torture Under the European Convention on Human Rights." *American Journal of International Law* 73:267–72.

Steffek, Jens. 2003. "The Legitimation of International Governance: A Discourse Approach." *European Journal of International Relations* 9 (2): 249–75.

Stiansen, Øyvind, and Erik Voeten. 2020. "Backlash and Judicial Restraint: Evidence from the European Court of Human Rights." *International Studies Quarterly* 64 (4): 770–84.

Stone Sweet, Alec, and Thomas L. Brunell. 2013. "Trustee Courts and the Judicialization of International Regimes: The Politics of Majoritarian Activism in the European Convention on Human Rights, the European Union, and the World Trade Organization." *Journal of Law and Courts* 1 (1): 61–88

Van Pachtenbeke, Andy, and Yves Haeck. 2010. "From De Becker to Varnava: The State of Continuing Situations in the Strasbourg Case Law." *European Human Rights Law Review* 1:47–59.

Vaubel, Roland. 2006. "Principal-Agent Problems in International Organizations." *Review of International Organizations* 1 (2): 125–38.

Ventura Robles, Manuel Enrique. 2021. "Costa Rica y Perú: Un pasado de solidaridad, un destino común." *Revista Política Internacional* 129, Edición Bicentenario, 174–80.

Voeten, Erik. 2010. "Borrowing and Nonborrowing Among International Courts." *Journal of Legal Studies* 39:547–76.

Wildhaber, Luzius. 2007. "The European Court of Human Rights: The Past, the Present, the Future." *American University International Law Review* 22 (4): 521–37.

Windridge, Oliver. 2018. "Assessing Rwexit: The Impact and Implications of Rwanda's Withdrawal of Its Article 34(6)-Declaration Before the African Court on Human and People's Rights." *African Human Rights Yearbook* 2018: 243–59.

Zippel, Kathrin. 2004. "Transnational Advocacy Networks and Policy Cycles in the European Union: The Case of Sexual Harassment." *Social Politics: International Studies in Gender, State & Society* 11 (1): 57–85.

Index

Page numbers followed by *f* and *t* indicate figures and tables.

Sanoma Uitgevers B.V. v. the Netherlands,
126–27
Schalk and Kopf v. Austria, 174
Sébastien Germain Ajavon v. Benin, 161
Second International Human Rights Forum
(2021), 192
Senghor, Léopold Sédar, 78, 79
Serbia, personal integrity rights
case involving, 2
Serrano-Cruz Sisters v. El Salvador, 157–58
sexual orientation, protections against
discrimination based on, 167; ECtHR
jurisprudence on, 170–71; IACtHR
jurisprudence on, 179, 181
Shelton, Dinah, 47t
significant disadvantage criterion, ECtHR
jurisprudence and, 33
Šilih v. Slovenia, 147–48, 149, 150
Simmons, Beth, 7, 10
Simó, Alfredo, 68
Slovenia, personal integrity rights case
involving, 147–48
Smith and Grady v. the United Kingdom,
170–71, 180
social purpose, founding: of ACtHPR, 190,
195; changes in interpretation of, 22; and
contemporary jurisprudence, 192; of
ECtHR, 52, 56, 57, 58, 60, 99, 114, 154,
177, 191; geopolitical context and, 21, 50,
75, 76; of IACtHR, 75, 76, 90, 106, 108,
160, 191
Soering v. the United Kingdom, 96–97
Somalia, anti-LGBT discrimination in, 186
Somda, Jean Emile, 87, 88
Somoza family military dynasty, 64
South Africa, LGBT rights in, 186
Spain: admission to ECtHR, 30; amnesty law
in, lawsuits related to, 141, 149; personal
integrity rights cases involving, 149;
same-sex marriage legalized in, 173
Spano, Robert, 55
Spielmann, Dean, 169
state compliance: with ACtHPR judgments, 6,
87; challenges inherent to international
human rights law, 8; with ECtHR
judgments, 6, 27, 58; with IACtHR
judgments, 6, 27, 72; monitoring
and enforcement of, deferential vs.
interventionist courts and, 27, 46t, 48t
state consent: deferential courts' prioritization
of, 23; and legitimacy of international
organizations (IOs), 21
state sovereignty: balancing of regional human
rights courts' power and, 7, 8, 199;

Council of Europe (CoE) and concern
about, 51, 52, 56, 76; ECtHR and respect
for, 99. *See also* subsidiarity, principle of
Steffek, Jens, 12
Stevan Petrović v. Serbia, 2
Stiansen, Øyvind, 35
Stroessner, Alfredo, 64, 130
subsidiarity, principle of: deferential court and
use of, 45t; ECtHR's commitment to, 35,
57, 131, 151, 167; IACtHR accused of
subverting, 39; IACtHR jurisprudence
emphasizing, 132, 139
Sunday Times v. the United Kingdom, 100, 109,
121
Sweden: LGBT rights in, 170, 173; and right of
individuals to petition ECtHR, 205n19
Switzerland: freedom of expression case
involving, 100; LGBT rights in, 221n38

Talon, Patrice, 135, 136, 137, 138
Tambala, Duncan, 113
*Tanganyika Law Society, Legal and Human
Rights Center, and Rev. Christohper
Mtikila v. Tanzania,* 110–11
Tanrikulu v. Turkey, 145
Tanzania: ACtHPR's headquarters in, 17,
42, 197; freedom of expression case
involving, 110–11; personal integrity
rights cases involving, 42, 160–63;
withdrawal of individual access to
ACtHPR, 41, 42–43
Teitgen, Pierre-Henri, 51, 52
temporal jurisdiction *(ratione temporis),* 57;
ACtHPR's interpretation of, 6, 86, 110,
111, 112, 114, 143, 161–62, 163, 165, 191,
217n30; deferential court's interpretation
of, 26, 45t; ECtHR's interpretation of, 6,
57, 97–98, 142, 146, 147–50, 154, 164,
217n30; IACtHR's interpretation of, 71,
105, 106, 107, 108, 143, 157–58, 159,
164; interventionist court's interpretation
of, 26, 47t; variation in regional courts'
interpretation of, 6, 26, 142
Thompson, Elsie Nwanwuri, 113
Tibi v. Ecuador, 156–57
torture: ACtHPR jurisprudence on, 161;
ECtHR jurisprudence on, 92f, 94, 95;
IACtHR jurisprudence on, 92f, 93,
106–7; Mexican government's use of, 64;
prohibition of, American Convention
and, 105; prohibition of, as *jus cogens*
principle, 143; Uruguay government's
use of, 63–64; violations of prohibition
of, 142

www.ingramcontent.com/pod-product-compliance
Lightning Source LLC
Chambersburg PA
CBHW030359270326
41926CB00009B/1178

9 781501 785535